D1592523

The Opera Houses of Iowa

The
Opera Houses
of
Iowa

By

George D. Glenn and Richard L. Poole

Iowa State University Press / Ames

792.5
G487

George D. Glenn is professor, Department of Theatre,
University of Northern Iowa, Cedar Falls, Iowa.

Richard L. Poole is associate professor and chair, Department of Speech and Theatre,
Briar Cliff College, Sioux City, Iowa.

♾ Printed on acid-free paper in the United States of America

First edition, 1993

Library of Congress Cataloging-in-Publication Data

Glenn, George D.
    The opera houses of Iowa / by George D. Glenn and Richard L. Poole.—1st ed.
        p.   cm.
    Includes bibliographical references and index.
    ISBN 0-8138-0984-3 (acid-free paper)
    1. Theaters—Iowa—History—19th century. 2. Theaters—Iowa—Stage-setting and scenery—
History—19th century. 3. Theater and society—Iowa. I. Poole, Richard L.
II. Title.
PN2275.I8G58 1993
792.5'09777—dc20   93-22793

Contents

Preface

IN 1982 the Mid-America Theatre Conference, a regional theatre organization comprising members from the seven states of Minnesota, Iowa, Missouri, North and South Dakota, Nebraska, and Kansas, decided that it would be a good idea to compile a comprehensive listing of the resources for the study of theatre history in our region. The resulting study began life as the MATC "Frontier Theatre Inventory," and the involvement of George Glenn and Richard Poole as the co-chairs for Iowa ultimately led to the publication of this book.

Originally we hadn't necessarily planned to concentrate on opera houses, but, like Topsy in that perennial favorite of the opera houses— *Uncle Tom's Cabin*—our interest and involvement in Iowa's opera houses "just growed." To be honest, at the beginning we didn't realize the extent and richness of Iowa's opera house heritage. George remembers the first "find" that was ultimately to send Richard and him on their statewide odyssey—the CSPS Hall in Vining. George had been talking about the MATC project in one of his theatre history classes one day when a student volunteered that he knew of an old "dance hall" in the small town of Vining, near his hometown: "Yeah, it still has scenery and stuff in it." So on a beautiful spring afternoon George found himself heading south out of Cedar Falls to Vining.

The problem was how to find the people in Vining who might know something about the hall. Arriving in Vining George located the combination bar/grocery store, went in, sat at the bar and ordered a beer from the lady storekeeper/bartender. Sipping his beer he looked around the bar, nodding to the three or four seedcorn-capped men of various ages nursing beers at a couple of chrome-legged tables in the back.

While he was trying to decide on a conversational ploy, a lady came in to deliver some homegrown carrots to the grocery store. A corkscrew-shaped carrot stimulated a general conversation. At an opportune moment George asked if anybody knew anything about the old hall, and whether it would be possible to see the interior. "Oh, hell, yes," answered a young man. "Do you want to see it? Let's go," said another.

So George followed the two men outside to their trucks, and the three drove the block to the edge of town and the large, white, single-story wood-frame CSPS Hall. Obtaining the key from a lady in the house across the street, the three entered the building. George immediately realized that he had found treasures. There was a large, hardwood-floored hall filled with long tables and bentwood kitchen chairs. Wide-bladed fans hung at intervals from a pressed-tin panel ceiling. A couple of corners held potbellied wood-burning stoves. At the far end was a velour-curtained stage; opening the curtain revealed stacks of old scenery, a wonderful amateur advertising roll drop, and a street scene roll drop. An hour or so spent examining the hall, the stage, and the scenery convinced George that the place was worth further study. (The next fall he did return with a group of students to examine, measure and photograph the hall and its contents.)

As he drove home George remembers thinking, "If there's one such old opera house so close, the odds are that there are more still standing elsewhere in the state. I'll bet there might be as many as twenty or thirty still around." To find out, George and Richard devised a questionnaire to be sent to every Iowa city and town: the questionnaire asked in essence, "Do you still have an opera house, and if not, did you ever have one?" and, "If you don't know, will you pass this on to a local citizen who might know?" This questionnaire was sent to the librarian of every town library, to every local and county historical society, and in the absence of any of these institutions, to the local postmaster. It is an understatement to say that we were stunned as the questionnaires began to return and the positive responses mounted into the hundreds. We began to appreciate the enormity of our task as it occurred to us that we were pledged to visit, document and photograph every extant opera house in Iowa. It hadn't seemed to be much of a chore back when we were anticipating perhaps thirty positive responses, but we knew we had our work cut out for us when it was clear that the response was ten times our original estimate. Ultimately we documented over three hundred extant Iowa opera houses and identified over seven hundred non-extant opera houses by name.

We spent the next few summers travelling around Iowa from opera house to opera house, generously assisted by grants and leaves provided by our respective schools, the University of Northern Iowa and Briar Cliff College. Since Richard was based at Briar Cliff he took everything west of Interstate 35, while George, at Northern Iowa, covered the eastern half of the state. It was nothing to put 5,000 miles on a car in a summer and never get more than two hours from the home base. We would plan an out-and-back route that we thought we could cover in a day, call our contact people in each town we planned to visit, and hit the road early in the morning. We developed a travel kit that included a camera bag filled with camera, lenses, film, and record-keeping photo log; a cassette tape recorder; a clipboard with a stack of information-gathering forms we devised; a folding rule and a 100' tape measure; a flashlight; a hardhat; and the solace of the Iowa traveller, a plastic yellow and red Casey's coffee mug (refills $0.10) affixed to the dashboard.

We discovered that Iowa has an abundance of excellent, little-travelled secondary and county roads, and an equal abundance of friendly, helpful people. The ones we met may sometimes have been more than a little bemused by our fixation on old theatres and anything remotely connected to old theatres, but they kindly stifled their opinions and gave freely of their time and information.

Our usual procedure on arriving at a town and locating our contact person and the opera house was to begin by measuring and photo-graphing the exterior. If the interior had not been totally altered to a nontheatrical configuration we would next thoroughly measure and photograph the interior, including stage, scenery, and decorations, as well as such artifacts as remained, like playbills and posters pasted to the backstage walls. If time permitted we would check the local library, newspaper, or historical society for further information on the opera house. We might be so fortunate as to obtain an interview with a local resident who had personal recollections of the opera house in its heyday or who had perhaps even acted with a company that had performed in the old opera houses.

We had fun. There was a continuous feeling of excitement and anticipation as we would drive from town to town, never knowing for sure what we were going to find next, but knowing that it would be interesting. And sometimes we ran into conditions that few other researchers in theatre history have had to face. George remembers at least two long-abandoned second-story opera houses where the accumulation of pigeon droppings was so great that he had to wear a dust mask just to move around, and where he couldn't walk without stepping on a pigeon skeleton. But Richard had two experiences that topped that.

Once in southern Iowa, where there was no direct access to the second-story hall as the outside staircase had been removed (a condition we encountered on more than one occasion), Richard had to climb a ladder to the roof of an adjacent structure, cross that roof, and then climb through a window to get into the opera house. As he got closer to the window he noticed that it seemed to be pretty dirty. Then the dirt started to move! The owner, who went up with him, assured

Richard that the bees that covered the window were pretty groggy at this time of day and that if he "moved quickly" they probably wouldn't sting! So Richard moved quickly, diving headlong through the window being held open by the owner, hoping and praying that the owner was right and the bees were groggy—or friendly—or both. The owner was right, and Richard got his pictures and measurements while avoiding what could have been the stings of outrageous fortune.

At another opera house in southern Iowa, Richard had to climb up through a false ceiling to take pictures of some roll drop scenery. Noticing some dead bats as he climbed didn't give him a lot of confidence. The ladder he was climbing was vertical, and he had to take flash pictures holding the camera in one hand and the ladder with the other. The day was hot, the enclosed space was hotter, and the thought of being dive-bombed by rabid bats (Richard has an active imagination) produced such a cascade of sweat that Richard's glasses fogged and it was a miracle that he got safely back down the ladder, much less successfully getting the photographs he wanted.

With all the hazards and inconvenience of bees, bats, dust, cobwebs, and pigeon dung, most of the time our explorations were uneventful, except for the excitement of discovery, which was always with us. We had our frustrations and disappointments as well, of course. Occasionally we would arrive at a location to find that we had been misinformed and that the structure had never been an Opera House, or had always been just a movie theatre. A number of times we were simply too late: the opera house had been torn down, or as happened twice, had burned down the week before we visited the town. Similarly, a number of times we found the opera house only to discover that loads of scenery and artifacts—"junk" to the owners—had been carted off to the dump just recently.

We were lucky, too. A number of times we completed our investigation and acquired our photographs, only to have the opera house burn down, fall down, or be torn down at a later time—the Clarksville Opera House burned only a week after George had been there. Although we lamented the destruction of these wonderful buildings, our feelings of loss were tempered by the knowledge that at least we had a pictorial record of the opera house interiors, the scenery, and the artifacts.

Sometimes we were denied access to the opera house. At least twice we encountered a building owner who, for whatever reason, was unable or unwilling to overcome his doubts as to our true motives for our desire to see his opera house. George, for example, three times made an appointment to visit an eastern Iowa opera house some three hours away, only to be "stood up" all three times. He finally conclud-ed that the owner simply didn't want him in the building, so that particular opera house is missing from our records.

There is a sign outside of Readlyn, Iowa, which says something like "The home of 858 wonderful people and one old grouch," and this is really the story of our research. For every "old grouch" we ran into there were hundreds of people who gave unstintingly of their time and memories; who said, "Here's the key, there's the opera house, bring the key back when you're finished"; who showed us with great pride what remained of their opera house; who took hours out of their busy schedules to show us around, talk with us, and introduce us to even more friendly people, and who later wrote to us and described with great affection how their opera house was the center of their lives. To all those wonderful people we can only say "Thank you." Anything good in this book is due to them; we simply could not have undertaken or completed this project without them.

We hope you will find this exploration as exciting as we did. We are delighted to be able to share this rich portion of Iowa's heritage with you. And please help us keep this project alive and ongoing. If we have made mistakes (and we surely have), please correct us. If we have left out your town or opera house, it was inadvertent—we simply didn't know about it. By all means let us know. We know there are more out there to be found, and we'd love to visit you and your opera house, and continue to expand our knowledge of Iowa's wonderful theatrical past.

Finally, we have great ambitions for this book. No other state can boast of such a chronicle. We believe it provides an accurate, clear, and complete record of a fast-disappearing theatrical heritage and demonstrates the richness and diversity of that presence. Further, we hope it will stand as a research model for other states and be used as a scholarly secondary resource. Perhaps most important, we want it to be an interesting book; one that both the scholar and casual reader will find absorbing and fascinating. If it even begins to fulfill these goals, then ten years of hard work will be amply rewarded.

Acknowledgments

THIS PROJECT could not have been undertaken or completed without the generous assistance of a great number of people, particularly those who allowed us access to their opera houses. They are too numerous to thank individually—they know who they are.

The authors particularly thank their respective institutions: the University of Northern Iowa for providing George Glenn with a Summer Research Grant (1983) and a Professional Development Leave (fall 1988) to enable him to initiate and complete his work on this project; Briar Cliff College for providing Richard Poole with a sabbatical leave (fall 1985) and for administrating a Kellogg Grant which allowed him to visit opera house sites, and the Faculty Development Committee which provided him with funds to perform basic research.

Richard Poole thanks Professor William Hewitt of the West Chester University History Department, who provided encouragement and support in those dark days when people said, "You're working on what?" He also thanks the staffs of the Sioux City Public Library and the Briar Cliff Library for their prompt, courteous, and efficient service in getting essential books and materials. A special thank you to Scott Sorensen and the Sioux City Museum and Historical Association for their help. Also, special thanks to Scott Heim, who was always there when Richard needed him (and he needed him a lot), to explain the intricacies of word processing.

George Glenn thanks the many theatre students in the Department of Communication and Theatre Arts at the University of Northern Iowa, who put up with his opera house obsession over the years, and in particular Timothy Crawford and John Hosier, who put in long hours assembling and tabulating questionnaires and doing research; others are Andrea Boesen, Chelle Budrevich, Allen Coleman, Mary Delaney, Leann Diercksen, Lori Finch, Steven Giannoble, Terry Gustafson, Scott Hansen, Tina Hantula, John Hogan, William Ivey, Neal Jacobs, Karen Mitchell, Thomas Neville, Douglas Nichols, Lisa

Paulsen, Gregory Schrader, Sheila Staebler, Diane Stevenson, Jodie Stockberger, Devin Thompson, Derek Voy, Michael Wilhelm, Todd Williams, Allison Wheeland, and Stephen Young. Especial thanks go to his colleagues at Luther College, Robert Larson and Rod Van Loh, and his colleagues at the University of Northern Iowa; Peggy Sannerud, Bruce Brockman and Charles B. Scholz of the Department of Communication and Theatre Arts and Nancy Hinshaw of the Educational Media Center. Special thanks to Paul Sannerud, Department of Theatre, for his drawings of typical opera house structures.

The authors thank their many professional friends and colleagues throughout the country who have expressed interest in and encouraged their work; the staff of the Iowa State Historical Society for their help in providing research materials and encouragement, and particularly to the Museum of Repertoire Americana and the Society for the Preservation of Tent, Folk, and Repertoire Theatre, Mt. Pleasant, Iowa. The museum is unique to Iowa and possibly to the nation in its unparalleled collection of opera house and tent show artifacts, memorabilia, and research materials. This project could never have been what it is without the help of Curator Caroline Schaffner, Assistant Curator Joe Mauck, Secretary Billie Turley, President Emeritus Jimmy Davis (who has already put our Iowa opera house list to work in booking his revival of the Schaffner Players), and the many former troupers who gather for a reunion each year at the museum, and who have welcomed us into their society.

Finally, the authors thank their wives, Sandra Glenn and Marcia Poole, and their children, Stephanie Glenn, Laura Sorensen, David Glenn, Gerald Poole, and Alexander Poole, for listening to our ravings, patiently enduring our obsession, and even visiting opera house sites with us. Thanks to us, none of them can pass through a town without gazing at the tops of buildings hoping to find that magic sign—*Opera House*.

The Opera Houses of Iowa

1

Opera Houses in Iowa

he Opera House. Its name conjures up images of glamour, splendor, excitement, European sophistication, and the big city. These images were not restricted to the big city, however. In the not too distant past virtually every city and town throughout the length and breadth of Iowa had a place called "the Opera House." But the day is long since past when the local Iowa opera house was the hub of community and entertainment. The building where people saw the latest big city production (or some version that resembled it!); thrilled to the histrionic talents of a famous performer; heard a church sermon; participated with their friends in a home talent show; rollerskated with their family; danced with a sweetheart or wife; were enthralled by the medicine show pitch of the Great Dr. Balthazar T. Archimedes, has now been reduced to a run-down movie house, a block of aging apartments, a feed and grain storage warehouse, or a decrepit eyesore destined for the wrecking ball if it hasn't already fallen down, been knocked down, burned down, or blown down by the cyclone of 1948.

Between 1850 and 1915, all types and sizes of Iowa communities had their opera house. A town could not call itself civilized unless it could advertise programs in its very own opera house. But what were opera houses and where did the idea come from?

Origin of the "Opera House" Euphemism

England originally provided the models for North American entertainments and the structures that housed them. By the 1750s, when the first professional theatres were being built in the English colonies in America, England had a number of theatres called opera houses that were devoted to the performance of Italian and English opera, as well as other forms of light entertainment. However, the term opera house did not appear in America until 1787, and then it occurred in conjunction with a subterfuge. According to Arthur Hornblow, "when in 1787 a Philadelphia law prohibited theatrical performances, the Southwark Theatre was advertised as the Opera House Southwark" (Hornblow 1965, 172–73).

Although theatre was welcomed in some parts of America in the eighteenth century, particularly in the mid-Atlantic and southern colonies (and states), authorities in other areas such as New England and Quaker-dominated Philadelphia frowned on the theatre as an immoral activity, and prohibited it whenever they could. Theatre managers and performers cleverly circumvented the restrictions with a number of subterfuges. Plays were disguised as something else: a performance of *Othello*, for example, would be advertised as a "Moral Dialogue on the Effects of Jealousy, in Five Parts." And the performance space was disguised by calling it a "Museum," an "Academy of Music," an "Athenaeum," or ultimately, an "Opera House."

Early American censors were thus caught in a massively illogical posture: on the one hand they allowed the promotion of entertainment in a place called an opera house. On the other, they prohibited the same entertainment in a place called a theatre. Of course, to them it made perfect sense. The authorities obviously thought that an opera house and what occurred there (supposedly opera or at least something musical) was somehow more reputable and less damaging to its citizens than *anything* which was presented in a building called a theatre. By 1870, particularly throughout the Midwest and West, the euphemism of choice more often than not was "Grand Opera House," "Opera House," or "Opera Hall," although "Academies of Music" were still to be found, and there were always the generic "Town Halls" or "Community Buildings."

A great building boom in entertainment facilities occurred between 1870 and World War I, when thousands were built in the Midwest and the West (Slout 1972). In Iowa alone, more than 300 such structures still stand and we estimate that four times that many originally existed (see Chapter 4). Many things contributed to this proliferation. Three were paramount. First, railroad track mileage increased from 35,083 miles in 1865 to 243,013 in 1897 (Census, *Historical Statistics*, 200–202). This vast connecting network of railroads meant one could literally go to anywhere from anywhere. Indeed, according to Jack Poggi in *Theatre in America: The Impact of Economic Forces, 1870–1976,* "the development of the railroads seems to have been a technological advance as significant to the theatre as the later inventions of the motion-picture camera and the electronic tube" (Poggi 1968, 6). Second, as a result of improved means of transportation, traveling theatre companies from New York and other big cities increased dramatically and by 1896 their numbers were estimated at 1300 (Slout 1972, 2). Third, the local performance facility became a community symbol of progress and civilization. Many towns, particularly those just emerging from a frontier condition, built performance structures to proudly advertise their newly-achieved status as a civilized metropolis. In some instances, local businessmen either bought and upgraded the existing entertainment facility, or built a new one. They were financed through the patronage of wealthy citizens, or through the sale of stock to the general public, or both. But these facilities were almost never called theatres: most of the time they were called opera houses.

The opera house building boom did not go unnoticed by the *Dramatic Mirror*, the premier theatrical newspaper of the day. In a 7 March 1885 article entitled "The Name Opera House," an anonymous author attempted to explain the origination and current use of the name opera house. The author contended that buildings called opera houses were originally devoted completely to music and especially opera. For some reason they were financial disasters and most of the facilities became theatres:

> Thus it comes that we have Opera Houses—Grand Opera Houses at that—in which opera is never heard. But the name "Opera House" has another significance. To some extent it overcame the scruples and deadened the consciences of those who cared not to build or to attend "Theatres." The Academies of Music having become exhausted, and the name grown rusty, how fascinating to turn to the elegant Opera House! . . . The foreign actor or artist making a first visit to our shores must marvel at our brilliant array of Opera Houses. But after he has traveled a few weeks the sham is exposed. He finds that they are only theatres, after all, and some of them shambling rookeries at that.
>
> Still, with all this mushroom growth of Opera Houses during the last ten or twelve years, the greater number are substantial, well-kept edifices, and some of them stately piles of architectural beauty. We number our Opera Houses by the

thousands. The towns of 2,000 inhabitants and upward without an Opera House, Grand or otherwise, are few and far between—especially in the west (*Dramatic Mirror* 1885).

Other writers reinforce the *Dramatic Mirror*'s assertion that theatres were called opera houses to overcome "the scruples and . . . consciences" of the local population. Jere Mickel, in *Footlights on the Prairie*, contended that many Americans had considerable prejudices against anything theatrical because in their minds theatre was associated with "aristocratic sexual immorality, drunkenness, and any other kind of social misconduct that could arise from the apparent instability of the life of the theatre." Actors were vagabonds. They did not do honest work—"they played." Since "music had for centuries been a respectable art as it had always been associated with the worship of God," and since "Opera is music," therefore, as "strange and unintelligible as it is to most people, the term opera house came to be applied to any place devoted to shows" (Mickel 1974, 48).

Willis F. Dunbar substantiates this point of view in his article "The Opera House as a Social Institution in Michigan." Dunbar asserts that the Protestant Church exerted enormous influence on small-town activities and did not approve of theatres or what went on in them (Dunbar 1943, 661–72). Most amusements had to be approved by the local religious community before they could occur. Some of them, such as "singing schools, spelling bees, lyceum lectures, temperance meetings, and even circuses were defended as being 'educational,'" and therefore easily approved. No good education ever occurred in theatres.

In 1916, Dunbar, then a young lad in a Michigan town, "regarded the Opera House and the things that went on there as slightly devilish." It came as a great shock to him to see a minister and his wife enter the place to attend a lyceum lecture! Dunbar concluded that this only could have taken place because the Opera House owner (who was also the manager) "insisted that the newspaper always refer to it [the opera house] as the 'Academy of Music.'" He concluded that even though the term Opera House might have reflected the ambitious nature of the owner, the use of the term more than likely "was used instead of 'theatre' as being less offensive to church people" (Dunbar 1943).

Opera House Categories

In spite of opposition or managerial guile, the nineteenth century witnessed the development of opera houses in virtually every city, town, and village in the hinterlands. Because the term was generic, opera houses came in a bewildering variety of sizes and types and fulfilled a wide variety of similar functions. The problem for the theatre historian became one of classification. In the recent past scholars have given much thought and effort into formulating an opera house taxonomy, setting up categories of architectural and functional characteristics into which various opera houses have been placed.[1] Beginning with Joseph Donahoe's study "Theatres in Central Illinois—1850-1900" in 1953 and continuing with Cunning's *Opera Halls and Opera Houses: Evolution of Stage-focused Structures in Iowa* in 1987, they have attempted to conform past and existing structures into a definition of types. The types have their basis in a chronology concomitant with an evolving architectural complexity. Opera house structures, therefore, have been defined as "general utility halls," "opera halls," "opera houses," or "grand opera houses." Allegedly, the general utility hall came first in the chronology, to be replaced or supplanted by more complex and ornate structures as the community or region increased in population, wealth, and cultural aspirations.

Further, each type is seen as being distinct in its form and function. The general utility hall is described as being typically a plain, rectangular hall on the second floor of a commercial establishment. The stage is small and poorly equipped, the auditorium is small and not "stage-focused": that is, the floor is flat and the seating is removable to allow the space to be used for a multiplicity of non-theatrical functions. There are limited support facilities for both audience and performers. Opera halls are a step up from the general utility hall, although they also tend to be second-story halls in commercial buildings. They are larger, with bigger and better equipped stages; their auditoria are larger and are stage-focused, with permanent, stage-oriented seating (including balconies, galleries, and boxes), and they provide more audience and performer support in the way of lobbies, rest rooms, central heat, dressing rooms, and offices. Opera houses are still more advanced, and tend to be buildings that are built primarily for theatrical use although they may contain commercial establishments within them. They are identifiably

---

1. Donahoe 1953; Allen 1981; Cunning 1987; Frick and Ward 1987; Zivanovic 1988.

"theatres" on the exterior, and serve only theatrical functions inside.

The problem with these categories is that often they simply do not accurately describe Iowa's opera houses. Each classification is sometimes given several subclassifications. For example, Allen and Cunning divide the "opera house" category into three subtypes: "transitional opera houses," "regular opera houses," and "grand opera houses." This division is both cumbersome and confusing, particularly when attempting to fit an existing structure into a category or subcategory. Allen based his study for the most part on an examination of nonextant opera houses, examining contemporary accounts and newspaper records for his information. He apparently never examined an opera house *in situ*. Attractive as it may have been to attempt a scientific categorization of opera house types, their categories were imposed rather than revealed. Our ancestors were building *opera houses*, not general utility halls or opera halls. They built small opera houses and big ones; they built small single-story wood-frame opera houses, and second- and third-story opera houses in frame, brick, or stone buildings; they built small, medium, and large "stand alone" multistory opera houses. And they didn't pay any attention to chronology: they built what they needed and what they could afford when they needed it, whether it was a "general utility hall" in 1910 or a "grand opera house" in 1870—and they were all called "opera houses" by the people who built them, ran them, performed in them, and attended them.

We have wrestled with this problem of categorization in order to determine the best way to describe the great variety of opera houses built in Iowa, so many of which are still standing. We have decided that we will use the term "opera house" as our ancestors did—to refer to structures that included stages and were used, even if only occasionally, for the performance of live theatre. Any further distinctions will be clear from the descriptive context. We will progress in our examination from small and insignificant to large and magnificent, and we will wrestle with the wonderful variety to be found in Iowa's opera houses, so representative of the variety characteristic of every aspect of the state itself.

Single-Story Opera Houses

The most popular and widespread opera house structure was the small, rectangular, usually single-story, wood-frame or brick opera houses so common in the small towns and villages throughout Iowa. For a community that was eager to bring the cultural advantages of the larger cities to its citizens, the small, single-story opera house was the obvious solution. It was simple in design, easy to build, and relatively inexpensive. And when it wasn't needed to fulfill its theatrical function, it could double as town meeting hall, lodge or association hall, basketball court, roller rink, and ballroom (Fig. 1.1).

It was easy to design and build: a simple frame structure about 30 feet wide by 90 feet long; at one end a raised stage about 20 feet deep fronted by a proscenium arch with an opening about 16 feet wide by 12 feet high; at the other end a vestibule with a box office. A small balcony easily could be added opposite the stage, and, if necessary, extended along the sides. Flat hardwood served as the auditorium floor. Audiences sat on individual chairs or rows of four or five joined at the bottom or back. Interior decoration probably consisted of pressed-tin panels for the ceiling and walls, commonly used in conjunction with stencilled decorations. Because stage ceilings were seldom higher than 12 or 14 feet in these opera houses, the stage could handle only simple and uncomplicated scenery (see Chapter 2 for a discussion of opera house scenery). It was a simple, utilitarian design, practically unchanged from the small theatres of the English Restoration and the early colonial playhouses.

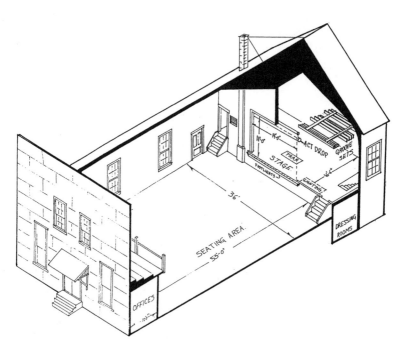

1.1 *Cut-away view of a typical single-story opera house, based on the Westgate Opera House. Drawing by Paul Sannerud.*

By 1900 virtually every small town and village in Iowa had such a structure, so many examples should have been available for examination. Unfortunately, single-story opera houses suffered a high mortality rate. Always susceptible to fire and wind, their wooden construction deteriorated so rapidly that many were torn down when the opera house period ended. Their utilitarian design also meant that they could be easily converted to other, nontheatrical uses. Those still existing serve such nontheatrical purposes as storage sheds or welding shops. Because their exteriors did not automatically indicate "theatre," there may be many undiscovered opera houses in Iowa whose theatrical history is forgotten and unsuspected.

A prime example is still recognizable as a theatre inside: the opera house in Westgate (Fayette County), population 263. The Westgate Opera House (ca. 1900) is unusual in that it is sheathed in tin inside and out but otherwise is representative of the single-story opera house (Fig. 1.2). The building is 36 feet by 80 feet; the false front facade contains four windows and a double entrance door protected by a projecting porch roof. There is a small lobby and a box office window just inside; the auditorium measures 34 feet 6 inches by 53 feet. The floor is flat with no permanent seating; it is painted for a basketball court. There is a small balcony, 35 feet 2 inches by 10 feet 5 inches with a gentle rake; hanging below the balcony and in front of the proscenium opening are basketball

1.2 *The tin-sheathed Westgate Opera House, Westgate (Fayette County), Iowa.*

backboards and hoops (Fig. 1.3). The proscenium opening measures
14 feet wide by 11 feet high; the curtain line to the back wall
measures 16 feet 6 inches with 9 feet 6 inches of wing space offstage
right and left. Attached to the stage ceiling are four sets of grooves
for wing and groove scenery and the rigging for roll drops. The stage
has one trap, stage center.

The stage is equipped with simple overhead strip lights and a
primitive control board off left stage. Also off left is a remnant of the
old gas lighting equipment: a device on the wall was made by the
"Perfection Lighting System, American Gas Machine Co., Albert
Lea, Minn., Style A, No. 3" (Fig. 1.4).

The theatre also contained examples of typical small opera
house stage scenery, now in the collection of the Museum of
Repertoire Americana, Mt. Pleasant, Iowa. There were nine interior
flats, 10 feet high by 5 feet wide, made by the Kansas City Scenic
Studio; this collection included a door flat and a window flat. In
addition there was an advertising front roll drop, painted by an
unskilled hand (see Figs. 1.3 and 2.26), and a "Westgate Street" roll
drop (as identified on the back of the drop) painted by the Kansas
City Scenic Company (see Fig. 2.14). The latter is addressed on its

1.3 *The proscenium arch of the Westgate Opera House, with the advertising
front drop curtain in place. The multiuse
nature of small opera houses is indicated
by the basketball hoop and backboard
suspended in front of the stage.*

1.4 *A control mechanism (?), part of the original gas lighting system in the Westgate Opera House. It was a Perfection Lighting System, Style A, Number 3, manufactured by the American Gas Machine Company, Albert Lea, Minnesota.*

roller to "E. W. Lusby, Mgr." An unidentified newspaper clipping dated 1905 supplied by Mona Ladwig, coordinator, Fayette County Historical Center, identifies Lusby as the new druggist in Westgate. Ms. Ladwig also reports that the Fremont Township census of 1910 lists Edwin W. Lusby as being 36, born in Missouri, and married for eight years to Elizabeth. They had one daughter, Helen. There is no indication as to when Lusby took over management of the opera house, but the "Westgate Street" drop must be circa 1910.

Obviously, these small opera houses were multiple-use facilities: the inclusion of basketball courts alone would indicate that. But sometimes the buildings were designed as multiple-use facilities in another way, by combining the function of opera house and lodge or society hall. Many Masonic Temples have theatres in them, although they tend to be used exclusively for Masonic ritual. Other common opera house/lodge combinations were: Odd Fellows' halls, Czechoslovakian society halls, German Turner halls, and Scandinavian society halls. While some of these are fairly elaborate structures, many fall into the single-story category.

Upper-Story Opera Houses

Other simple, multipurpose halls were housed in two-story or three-story buildings (Fig. 1.5). As with single-story opera houses, there is a great variety among the two- and three-story opera houses of Iowa. Most of them were built as combination commercial establishments/opera houses. While some of them were "stand-alone" buildings, many were built as business "blocks" on a city street of continuous business buildings. Also, these multiple-story structures varied considerably in their size and theatrical complexity. Significantly, some of these opera houses were named after an individual rather than the community in which they were built.

More of the multiple-story opera houses have survived than have the single-story opera houses, although their function has typically been altered to nontheatrical usage. It is precisely because a theatre is basically a large empty space, easily alterable, that these large, primarily brick buildings have survived past their theatrical usefulness. Most of the oldest surviving examples of Iowa opera houses are of this brick, multiple-story type.

An example of a small town business block with a second-story opera house is Brown's Opera House, above what is now Lenth's Feed Store, in Riceville (Howard County), population 877. The 67 foot by 80 foot brick building was built around 1902 (Fig. 1.6). The stairway to the opera house enters the side of the hall, where a small box office is located. The flat main floor measures 62 feet by 57 feet

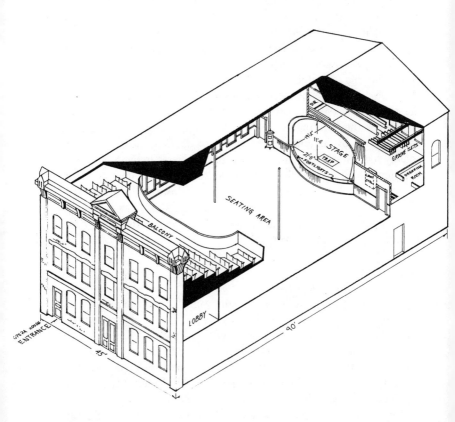

1.5 *Cut-away view of a typical upper-story opera house, based on Brown's Opera House. Drawing by Paul Sannerud.*

6 inches. The elaborate stencilled and painted decorations on the walls and ceiling of the auditorium gave the opera house its nickname of the "Rainbow Hall." There is a sailboat mural flanked with painted columns on the stage right side of the stage (Fig. 1.7), and a mountain/waterfall mural, also flanked with painted columns, on the stage left wall (Fig. 1.8). The murals are signed "M. Smith." The painted columns extend on all the walls, with an elaborately stenciled ceiling border and ceiling, in a color scheme of rose, lime green, and pink (Figs. 1.9–1.11). The original potbellied stoves that heated the hall are still in place (Fig. 1.12).

Most notable is the stage with its elaborately painted proscenium arch which proclaims "All the world is a stage" (Fig. 1.13). The proscenium is also decorated with nine small lamps around its edge. The proscenium opening measures 21 feet wide by 11 feet high; curtain line to back wall is 19 feet 2 inches, with a 4 foot 6 inch curved apron containing 12 footlights. There is a trap door, center. There is 14 feet of wing space stage right, and 12 feet stage left. Two dressing rooms flank the stage: one is 9 feet by 8 feet 8 inches; the other is 9 feet by 10 feet 6 inches. A curtain track for a draw curtain hangs above the proscenium (Fig. 1.14); there is also rigging for roll drops in the stage ceiling. A simple switch board with knife switches (marked variously "stage," "foot," and "house") is framed into the wall stage left. A bill for *The Royal Slave* is still on the inside of the hinged light board cover (Fig. 1.15). There are a few old flats in a

1.6 *Brown's Opera House, Riceville (Howard County), Iowa. The opera house was on the second floor.*

1.7 *The stage right sailboat mural in Brown's Opera House.*

1.8 *The stage left waterfall mural in Brown's Opera House.*

1.9 *A portion of the side-wall stenciling and decoration in Brown's Opera House.*

1.10 *Part of the stenciled ceiling in Brown's Opera House.*

1.11 *The central ceiling decoration, complete with cherubs, in Brown's Opera House.*

1.12 *One of the original wood- or coal-burning stoves that heated Brown's Opera House.*

1.13 *The unique original proscenium arch in Brown's Opera House, with its motto: "All the world is a stage" (a misquotation of the original Shakespearean line, "All the world's a stage").*

1.14 *The original draw-curtain track immediately upstage of the Brown's Opera House proscenium arch.*

frame on the up-stage back wall.

Brown's Opera House is unique because some of the original roll drop scenery was restored and preserved in an unusual way. A new addition to the Riceville Public Library was built to hold a small meeting room with a replica of the original proscenium arch, behind which hang the restored drops (see Fig. 2.20). The four drops will be discussed in more detail in Chapter 3; they consist of an advertising front drop and a main drop (both 13 feet 6 inches by 23 feet 6 inches), and three drop scenes (all 13 feet 6 inches by 20 feet)—a street scene, a country lane, and a mountain pass (see Figs. 2.7, 2.8, 2.11, and 2.20). None had any identification as to what scenic studio produced them, although their quality indicates that they were professionally painted. In fact a comparison of the Riceville street drop with a street drop painted by Jesse Cox from the Smithland Opera House raises a strong supposition that the Riceville drops were in fact painted by the Jesse Cox Studio (compare Figs. 2.11 and 2.12).

One of the oldest and best-preserved three-story brick opera house is Steyer's Opera House in Decorah (Winneshiek County), population 7703 (Glenn 1988). Built in 1870 by Decorah tavern owner, Joseph B. Steyer, (architect F. G. Brandt of Dubuque) the three-story brick building at 102 West Water Street originally was planned to hold commercial establishments on the first floor,

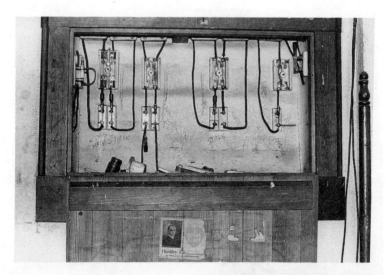

1.15 *The original knife-switch electrical control board, backstage left in Brown's Opera House.*

apartments on the second floor, and the opera house on the third floor (Fig. 1.16). Although the businesses have changed, and the opera house has not been used for over sixty years, commercial establishments still occupy the first floor, and the second floor is apartments. The old opera house is now used as storage for the second-floor apartments.

Steyer remodeled his opera house in 1875, enlarging the stage and moving it from an end wall to a side wall, and extending the three-tiered balcony around the other three sides. It is this configuration that exists today. In addition, Steyer hired a Chicago scene painter, Harry Dressel, to construct and paint new scenery for the larger stage.

Access to the hall is by way of a narrow stairway in the front of the building, although a blocked off stairway and remnants of a cloak room can be found at the back of the hall. The interior of the hall is decorated with embossed-tin ceiling and wall panels, and embossed cornices and decorations for the two elaborate stage doors, balcony facings, and the proscenium arch (Fig. 1.17). The auditorium was originally lighted by five chandeliers, although at present only a single, elaborate center chandelier remains. The flat main floor measures 42 feet by 81 feet: the seating capacity was 700–800. A few of the original movable seats remain. The proscenium width is 28 feet 6 inches, and is 12 feet 7 inches high. The stage measures 19 feet

1.16 *Steyer's Opera House, Decorah (Winneshiek County), Iowa, was located on the third floor of the 1870 brick business block.*

1.17 *One of the pair of ornate stage doors in Steyer's Opera House.*

from the curtain line to the back wall; there is a curved 4 foot apron which contains covered footlight troughs (Fig. 1.18). There is one 2 foot by 2 foot trap, center. There is 17 feet of wing space offstage right, and 12 feet offstage left. There are offices, dressing rooms, and storage lofts offstage left and right. One 20 foot by 14 foot room, which may have been a men's dressing room, is offstage left, with a storage loft above it. Offstage right is a women's dressing room, 10 feet 6 inches by 13 feet six inches, with a 5-foot wide passage way in front of it leading to a 24 foot by 19 foot 3 inch office or green-room.

The stage is still rigged with four sets of overhead grooves for wings and flats (Fig. 1.19). The downstage set has four grooves, the middle two sets have six grooves each, while the upstage set has eight grooves. Attached to the stage ceiling are numerous wooden blocks for roll drops and other scenery. Remnants of the main front roll drop were still attached above the stage; the rest of the drop, which was ripped off, had been rolled up and stored elsewhere in the hall. It has subsequently been repaired, and now hangs in its old place above the proscenium arch. A double winch, counterweights, and a

1.18 *The stage of Steyer's Opera House much as it was after interior redecoration in 1875.*

1.19 *The original four sets of overhead grooves backstage in Steyer's Opera House.*

counterweight chute are located offstage left.

It is rare to find an opera house this old with such a wealth of surviving details, and Steyer's would be remarkable if this were all, but also stored in the hall are several complete wing and groove sets, with a number of miscellaneous scenery pieces. Some of these sets are signed by the 1875 scene painter, Harry Dressel. It is reasonable to assume that this scenery is the original 1875 scenery. We will examine it in more detail in Chapter 3.

Steyer's Opera House was the only performance space in Decorah until 1896 when the new Grand Opera House was built. The Grand is long gone, but Steyer's remains, replete with the ghosts of such past performers as Ole Bull (1872), Mme. Janauschek (1875), and according to graffiti on the backs of the scenery: the Bum-Duprez & Benedict's Minstrels; George Brooks & Percy Spanks, Song and Dance Artists; and the Wallus Comedy Co., among others. Also in the hall, found wadded up in the storage loft, is a three-piece banner made from pasting up posters advertising Mason and Morgan's *Uncle Tom's Cabin* Company.

Stage-Oriented Upper Floor Opera Houses

There is a "subclass" of the multifloor brick opera house that accommodated a stage-oriented theatre on the upper floors (Fig. 1.20). A good example is McHaffey's Opera House in Eldon (Wapello County), population 1255 (Fig. 1.21). Built in 1891 the three-story 45 foot by 90 foot building has a raked and tiered auditorium facing a curved stage front with two proscenium doors and a 19 foot 6 inch by 12 foot proscenium arch (Fig. 1.22). The stage is 15 feet deep, with a 4 foot 6 inch apron that masks a footlight trough. There is 10 feet 6 inches of wing space on either side, with dressing rooms offstage right and left.

There is no fly loft, but the stage ceiling still retains remnants of rigging and lighting instruments, and some old woodland flats. The backstage potbellied stove is still in place (Fig. 1.23). The backstage walls are covered with graffiti and theatrical posters. The stage curtains are in the collection of the Museum of Repertoire Americana. The original seats are still in the auditorium.

Grand Opera Houses

Grand opera houses were built exclusively for a theatrical purpose (Fig. 1.24). They are often "stand-alone" multistory structures, and their auditoria are permanently stage-focused. They have identifiable stage houses with fly lofts and fly galleries/pinrails. From

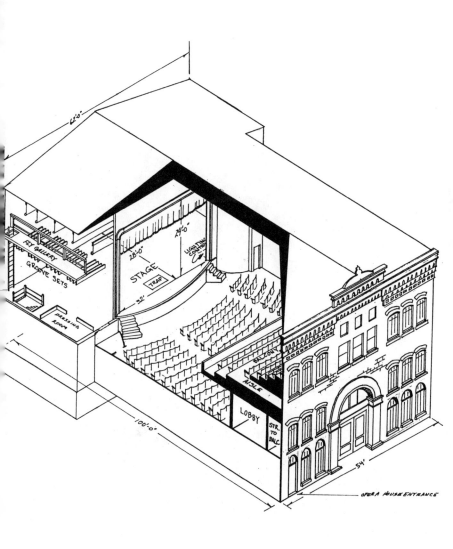

1.20 *Cut-away view of a typical upper-story, stage-oriented opera house, based on McHaffey's Opera House. Drawing by Paul Sannerud.*

1.21 *McHaffey's Opera House, Eldon (Wapello County), houses a stage-oriented opera house in its second story.*

1.22 *The stage and a portion of the raked-floor auditorium in McHaffey's Opera House.*

1.23 *The stage was kept warm by the typical backstage stove in McHaffey's Opera House.*

their exteriors and interiors they are immediately identifiable as "theatres" to most people. Most, if not all of the extant examples have been converted to movie theatres: it is this easy and natural conversion that has ensured the survival and continuous use of this category of opera house. Some have even transcended their conversion to movie theatres to begin a new life reconverted/restored to legitimate theatres. As with the other categories we have examined, there is a great deal of variety in the grand opera house category; some structures are relatively small and simple in design, others are large and splendid in design. As we shall see, however, these differences are not necessarily keyed to chronology.

The earliest grand opera house that we shall examine is the De Witt Opera House in De Witt (Clinton County), population 4512. Built in 1876 by the De Witt Opera House Association (Fig. 1.25), this stucco building measures 44 feet 6 inches by 86 feet. Originally the opera house had an elaborate cupola surmounting it (Fig. 1.26); this has since been removed, and the original arched main entrance has been modernized with the addition of a porch roof (Fig. 1.27). The

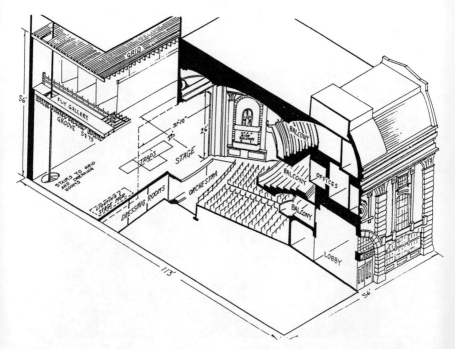

1.24 *Cut-away view of a typical grand opera house, based on the Majestic Theatre. Drawing by Paul Sannerud.*

stage has been remodeled to hold a removable movie screen: the proscenium is currently 32 feet wide by 13 feet high, and the stage is 32 feet deep from the curtain line (Fig. 1.28). There is four feet of wing space on either side. The trap is covered over. Dressing rooms are located below the stage. The stage has been ceilinged over, and it was impossible to discover if anything remained above it. It is doubtful that at this early date there was anything like a modern fly loft; the exterior shows no evidence of a stage house.

Judging from an early twentieth-century photograph of the stage the proscenium opening appears to have been narrower, approximately 26 feet (Fig. 1.29). This photograph is valuable for showing a portion of the original advertising front roll drop curtain, and a wing-and-groove setting with a Center Door Fancy roll drop upstage. There also seems to have been a large apron in front of the proscenium.

The auditorium, with its raked main floor, now seats 186 on the main floor and 39 in the balcony. It is almost certain that seating capacity has been reduced over the years with modernization of the auditorium, particularly with the addition of a projection booth in the balcony.

Built in the heyday of the multistory business block opera houses, only six years after Steyer built his opera house in Decorah, the De Witt Opera House must be one of the earliest examples of

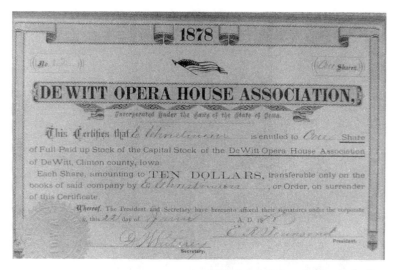

1.25 *An original stock share in the De Witt Opera House Association.*

"stand-alone" grand opera house construction in Iowa.

The 1893 Masonic Opera House in What Cheer (Keokuk County), population 803, is our first example of a grand opera house that has retained its theatrical function, although the stage has been much remodeled. The three-story brick building measures 48 feet wide by 94 feet long (Fig. 1.30). The auditorium seats 383 in the parquet and dress circle, and 217 in the raked horseshoe balcony (Fig. 1.31). The stage is fronted with an orchestra pit; behind the 6 foot curved apron is a 21 foot 9 inch wide by 19 foot high proscenium arch. The curtain line to the back wall is 20 feet, with 12 feet of wing space on either side. The stage floor has one center trap, 6 feet 6 inches by 4 feet 10 inches. The grid is 25 feet above the stage, with a fly gallery and pinrail on each side of the stage. There are two 8 by 11 foot proscenium dressing rooms on each side of the stage. Many old theatrical posters remain on the back stage walls, including a series for a production of *Quo Vadis* (Fig. 1.32). There is an 8 foot 6 inch by 14 foot foyer in the front of the theatre; the third floor is devoted to lodge meeting rooms.

1.26 *The original appearance of the De Witt Opera
House, from an old photo-
graph in the theatre.*

1.27 *The De Witt Opera House, De Witt
(Clinton County), as it appears today.
Built in 1876, it is the earliest stand-
alone grand opera house that we have
examined.*

1.28 *The stage of the De Witt Opera
House as it appears today.*

The What Cheer Masonic Opera House is somewhat of an anomaly in that it is a fairly large grand opera house in a very small town. Most of the larger theatres were in the larger communities. The Majestic Theatre in Dubuque (Dubuque County), population 64,336, was built in 1910 as one of the grandest of the grand opera houses. Now restored and part of the Five Flags complex, the six-story brick Renaissance revival theatre was designed by the Chicago architectural firm of C. W. and George L. Rapp (Fig. 1.33). The theatre is 65 feet wide and 113 feet long. The interior is replete with gold leaf and plaster moldings (over $10,000 of gold leaf was used in the restoration). The orchestra seats 322, while the dress circle of 38 "na celle" boxes and a second balcony seats 357 (Fig. 1.34). A third balcony, or Family Circle was walled off in the 1940s, and awaits restoration. There are large proscenium boxes on either side of the stage (Fig. 1.35). The huge proscenium opening measures 31 feet 10 inches (boxcar width) by 26 feet high, and is surmounted by the coat of arms of Julien Dubuque (Fig. 1.36). There is an 11 foot deep apron, and the stage is 28 feet deep. There is 11 feet of wing space off right, and 7 feet off left. The grid is 56 feet above the stage, and there is a modern pinrail—in fact, the entire backstage area has been thoroughly

1.29 *This old photograph shows the original stage of the De Witt Opera House.*

1.30 *A grand opera house in a small town: the New Masonic Opera House in What Cheer (Keokuk County), Iowa.*

1.31 *The partitioned main floor and horseshoe balcony of the New Masonic Opera House.*

1.32 Quo Vadis *was touring in 1902 and must have visited What Cheer then. This is one of several* Quo Vadis *posters backstage.*

1.33 *The Renaissance revival exterior of the Majestic Theatre, Dubuque (Dubuque County), Iowa.*

1.34 *The gold-leaf-decorated balcony facings in the Majestic Theatre.*

1.35 *The gold-leaf-decorated side boxes in the Majestic.*

modernized. The stage floor has five trap doors. The Majestic, now the Five Flags Theatre, remains as a prime example of the kind of restoration that can be done.

The rich and varied opera houses that we have examined in this section are only a very small sample of the opera houses that are still standing throughout the state, as well as all the opera houses long gone that once graced the main streets and courthouse squares of virtually every Iowa community.

In the next chapter we will look at some examples of the scenery that was designed for these wonderful buildings. Like the opera houses, the scenery ranges from the simple to the complex, from the plain to the beautiful. Our examples include scenery that would have fit quite nicely on the stages of the eighteenth-century English and American playhouses as well as scenery that would not seem too out of date on today's stages.

1.36 *The elaborately decorated high proscenium arch in the Majestic, with the coat of arms of Julien Dubuque surmounting the stage.*

2

Opera House Scenery

n the last chapter we looked at a variety of opera house structures, from simple to complex, from small to large. Now we intend to examine some important parts of the theatre machine—the various kinds and types of scenery that were used in Iowa's opera houses, small and large.

Most opera houses maintained at least a small stock of scenery for the use of their own amateur or community productions, or for the companies that toured without their own scenery. While some opera houses in Iowa may have housed resident acting companies, most of Iowa's opera houses were built after "the Road" had been established, and communities were dependent for their entertainment on that broad network of touring shows and combination companies. The bigger and more important companies often toured with their own scenery, particularly if they were touring a single play, but most opera houses and repertoire companies had a stock of "standard" sets that would suit almost any dramatic necessity.

Iowa-Based Scenery Designers

Although many Iowa opera house owners went to firms in Chicago, Kansas City, and Minneapolis for their scenery and stage

equipment, there were some native-Iowa designers and scene painters as well. Our research has uncovered at least three men from Iowa who painted and/or designed stage scenery professionally. There may have been others and, of course, there were a host of amateurs. The professionals were J. F. Briggs of Waterloo; Louis Syberkrop, Sr. of Creston; and Jessie Cox of Estherville.

J. F. Briggs

The *Sioux Valley News* for Thursday, 17 November 1892, carried an article on the impending opening of the new Correctionville opera house, the Columbia. J. F. Briggs of Waterloo had been painting scenery for about a month and a half. According to the article "there were seven complete changes representing woodland, ocean, street, kitchen, parlour, and prison scene, and the curtain which represents a boat house and a number of boats anchored in the harbour. The walls will also have landscape scenes." Briggs may have been an artist and/or a sign painter or house painter as well, but we include him in our "professional" ranks. First, he is mentioned prominently in the article. Second, it does not make sense for an amateur to come clear across the state just to paint an opera house for fun.

Louis Syberkrop

According to *The History of Union County*, Louis Syberkrop, Sr., a Dane who came to the United States in 1871, settled in Creston in 1881 and was a decorator and scenic artist. He managed the Creston Opera House for seven years but decoration rather than scene painting or opera house managing was his real profession and he "gave up show business to more earnestly buckle into his life's work." Primarily he was a church decorator but he painted "many theatres, lodge rooms, private dwellings and how many theatrical scenes he painted we are not aware, but it would foot up a goodly number. . . ." He worked not only in Iowa, but in Nebraska, Missouri, Colorado, and Oklahoma. We assume that in some of those states he painted scenery and theatres as well as engaging in his primary profession as a decorator. He supposedly decorated over 300 churches and was an outdoor sign painter as well (Ade 1908, 257–58; Wilson).

Jessie Cox

The most famous and prolific Iowa-based scenic artist was Jessie Cox of Estherville. He was responsible, according to several newspaper articles, for two very important scene painting innovations. First, he allegedly invented a "Diamond Dye" process which enabled painted scenery to be packed, rolled, shipped and then unrolled without cracks or wrinkles, an essential condition for limited-budget small touring troupes. Second, instead of painting highlights on scenery, a common technique used to simulate three-dimensionality on a flat surface, he let the unpainted (or undyed) scenery canvas act as a highlight. His scenic studio painted literally hundreds of scenes for rural opera houses and traveling companies based in the Midwest and the Upper Midwest. His scenery was known all over Iowa and throughout the country. He also published the *Opera House Reporter*, a nationwide theatrical trade magazine catering primarily to small town opera house managers and traveling repertory theatre troupes. A 1910 advertisement in the *Opera House Reporter* touted the Cox Scenic Studios as "The Largest and Best in the West." Claiming 5,000 satisfied customers, the studio built "scenery for Theatres, Halls, Airdomes, Tent Shows and Vaudeville Acts." Boasting "no job too large or small for us," they provided scenery and fixtures for new and remodeled theatres. Warning potential customers not to "hand out your advertising curtain to tramp artists," they offered to "take old scenery in payment for new." Jessie's brother, James Cox, was also a publisher of the *Opera House Reporter* and a theatre architect (*Estherville Daily News*, 3 October 1966, 29 October 1968; Deemer 1980, 115; *Opera House Reporter*, 21 October 1910).

Standard Opera House Scenery

Although some of the larger opera houses employed their own scene painters, the majority of surviving opera house scenery was painted by one of the many professional scenic design studios or by individual professional scene painters. In Iowa we find examples from such major studios as the Twin Cities Scenic Company (Minneapolis), the Kansas City Scenic Studio, the Omaha Scenic Studio, and Sosman and Landis (Chicago), as well as from Iowa's own Jesse Cox Scenic Studio in Estherville. Occasionally one finds scenery that was obviously painted by an unidentified professional. And, despite Jesse Cox's warning against utilizing "tramp artists," one finds numerous examples of their work as well.

According to Mrs. Caroline Schaffner, curator of the Museum of Repertoire Americana, four settings were sufficient to mount most plays: "Front Room," "Back Room," "Timber," and "Town." No matter what the scenic requirements of the play, they could probably be met by these four settings, and many of our extant examples, some dating back to the 1870s, fit into one of these categories.

Front Room Settings

Among the 1875 scenery preserved in Steyer's Opera House in Decorah is a set of Front Room wings and flats. Like all the wings and flats preserved in Decorah, each of the two flats is 11 feet 6 inches wide by 13 feet 1 inch tall. When joined together on stage, the flats form a background 23 feet by 13 feet 1 inch. Each flat has a practical door in its center, measuring 2 feet 6 inches by 6 feet. Accompanying the flats is a pair of wings, each measuring 5 feet by 13 feet 1 inch. This setting is painted in wide alternating vertical stripes of light and dark green, with painted moldings at top and bottom. The doors in the flats are painted to resemble panelled doors. Unless some wings are missing from this setting it was designed to be a shallow setting, placed in the second grooves. It is an attractive setting, but is generalized enough to serve for virtually any fancy interior that might have been called for.

When roll drops replaced pairs of flats as backgrounds, they still were often paired with matching wings. An example is the Center Door Fancy setting found in the ZCBJ Hall in Clutier. The roll drop, with a practical door opening in the center, hung in an upstage position, flanked by a single, angled groove which held a pair of matching wings (Fig. 2.1). Drop and wings are painted gold, with

2.1 *A Center Door Fancy with a cut-out doorway, flanked with two matching wings, from the ZCBJ Hall in Clutier.*

42

decorative medallions circled with vine leaves and flowers. Gray painted moldings, complete with painted decorative plasterwork and painted shadows, are at the tops and bottoms of drop and flats, and surround the center doorway in the drop. This doorway is also surmounted with a painted arched pediment. It is not clear whether the center door was always practical, or whether it was cut out at some later time: Center Door Fancy drops are found both ways, as well as having a nonpractical center door painted in. Of course, once a practical door is cut into the center of a drop, it must be backed with something. In Clutier it was probably a neutral drop or curtain, since no matching interior backing piece was discovered. This setting is currently in the collection of the Museum of Repertoire Americana.

By 1900 roll drops in rural opera houses were being supplanted by free-standing flats which could be joined together to form the modern "box set," which simulates three walls of a four-walled room (the "fourth wall" being the proscenium opening—thus the well-known "fourth-wall convention" of modern Realism). In addition to the Center Door Fancy wing-and-drop setting, the ZCBJ hall in Clutier also had a Front Room set of half-a-dozen flats which could be lashed together to form a fancy interior (Fig. 2.2). The set, by the Universal Scenic Studio (Minneapolis), consists of two wall flats; two narrow

2.2 *A Front Room setting composed of individual flats from the ZCBJ Hall in Clutier.*

"filler" flats, or "returns"; a window flat with a practical, double-hinged window; two door flats with practical door openings; a French door flat with practical open-work French doors; and a fireplace unit. The functional nature of this scenery is indicated by the fact that, aside from the returns, the flats are all the same width, which means that they can be fastened together on stage in any order, thus varying the spatial arrangement as needed. The set is painted a combination of cream molding, panels, and trim, with light blue walls. The tops of the flats are decorated with painted bosses with hanging vines and pendants. The fireplace is painted with a red brick interior framed with black marble flanked with pillars with gold pediments. The painted mantle is adorned with gold plaster decorations. The window is backed by a blue flat, but the French doors are equipped with practical windows which must be backed with something: in this case there was a formal garden drop (Fig. 2.3). This setting is now in the collection of the Museum of Repertoire Americana.

Back Room Settings

Back Rooms were as necessary as Front Rooms. Back Room settings could serve as kitchens, cottages, or hovels, as the occasion

2.3 *The landscape roll drop from Clutier, which served as backing for the Front Room box set.*

required. The Back Room set of flats and wings in Steyer's Opera House is representative of this type. The set consists of a pair of flats and two pairs of wings. Each flat has a 2 foot 6 inch by 6 foot door positioned 5 feet in from the offstage edge (Fig. 2.4). The flats and wings are painted with brown wood wainscotting, door trim, and cornices. The doors are painted to resemble brown wooden cross-buck construction. The walls are painted to look like grayish-tan plaster, complete with cracks and missing pieces revealing the lath underneath. The flats and wings have sustained some water damage, and the stains contribute to the dilapidated appearance of this setting. Also visible on the flats are the outlines of the 1″ by 3″ cross-braces of the flat construction, caused by being stored for many years in a pile on the floor of the hall. This setting is unusual in that it is double-faced: the opposite side is a prison scene (discussed later).

The Museum of Repertoire Americana holds examples of Back Room roll drops; one for instance which contains a practical cut-out window (Fig. 2.5). There are not as many extant examples of Back Room settings as there of Front Rooms; there are, by comparison, more surviving Timber and Town settings and drops.

2.4 *The wing-and-groove Back Room setting from Steyer's Opera House.*

2.5 *This Back Room roll drop contains a practical cut-out window (the chair sitting in front of the drop is, of course, real).*

Timber Settings

As we have mentioned, Front Room and Back Room settings were intended to be generic, satisfying the location requirements of any play, as were exterior Timber and Town settings. Timber sets could represent actual wooded areas, or, more generally, any other outdoor, nonurban setting. Scenery in Steyer's Opera House provides an example of a wing-and-groove Timber setting, along with several pairs of flats and other scenery which could be used in conjunction with it.

The main component of this setting is three pair of profiled wings painted to resemble trees. The wings are the same size as the others already mentioned, with the addition of thin deal sculptured profiles attached to their edges by half-round stiffeners. Each wing is numbered to indicate its position in the proper groove, such as "2L," "2R," etc., painted in the corners. These designations indicate that the wings were painted with perspective in mind. The wings could be used with either of two pairs of flats: one pair which originally depicted a wooded area with a small pond (only one flat of the pair seems to be extant); the other showing a country scene with a large tree in the center foreground, fields on the stage left side, and trees and a pond on the stage right side (Fig. 2.6).

There are many roll drops showing a variety of rural scenes. Two of the finest are from Brown's Opera House in Riceville and are displayed in the Riceville library. One depicts a rural lane winding into a plain with scattered trees in the center distance, framed on either side by small trees, under a blue, cloud-filled sky (Fig. 2.7). The other shows a high Rocky Mountain lake, with rocks, pine trees, and fallen trees in the foreground and towering, snow-capped mountains in the background (Fig. 2.8).

Town Settings

As much variety as there is in the Timber settings, there is as much or more in the Town settings and drops, which depict urban street locales. Steyer's has a somewhat deteriorated and water-stained pair of flats showing a city street receding into the center distance. The stage right side of the street has a large classical-style building with a columned facade in the foreground; the stage left side features a domed building in the middle ground. No vehicles or persons are seen

2.6 *One of a pair of Timber flats in Steyer's Opera House.*

2.7 *A Timber roll drop from Brown's Opera House, Riceville.*

2.8 *A Rocky Mountain roll drop from Brown's Opera House.*

on the street, but gas street lamps are visible on each corner. The stage right buildings, in shades of blue and gray, are in shadow. The brightly sunlit stage left buildings are red brick. A blue sky with a few white clouds is in the background. The single-point perspective of the buildings and receding street is classical in its design, and is reminiscent of the one-point perspective scenery of the Renaissance (Fig. 2.9).

2.9 *This pair of Town flats comes from Steyer's Opera House, Decorah.*

One of the roll drops discovered above the stage in the Oxford Junction ZCBJ Hall turned out to be a Town drop from the Sosman and Landis studio in Chicago when it was recovered by the Museum of Repertoire Americana (Fig. 2.10). Unlike the Steyer's set, but more typical of turn-of-the-century roll drops, it is painted in angled perspective. We find ourselves looking down the stage left side of the street as if we were standing on the sidewalk. We can barely see the fronts of the buildings as they recede into a misty distance, but there are store signs and awnings projecting from the buildings. The other side of the street (the stage right side), is comprised of a number of brick and stone buildings, lit by the sun, which comes from the front right. A church steeple towers in the middle of the block. There are some trees on the corner, and the street has tall, four-globed street lamps. The gray sky is filled with darker gray cumulus clouds.

The Riceville collection includes a simpler but similar Town drop, also in angled perspective (Fig. 2.11). Again we find ourselves on the stage left corner, but this time a stone wall and trees obscure almost all of that side of the street, although we can see some of the street which parallels the front of the stage. Looking across and down the street we see trees in the foreground behind a walled corner, with some buildings and a church with steeple in the middle distance. There

2.10 *The Chicago studio of Sosman and Landis produced this Town roll drop for the Oxford Junction ZCBJ Hall.*

2.11 *The Town drop from Brown's Opera House, Riceville. Comparison with the Jesse Cox drop in Fig. 2.12 suggests that this drop is also from the Jesse Cox studio.*

are hitching posts on the corners and in front of the buildings, and the street is equipped with single-light street lamps. A comparison of this drop with the almost identical Jesse Cox Studio Street drop found in the Smithland Opera House is convincing evidence that the Riceville drops were also painted by the Jesse Cox Studio (Fig. 2.12). Note the similarity of the layout of the scene, with the street corner and wall on stage left, the identical treatment of the sidewalk with hitching post, lamps, and merchandise on the walk, the walled yard with trees on stage right, and the church steeple in the background.

The CSPS Hall in Vining contains a Town drop very similar in its design, if not in its details (Fig. 2.13). We have the same angled perspective, the same stage left street corner with a portion of the fronting street visible. The buildings, however, are larger and more elaborate. One building on the stage left side of the street extends past the top of the drop. A large corner building dominates the stage right side of the street, and the last discernible building on that side of the street is the ever-present church and steeple. Again, the sun comes from the right; the street has sidewalk signboards and globed street lamps.

The "Westgate Street" roll drop from the Westgate Opera House, now in the collection of the Museum of Repertoire Americana, is also in angled perspective (Fig. 2.14). Like the other drops we have examined, the vanishing point is towards stage left, but in this drop we

2.12 *This Jesse Cox Town drop was found in the Smithland Opera House.*

2.13 *This Vining CSPS Hall Town drop is also very similar to the Jesse Cox drop, and it, too, may be from Cox's studio.*

2.14 *The "Westgate Street" roll drop was painted by the Kansas City Scenic Studio, and comes from the Westgate Opera House.*

appear to be standing on the stage right corner looking across and down the stage left side of the street. The corner building on stage right is identified as a drug store, with windows full of bottles, and nice cast-iron pillars and decorations. The second floor boasts a projecting sign which advertises "The Finest Pool Hall in the City." A sidewalk signboard advertises "Cigars—News." Street drops painted by professional scenic companies, as all our examples were, often included blank signs in their design so that the names of local businesses could be painted in later. When one remembers that Lusby, the manager of the opera house, was also the town druggist, the choice of the corner building as a drug store, and the advertising signs, becomes understandable. The building on the corner across the street is identified as the "Hotel Minniapolis" [sic], showing that the Kansas City Scenic Studio, which painted this drop, was not too careful or knowledgeable about upper mid-west geography. The Twin Cities Scenic Studio in Minneapolis would have gotten it right.

Other Town drops reflect changing times. Instead of hitching posts along the street, the badly deteriorated street drop from Remsen has an early motor car parked on the stage right side. Other than this modern addition, the drop displays all the other characteristics of the earlier designs.

Other Localized Settings

Of course not all scenery fit into the four categories of Front Room, Back Room, Timber, and Town. Other generalized locales were useful, and many productions required specialized or particularized locales. For example, the reverse side of the Steyer's Back Room set depicts a room constructed of large, gray-tan sandstone blocks (Fig. 2.15). The doorways in the back flats are framed with large, round columns supporting arches over the doors. These arches appear to extend offstage right and left. Above the doors are small, arch-shaped barred openings. The remnant of the actual door is painted to resemble a riveted iron door with a small grilled window. The location is obviously a dungeon, suitable for any Gothic melodrama, but the setting could also be an interior in *King John* or *Macbeth* as well.

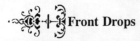 **Front Drops**

There were two other types of drop that every opera house had: a fancy front drop and an advertising drop. Very often the "ad" drop doubled as a front drop. When an opera house had a separate front

2.15 *The reverse of the Back Room wing-and-groove setting from Steyer's Opera House reveals this Gothic dungeon setting.*

drop it was invariably very fancy, with painted drapery and/or pillars framing some exotic scene. The oldest drop of that type we have found comes from Steyer's Opera House (Fig. 2.16). When discovered, the roll drop had been ripped away from its mounting above the stage, leaving about an 18-inch strip still hanging. The rest of the drop was rolled up and discarded in a corner. At some time it had had a panel of green cardboard attached to the lower edge. When it was unrolled, repaired, and re-rigged, the drop displayed much of its former grandeur.

The center of the drop is painted with an exotic tropical scene, perhaps representing a stretch of the Nile. Behind a stretch of green marble steps spanned in the center by a red and gold carpet, a broad river winds its way towards low mountains in the background. The banks of the river hold palm trees, ferns, and other luxuriant foliage; on the stage right bank a monumental building, perhaps a temple, can be seen, with a ceremonial barge in the river before it. On the stage left bank, half-hidden by the foliage, is a rock tomb or grotto, with stone steps leading up to a path which heads towards the spires and domes of a city in the background. This scene is flanked on each side by three sets of painted drapery and marble columns. Farthest to the side is a beige draw curtain, which is in front of a swagged red drape, trimmed at the bottom with a wide band of blue, a narrower band of

2.16 *The restored main front roll drop curtain from Steyer's Opera House.*

gold, and with long gold fringe at the bottom. This curtain is tied back with a golden tasseled cord. Behind this curtain hangs another beige curtain trimmed with a castellated design on the edges and bottom. Behind it stands the marble pillar on the marble steps which span the drop from side to side. Completing the impression of actual drapery, a knotted, tasseled rope hangs from the top center, trailing off to the stage left steps. The whole effect is representative of the day when theatres—even small town opera houses—were intended to be sumptuous settings for the art of the theatre.

An unusual fancy front drop was found above the stage in the ZCBJ Hall in Oxford Junction, now in the collection of the Museum of Repertoire Americana (Fig. 2.17). Painted red drapery has been pulled back with tasseled ropes on either side to reveal a massive gold painted picture frame enclosing a landscape of a city as seen from across a river. In the foreground we can see the reeds that line the river bank; in the distance, under a blue sky, is a vista of white buildings with red roofs, trees, and a glimpse of countryside. The scene is identified on the drop below the picture as *"Praha Pohled Na Stare Mesto,"* which we understand translates to "A View of Prague."

The Lyon Theatre in Rock Rapids holds a fine Twin Cities Scenic Company front drop (Fig. 2.18). A semicircular marble arch supported by double marble pillars on each side frames a mountain

2.17 *"A View of Prague" by the Sosman and Landis Studio in Chicago; used to hang in the ZCBJ Hall in Oxford Junction.*

2.18 *This fine front drop from the Lyon Theatre in Rock Rapids was painted by the Twin Cities Scenic Company.*

lake scene. The top of the arch is obscured by painted swagged red velvet curtains.

Another exotic scene is depicted in the front drop from the Remsen Opera House (Fig. 2.19). A large gold frame surrounds a Moorish-looking city scene. A palace or public buildings with red-tiled roofs sit on the bank of a river or canal on stage right, with a boat with a red-striped awning moored at the bank below. The river is spanned in the middle distance by a series of arched bridges; on stage left, also in the middle distance, is a round castle. Large domed buildings occupy the background. At the top, the frame is covered with painted red drapery.

The front drop of Brown's Opera House in Riceville is another example of a fine, professionally painted drop; although it is not identified as such, it is probably a Jesse Cox drop (Fig. 2.20). Painted, swagged, blue-green, ball-fringed drapery frames a background of formalized flowers and birds, with a large, circular medallion of bas-relief oak leaves. Superimposed over the medallion is a rectangular panel which is painted and shadowed to appear as if it were suspended in the air. This panel depicts an exotic river or harbor scene, with two dhows with brightly painted sails in front of a misty vista of a distant city of minarets and domes. This drop is fully in the tradition of exotic-scene front drops.

2.19 *The Remsen Opera House front drop presented a fanciful view of the Tiber River in Rome.*

2.20 *The main front drop from Brown's Opera House, Riceville.*

Advertising Front Drops

Perhaps most characteristic of any opera house scenery was the advertising front drop. Here was the chance for an opera house to have a decorative front drop that was uniquely its own, and at the same time bring in some needed revenue through selling advertising space on the drop to local merchants. The drops were usually professionally painted, but were sometimes the work of local amateurs or itinerant artists.

Dr. Lance Brockman of the University of Minnesota has discovered in the artifacts of the Twin Cities Scenic Company many examples of watercolor renderings and sketches of a variety of standard designs for advertising front drops (Fig. 2.21). Salesmen from the studio would carry these designs with them when they visited opera house managers. The managers would choose a design, sell the ads, and the studio would paint the drop, "filling in the blanks" with the local advertising copy.

We suspect that most of the extant ad drops date from the early twentieth century, although to date them exactly would require extensive research in old city directories to identify the firms advertising on the drop. A rough dating can be achieved by noting the telephone numbers (or lack thereof) in the ads. Ads with two, three, or four digit numbers were common from the early years of the twentieth century to the 1940s. Drops can also be roughly dated by the

2.21 *A salesman's sample "fill-in-the-blanks" front drop design from the Twin Cities Scenic Company studio. (From the Twin City Scenic Company Collection, Performing Arts Archives, University of Minnesota Library, St. Paul, Minnesota.)*

kinds of businesses which advertised. Ads for automobiles instead of livery stables, for example, indicate that the drop is relatively recent.

The Brown's Opera House (Riceville) is apparently an early drop because it has no telephone numbers and has ads for livery stables and blacksmiths (Fig. 2.22). The rectangular advertising panel of twenty-six advertisements is framed with a painted gold frame, and is bordered by painted drapery. The center of the drop depicts a gold-framed painted scene of a lakeside castle, with boats in the foreground and low mountains in the background.

Similar in its design of a simple, rectangular picture frame surrounded by rectangular advertisements is the ad front drop from the Blakesburg Opera House (Fig. 2.23). It appears to be an early drop—at least, there are no telephone numbers or ads for automobiles. There are ads for harness makers, cattle breeders, laundries, banks, hotels, life insurance companies, and cigars and tobacco. These ads surround a lake or seaside scene. Two boats are drawn up on the shore in the foreground, while the shore curves around on stage right to meet a castle, some trees, and a curious natural rock arch extending into the water. This picture is unusual in that it contains two human figures: a man sitting on a rock on the shore, and a woman with a basket on her head walking towards him.

Two other fancy advertising front drops are so similar in design that it is logical to speculate that they were painted by the same studio, and perhaps from the same basic design. They are the ad drop from the Eldon, Iowa, opera house, now at the Museum of Repertoire Americana (Fig. 2.24) and the ad drop from the Lyon Theatre, Rock

2.22 *The Brown's Opera House advertising drop.*

2.23 *The advertising front drop from the Blakesburg Opera House.*

60

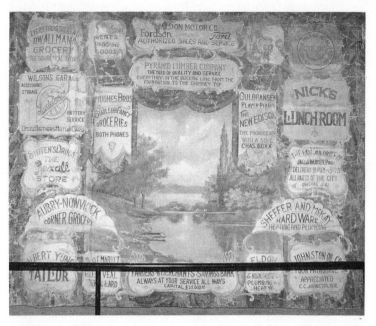

2.24 *The Eldon Opera House advertising front drop.*

Rapids, Iowa (Fig. 2.25). Both drops depict swagged red velvet curtains framing advertising panels in a variety of fantastic shapes such as shells, hanging banners, and baroque gold frames. It may be no coincidence that the bottom center panel in each drop is for the local bank, while the center panel immediately above the framed scene is for the local lumber yard. The framed scenes are different, but scenic companies had a variety of standard scenes that could be plugged into the standard frame. In this case the Eldon drop shows an idyllic country lake surrounded by trees with a distant landscape in the background. The lake shore is planted with flowers, and a small dock or diving board projects from the bank. The Rock Rapids drop depicts a formal garden with a marble wall and gate, potted plants and trees, and arbors over-arching the central path beyond the wall.

We have found almost as many amateur drops extant as professional ones. As might be expected, the amateur drops display a varying degree of artistic skill. Part of the fun in searching for opera houses and scenery is discovering relationships where none were expected, as was the case with the Jesse Cox street drops. When we found the amateur ad drop in the Westgate Opera House (Fig. 2.26),

2.25 *The Lyon Theatre, Rock Rapids, advertising front drop.*

2.26 *The Westgate Opera House advertising front drop.*

who would have expected that we would find two more drops obviously painted by the same untalented artist? Yet it is obvious that the ad drops from the CSPS Hall in Chelsea and the CSPS Hall in Vining are by the same anonymous amateur hand (Figs. 2.27 and 2.28). The Westgate and Chelsea drops are virtually identical, except for size and the content of the advertisements. Both drops contain rectangular ads, backed by flat red drapery decorated with ball fringe. The lower ads appear to be on gray stone walls and gateposts; a gray stone-flagged walk or drive leads past a pair of birch (?) trees to a white castle with a portcullis and five turrets. The Vining drop is different, but retains enough common characteristics with the other two to ascribe it to the same artist. The Vining drop has a green curtain with gold trim at the top, with advertisements on it and hanging from it; the wall and gate are of brown stone, and the gateposts are surmounted by large balls. The drive is of slabs of brown stone, and leads past a vista of pine trees to a brown two-turreted castle. The wall is fronted by a narrow strip of flowers (tulips?). The three drops apparently date from the early 1940s, according to the recollections of townspeople, although the ads list two-digit telephone numbers.

One final advertising drop provides an example of yet another type of advertising drop and is a symbolic indicator of the end of the opera house era: the ad drop from the Smithland Opera House displays the advertising panels surrounding a movie screen.

In this chapter we have examined the incredible variety of scenic elements not only available to, but used in Iowa's opera houses. No

2.27 *The Chelsea CSPS Hall advertising front drop.*

2.28 *The Vining CSPS Hall advertising front drop.*

matter what the size of the local opera house, every effort was made to make it as beautiful and splendid a place as possible. The exotic front drop scenes were thrilling to audiences not jaded by National Geographic specials on television. The scenery transported them to locales more wonderful than their own familiar surroundings. It didn't matter if the opera houses couldn't afford the services of the professional scenery studios or decorators; somebody would be found to do the best they could to provide the necessary scenery. There was probably more local pride in the homegrown amateur scenery than there was in the scenery from the big-city studio. The pride was similar to the pride felt by the community in the opera house itself—it was *theirs,* it was beautiful, it was bigger and better than anybody else's, it attracted better entertainment and served the community better. It was, after all, the "Opera House."

3

The Opera House as a Social Space: Performers and Performances

s we have seen in the last two chapters, nineteenth- and twentieth-century Iowa opera houses came in a variety of shapes and sizes. Virtually every village, town, and city had more than one; some as many as three. Most larger towns and cities had more than one. Regardless of size (one-story frame, multistory frame, one-story brick, multistory brick); location (first floor, second floor, third floor, parts of each floor, or parts of all floors); capacity (as few as 100, as many as 1300); ownership (a local doctor or saloonkeeper, the town itself, a far away insurance corporation, a consortium of businessmen); all Iowa opera houses fulfilled a similar purpose by providing space for a variety of functions. The Masons, Red Men, Good Templars, and Ku Klux Klan as well as the Catholic Fair, Evangelist Billy Sunday, the Welsh Singers from England and the latest Broadway hits (and sometimes stars) all met or performed at the opera house.

First and foremost, the opera house was a space. In Chapters 1 and 2 we dealt primarily with the physical space, focusing on exterior and interior design, and opera house scenery and artifacts. This chapter will focus on the opera house as a social space. As such, we

have identified several areas which either affected opera house use or were the result of it.

From the beginning these multipurpose structures were a meeting ground for all classes of people. The rural opera house was *the hub* of community activity and many nonentertainment activities occurred there. Our research shows that opera houses in Iowa, especially rural ones, were universally loved and when they were gone, were sorely missed. Without doubt they were the aesthetic, entertainment, frequently educational, and sometimes athletic focus of the community. Opera houses were considered an essential cultural attribute. Their value as a place, where all could meet and share experiences, was as important as the experiences themselves.

Iowa Troupes and Stars

Hundreds of acting troupes crossed and crisscrossed Iowa during the opera house era. Iowans could utilize homegrown theatre architects and scenic designers to build and equip their opera houses, and Iowa could supply the entertainment to fill them. Many touring theatrical troupes were Iowa based. Three of them were the G. D. Sweet Famous Players, Terry's *Uncle Tom's Cabin* Company, and The Trousdale Family Players.

George D. Sweet

There is not a great deal of information available about George D. Sweet (Holmes 1973, 161–62). Supposedly, he spent his earliest years around Early, Iowa, and was raised in Storm Lake, Iowa; he left town to marry an actress, and probably worked in small town opera houses and tent repertoire companies. Sweet and his wife, a singer and actress, played one night stands in opera houses before he founded The G. D. Sweet Famous Players, sometime between 1910 and 1920 and made Storm Lake his headquarters and winter home.

The Sweet shows were on the road in tents and opera houses for at least seventeen years until 1936 when Mr. Sweet died. Then the show was bought by Frank Gifford and he kept it going until 1941. The information is not clear about how many performers the Sweet show had in the 1920s and 1930s, but it did not seem to be an extensive company as almost everybody had a variety of duties to fulfill. The performers included Sweet's wife, her daughter Marjorie, his brother Lorenzo (also known as Bummer), Vincent Dennis, Frank Gallagher, Dixie Dow (Gallagher's wife), Roscoe Patch, and Harold

Holmes. Patch was from Hartley and had been a member of the Morgan Wallace Stock Company in Sioux City between 1915 and 1920. Holmes was from Storm Lake and was a tent rep player in the Midwest before joining Sweet in the late 1920s. There is no information about the others. Baldy Wetzel, a comic piano player, led the orchestra of five or six pieces. Sometimes, in the afternoon before the evening show, the musicians performed in a street parade in order to drum up business. Sweet himself almost never acted unless the cast called for a sheriff or some other small role. His main focus was as promoter, manager, and producer. Among the directors, who also acted, were Billy Lee and Frank Marlowe. The performances were called "Sunday school" shows because they were so clean—no "hells" or "damns" allowed. In the 1920s and 1930s they played a season of "Broadway Hits" as well as such then well-known pieces as *Deep Purple*, *Abie's Irish Rose*, and *Up in Mabel's Room*. They performed, were well known, and eagerly awaited in such Iowa towns as Ruthven, Newell, Fonda, Pocahontas, Laurens, Hartley, Sutherland, Spencer, Emmetsburg, Storm Lake, Sac City, Schaller, Moville, Denison, Correctionville, Holstein, Le Mars, Cherokee, Lytton and Vermillion, South Dakota.

Sweet himself was a showman. A large, imposing man, given to cigars and pearl-gray hats worn jauntily, he rode around Storm Lake in a big black Kissel automobile. Often his actors would also "do the town" in this impressive limousine. The car, allegedly on a par with a Cadillac, was a "showpiece in itself with its rich gray upholstery, its lace curtains and cut-glass vases that boasted fresh roses daily from Sam Kutz's greenhouse (Holmes, 1973)."

Since G. D. (as he was called) was not a performer himself, much of the company's acclaim went to his wife and daughter. Mrs. Guy Mills, of Sioux Rapids, saw a Sweet show at the Rossie Opera House in 1916 or 1917. She remembered that

> when Mrs. Sweet stepped out on the stage, the audience leaped to their feet and gave her such a warm welcome, because besides being an actress she was a very warm and gracious person. She would blow kisses to the crowd. Her daughter, Marjorie, was very much loved too. Often times the local people would decorate the stage with bouquets of lilacs or wild plum blossoms or other flowers in season (letter to Poole, 1 March 1983; see also Harold Holmes, interview with Poole, 8 June 1983).

O. Q. Setchell's Terry's Uncle Tom's Cabin *Company*

Terry's *Uncle Tom's Cabin* Company operated out of Little Sioux, Iowa, with various owners and casts from approximately 1893 until 1924. As far as we know it was the only "Tom show" originating out of Iowa at that time. *Uncle Tom's Cabin*, a novel by Harriet Beecher Stowe, was first dramatized in 1853. By the end of the century there were at least 500 touring *Uncle Tom's Cabin* companies (Henderson 1986). A staple of American theatre for 100 years, it provided white America with racially distorted images of black people, some of which, unfortunately, persist to the present day.

Little Sioux became part of the Uncle Tom history because O. Q. Setchell, a Barnum ringmaster and Little Sioux native, organized an *Uncle Tom's Cabin* Company in Lexington, Illinois, in 1870. He named it Terry's *Uncle Tom's Cabin* Company because he thought Terry, the name of his barber brother-in-law living in Little Sioux, would be a more memorable name. By 1893, the show was operating out of Little Sioux. Over the course of its lifetime, the company played tents and opera houses in Iowa, North and South Dakota, Minnesota, Wisconsin, Michigan, Illinois, and Indiana. In the beginning the company traveled by wagon. Later they traveled by train and truck. The first performance of the season was always given in Little Sioux in April. There would be a parade through the town in the afternoon preceding the evening performance. All the characters, on foot and on horse, took part. Some of the actors also served in one of the two bands which were part of the company. The black band had at least six members and the white one had at least 19. Originally, white performers portrayed the black characters in *Uncle Tom's Cabin* by "blacking up." That meant putting on black makeup and acting the part of black people in accordance with white stereotypes. A black man did not play the role of Uncle Tom in a serious production until 1878 when Sam Lucas portrayed him in one of the Frohman brothers' stock companies (Toll 1974, 217–18). This, however, was the exception rather than the rule. In Little Sioux, it was the rule rather than the exception. The Terry Uncle Tom was played by a black man from 1903 until at least 1928. *The Bicentennial History of Little Sioux Township* says it best:

> Terry's Uncle Tom, John Beecher, joined the show at St. Joseph, Missouri in 1903, as a roustabout. A few weeks later he was drafted for the role of Uncle Tom at the end of Act I to replace a Tom much the worse for gin. Beecher, or Bojangles as he was known in Little Sioux, was with the show for more than 25 consecutive seasons. He spent his winters in Little Sioux with the Dickey family, exercising the ponies, sometimes taking lucky children for rides and playing the trap drums and player piano for the movies at the Kerr Opera House. He was a quiet pleasant man and was generally accepted by the townspeople (1976, 46–53).

68

The Trousdale Family Players

The Trousdale Family Players were an Iowa institution for four decades. Originally from Estherville, Iowa, they performed in the Midwest, the West and Canada. According to Truly Trousdale Latchaw, daughter of one of the four Trousdale Brothers, the company began in 1895 in Estherville "as a family concert company with Swiss Bell ringing." From then until 1935, the four brothers, Winn Walton, Merle Mortimer, Earle Eugene, and Boyd Buckmaster, were involved in theatre. At one time they each had their own company. Sometimes they joined forces. They also acted with other companies. Accomplished musicians, they performed in standard plays, minstrel shows, musicals, and melodramas. They did three night stands, traveling repertory, and permanent repertory in Cedar Rapids. Also they have been credited with inventing the "Circle Stock" concept, where a company has a home base and performs one play in a circle of towns surrounding the home base for a week. The next week a new play was performed for those same towns and so on throughout the season. The Trousdales were immensely popular especially with their two most successful productions, *The Man on the Box* and *The Aviator*. When they played small town opera houses, they carried scenery with them made by Iowa scenic artist Jessie Cox, also of Estherville. According to Clarence A. Andrews, "they played in 235 towns in Iowa and in more than 50 in each of the following states: Nebraska, Minnesota, Wisconsin, and North and South Dakota" (Andrews 1982, 23–27). Finally, "as a family they brought clean wholesome entertainment to people in the midwest, who had no other means of finding it" (Truly Trousdale Latchaw, letter to Poole, 26 January 1983; see also Andrews 1982; Mickel 1974, 23–26).

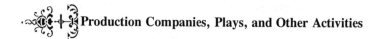 **Production Companies, Plays, and Other Activities**

Production Companies and Plays

The touring repertoire production companies were welcomed back year after year, particularly in small towns. Many times the performers were lodged with local citizens. They were greatly appreciated and even loved, and their appearances were eagerly awaited.

In the palmy days of "the road"—prior to World War I—when it was literally possible to get to anywhere from anywhere by railroad—hundreds of touring "combination" companies took to the rails every year. Later troupes took equal advantage of the automobile and paved roads to reach virtually every Iowa community.

Larger cities and towns, with the larger grand opera houses, would get the touring companies of the latest Broadway hits, or the companies of the great actors of the day. In the 1901–1902 season, Davenport, Waterloo, and Sioux City could have seen Hoyt's *A Texas Steer*, Bronson Howard's *Shenandoah, Ben Hur* (complete with double turntable for the chariot race), *Quo Vadis* (which even played in What Cheer), William Gillette's *Sherlock Holmes* with the author in the title role, as well as such great stars as ex-Augustan Daly star Ada Rehan, E. H. Sothern and Julia Marlowe, Ethel Barrymore, Henrietta Crossman, Sir Henry Irving, James K. Hackett (son of the great comedian James H. Hackett), Joseph Jefferson III (undoubtedly performing his *Rip van Winkle*), James A. Herne in his own hit play, *Shore Acres*, Maude Adams, May Irwin, Mme. Modjeska, Mrs. Leslie Carter, Minnie Maddern Fiske, Otis Skinner, and Richard Mansfield (Cahn 1901, xiv–xxv; Glenn 1988, 2).

Smaller cities, like Dubuque, Waterloo, Fort Dodge, Mason City, and Iowa Falls, might get some of the foregoing attractions, but were more likely to attract such secondary attractions as *Down on the Farm, Go-Won-Go Mohawk, Our New Minister, The Gay Mr. Goldstein*, and *The Katzenjammer Kids*, or perhaps such tried-and-true favorites as *Ten Nights in a Bar-Room, Uncle Tom's Cabin*, or *Way Down East* (*East Lynne* didn't seem to be touring from New York that year, but the odds are that a regional repertoire troupe was touring it) (Cahn 1901; Glenn 1988).

In addition to individual companies and stars, there were also many touring stock companies fanning out from New York, each company with a number of plays in its repertoire: in 1901–1902, for example, an opera house could have had for a week at a time such companies as the Alcazar Stock Company, the Bennett & Moulton Company, the Castle Square Theatre Stock Company, the Corse Payton Comedy Company (as well as the Corse Payton Stock Company and the Corse Payton Southern Stock Company—all Iowa-based but booking from New York), the Emergency Stock Company, and the Lyceum Stock Company, among others. All in all, over 300 combination companies and thirty stock companies were touring from New York that year. And if straight plays were not enough, there were in 1902 innumerable touring opera, extravaganza, vaudeville, and minstrel companies, with John Philip Sousa's Band to top it all off (Cahn 1901; Glenn 1988).

Small to medium sized houses, which couldn't afford a major New York company, or weren't located on a main rail line, were not bereft of entertainment and culture—there were many local and regional touring repertoire companies offering a wide variety of drama and comedy, often composed of old favorites and productions with a regional orientation. Iowans saw the Charles and Mary Slawson Players, the Trousdale Brothers (all of their troupes), the Al Gorel Company, the Hendersons, Tilton and Guthrie, G. D. Sweet Famous Players, Clint and Bessie Robbins, the Hatcher Family Players, Terry's *Uncle Tom's Cabin* Company, Rusco and Swift *Uncle Tom's Cabin* Company, Eilers *Uncle Tom's Cabin* Company, Hal Barber's Londale Theatre Company, Katherine Ridgeway and Company, the Hayward Celebrities, the Dick Ferris Company, Will H. Locke Company, the Tennesseeans, the Storm-Beaton Dramatic Company, Woodward Theatre Company, Beach and Bowers Company, Ford's Opera Company, Ralph Riggs Company, North Brothers Stock Company, the McNutt Sisters, the Cherry Sisters, Eugene Walters Company, Katie Putnam Troupe, Knapp Brothers—midget comedians, Andrews Opera Company, Worwicks Minstrels, the Spooner Company, and the Chase-Lister Company.

The repertoires of these companies included such favorite plays as *Mutt and Jeff in Panama, Sis Hopkins, Barriers Burned Away, Pecks Bad Boy, Si Perkins, Lena Rivers, Quincy Adams Sawyer, The Old Homestead, The Lost Heir of Linlithgow, A Bunch of Keys, Tony the Convict, Fruits of the Wine Cup, Ten Nights in a Bar-Room, The Count of Monte Cristo, Faust, The Wolf, The Girl and the Gawk, Gypsy Rover, The Home Seekers, The Rajah of Altara, Lena the Madcap, The Show Girl, The Candy Girl, The Wrong Mr. Wright, A Wise Member, Ole Oleson in Spiritland, The Warning Bell, The Royal Slave,* and *A Happy Night in Dixie.*

The Medicine Show

Another popular entertainment that frequently visited the Iowa opera house was the medicine show. It could be a one-man operation or an entire company. The driving force behind the medicine show was a pitchman who styled himself THE GREAT DOCTOR, a self-proclaimed appellation. This descendent of European mountebanks and smooth-talking quack doctors, pitched his wares in a loud and colorful voice. According to Brooks McNamara in his book *Step Right Up, An Illustrated History of the American Medicine Show*, the "natural home [of the medicine show] was the village square or a small town opera house, and the medicine showman's favorite audience a crowd of eager rustics" (1976, 16). Medicine showmen pitched such compounds as Lydia E. Pinkham's Vegetable Compound, Ayer's Sarsaparilla, or Kickapoo Indian Sagwa. These, and a host of other nostrums, were the stuff of which medicine shows were made. For the more modern and adventurous soul, Dr. Williams' Electric Pads were cures, it was claimed, for the following diseases and complaints: malaria, chills, biliousness, nervousness, rheumatism, sick headache, lung troubles, catarrh, palpation of the heart, wakefulness, piles, dyspepsia, liver complaint, pimples, female complaint, kidney disease, neuralgia, dizziness, indigestion, constipation, ague, and all diseases arising from impure blood or any imperfect action of the stomach, liver, kidneys or lungs. Incidentally, Dr. Williams', Electric Medicated Pads were made only by the Electric Pad Manufacturing Company of Brooklyn, New York (31).

According to the *Quimby 75th Anniversary Book*, medicine men sold boxes of candy containing "tiny prizes" which appealed to the children in the audience (146). Anita resident John Benham recalled that medicine showmen would sponsor a contest to see how much medicine town girls could sell. At the end of the week, the girl selling the most would win a prize which consisted of a bracelet, string of "pearls" or a cheap "diamond" ring (letter to Opera House Division, Iowa State Historical Department, 6 April 1978). Madge Peters of Lewis remembered that one medicine show also used a contest among local girls as a device to entice audiences to the show. The girls' names were posted and then at some point in the show the audience voted. Girls who received the most votes were given a prize. And "one young fellow was so determined to have his girl win that it got out of hand. 'Another 10 votes for Katy'—and again and again. It was a joke for years. I don't remember if she got the prize but she did marry the guy" (letter to Poole, 2 January 1984). Medicine show traditions continue in somewhat modernized form today with the "pitching" of over-the-counter remedies in countless newspaper and television advertisements.

Organizations

Organizations that met at the opera house or whose facilities either included an opera house or who included opera house activities (primarily entertainment) in their facility were: the Knights of Pythias, American Legion, Masons, *Germania Verein* (German organization to promote German culture and nationalism), *Denmarks Minde* (Danish Brotherhood), ZCBJ, CSPS (both Czechoslovakian societies), Modern Woodman, Elks, Eagles, Odd Fellows, Good Templars (primarily for young people), Red Men, Lions, Eastern Star, Rebekkas, Methodist Ladies Aid Society, Yeoman Lodge, Ku Klux Klan, the Woman's Christian Temperance Union, and the Camp Fire Girls.

Musical Programs

Opera house patrons could see home talent musicals, the Chicago Opera, Gilbert and Sullivan Company, Blind Boone—the Black pianist, the Philharmonic Company of Chicago, the Salisbury Orchestra of Chicago, and the Norwegian Violinists Ole Pheoboldi and Ole Bull. To a variety of bands they would square dance, waltz (regular, Home and Rye), two-step, cakewalk, quadrille (La Belle, Plain, Masonic, Cakewalk, Prairie Queen, Hot Time, and Sleigh Bells), Schottische, and Polka. They could also do something called the Fireman Dance.

Educational Programs

Many educational programs took place at the opera house. Often classes were held there when the old school house developed boiler problems, needed repairs or just did not have adequate facilities. Graduation exercises and high school plays were held in the biggest and fanciest space in town, the opera house, until the high school auditorium was built. Typically, graduation day exercises would take place on the flower-decorated stage of the opera house with the class motto on an overhead banner. The motto of the 1903 George, Iowa, graduation class was "Only a Commencement." That evening those graduating gave addresses entitled "American Statesman," "Woman's Hand in the Affairs of the World," "Nature," "Music," and "American Coal Fields." The whole program was interspersed with piano solos and male quartettes (*In and Around George* 1975, 70). The opera house also was the meeting place for the Farmers Institute, the Farmers Union, and the Domestic Sciences Institute. The Iowa State Extension Service Short Courses, Lyceum, and Chautauqua were all presented in the opera house.

Other Functions of the Opera House

We have listed a great many opera house activities. And this is just a sample! Unbelievable as it may seem, opera house space was used for still other things that did not fit in the above categories such as parties, roller skating, basketball games, wrestling meets, minstrel shows, temperance meetings, "Tom Thumb" weddings, speech contests, speakers of all kinds, magicians, hypnotists, wedding receptions, political rallies, home talent carnivals, knife throwers, box socials, magic lantern shows, trained animals, chalk talk artists, mind readers, church services, memorial services, election polling, silent movies and eventually talkies.

At the Alta Opera House, long-time resident Stella Kindwall remembered that "a room was provided in the basement [of the opera house] for a Rest Room for ladies from the country and their children to rest and wait for their husband while he did his business" (letter to Poole, 24 January 1983). The Knights of Pythias of Adair used to have an annual rabbit supper in the opera house. Churches were sometimes converted into opera houses (and vice versa). The Remsen Grand Opera House was originally St. Mary's Catholic Church. In Essex the opera house was originally a Baptist Church. The Wall Lake Opera House was a Methodist Episcopal Church until 1900. The Minden Opera House was used as a weather station, flying flags of different colors to indicate storm, wind, rain, and clear. And finally, at the Beaconsfield Opera House, Raymond Doty reported that, as a child, his parents would take him up to the opera house once a year on a lodge night. The other parents brought their children too. Hanging from the ceiling was a bunch of bananas. On the floor were crates of oranges. All the kids had to do was help themselves (Vera Lantz, letter to Poole, 1 September 1983).

Regardless of the various functions they fulfilled, opera houses were at the center of life, particularly in the rural areas of Iowa during the late nineteenth and early twentieth centuries. Dorothy Mills of Sioux Rapids recalled the impact of the Rossie Opera House:

These were the days before we had many cars and rather than miss a performance local people would walk or drive a team of horses not to miss one. If in winter they would have to dress warmly and overcoats were hung on nails at the back of the hall. When they would no longer hold them all they would pile them up on the floor. After the show what a scramble there would be to find the right overshoes, caps and coats.

When some of the larger companies came through some of the ladies attending would dress in the heighth [sic] of fashion and tried hard to make a good impression in front of those famous entertainers, even though they were just run of the mill country folks.

Romantically inclined young couples would seek the darker parts of the Opera House, so that the boy could casually slip his arm around his girl friend during some of the tender scenes of the play. Generally the girl had her mind on the dashing young hero of the play.

In between the acts the comedians took over and would tell some joke using the name of a local resident. This would always bring real belly-laughs from the men in the audience. But they always told good, clean jokes that were acceptable to the ladies present.

Boxes of candy kisses were sold during intermission. Many

boxes had small prizes and lucky were the ones that drew the large prize displayed near the stage.

No matter that the play was a serious drama, mystery or a comedy people were not ashamed to express their feelings by shedding a tear, laughing loudly, clapping their hands or cheering when patriotic scenes took place. They enjoyed and were carried away by the talents of these actors and actresses. The little curtain speeches always brought applause. The musicals brought the best of music and talented dancing girls as graceful and light on their feet performing many kinds of dancing, their dresses were beautiful all properly designed and their picture hats or be-flowered and ribbon hats would delight any maiden. The men wore straw hats and carried canes and could do many fancy steps leaving the echo of dancing feet always in your memory (letter to Poole, 1 March 1983).

Finally, Mrs. Edwin Seabury of Pisgah recalls her opera house days and the wonder and excitement of performances there:

Then there was the stage! I still see it in my mind's eye, as clear as the first day I appeared on it. Brightly painted scenery with local advertising. A roller front curtain, back and side scenery. Enough to delight the eye of one who was immersed in dramatic theatre as I was (my father's cousin "Mabel Eaton" was a Shakespearean Actress in New York City and Chicago—she was married to Wm. Farnum—prominent Stage and Movie star of Ben Hur fame, also "The Spoilers." I had photographs of her in different costumes which enthralled me!) Steps led up to each side of the stage from the hall and a large dressing room was built on the back of the Opera House. Even a small hole in the front curtain you could peek through, to see how big the crowd was. Excitement galore! A perfect set up for Professional and Hometown Dramatics!

As I look back at a rich and full life, doing the things I loved most, my mind goes back to where my love for the theatre started, "Our Pisgah Opera House" followed by the School Auditorium, sometimes Church, the neighboring town's Opera Houses and School Auditoriums and finally our "Little Theatre" at College and them back to the Opera Houses and School Auditoriums. They have played a big part in the lives of all of us! (letter to Poole, 19 August 1983).

The Decline of the Opera House

There were many reasons why the opera houses died. Traveling road shows and companies big and small had to face increased costs and competition from radio and movies. New school auditoriums made the once glamorous opera house look small, shabby and shopworn. Better cars and paved roads meant that small rural communities were no longer isolated and people could go to the county seats and even the big cities for their entertainment. And even in the big cities, once movies took hold, the decline was swift and merciless.

Now only a memory, the opera house served all the citizens faithfully and well. It was always more than just a space, particularly in those small rural communities when the actors came to town and the allurement was high. Respectful communication was the link between actors and audience. It seems fitting, therefore, that this chapter and our book should end with the following from Fred Oney Sweet, reminiscing in 1940 about the Hampton Opera House:

> The Rock of Gibraltar front curtain has gone the way of the fancy hitching post in front of the Harriman drug store. They built the movie theatre on the site where once stood the Phoenix Hotel. Modern youth need not pine for the next show to come along, for there is a new one every night, including Sundays. The films follow each other in such kaleidoscopic fashion that the plot of one is mixed with that of its predecessor. For scenery, the camera has caught everything that lies out of doors, and leading ladies smile photographically for the Hampton audience just as they do for those in the cities from coast to coast. Our romantic hero and heroines walked our streets, breathed our air, ate our food. They were not strips of celluloid packed tightly in tin boxes shipped to us from across the continent. (355).

4

A Catalog of the
Opera Houses of Iowa

he following is a listing by town and county (in parentheses) of all the known opera houses in Iowa, whether extant or not. The listing is certainly not comprehensive, for there are undoubtedly many more Iowa opera houses, both extant and nonextant, which are still unknown to us. This listing was compiled from a variety of sources, including: (1) information gathered through a statewide survey conducted by the authors and through additional correspondence; (2) on-site visitation and documentation of known extant opera houses by the authors; (3) information gathered from John B. Jeffrey, *Guide and Directory to the Opera Houses, Theatres, Public Halls, Bill Posters, etc., of the Cities and Towns of America,* 11 editions, Chicago, 1879–1890; Julius Cahn, *Julius Cahn's Official Theatrical Guide, Containing Information of the Leading Theatres and Attractions in America,* 13 editions, New York, 1896–1909; *The Cahn-Leighton Official Theatrical Guide, 1912–1913,* New York; *Gus Hill's National Theatre Directory, 1914,* New York; and *Julius Cahn–Gus Hill Theatrical Guide and Moving Picture Directory, 1921,* New York; and (4) information from the Iowa State Historical Society, the Museum of Repertoire Americana, and a num-

ber of county historical societies and museums, municipal libraries, city and county histories, and privately published histories and accounts.

In the following listing, the names of opera houses that are still standing are in **boldface**. Dates of construction or renaming are as precise as we could obtain; in most cases a "ca." date indicates the first (if not the only) year that the opera house was listed in one of the guides (Jeffrey, Cahn, etc.). Following the date of construction or renaming is the range of dates for which the opera house was listed in the yearly guides. When known, the manager and other personnel are listed at the end of the entry: some opera houses had more than one manager over the years during which the house was listed in the various guides. Other personnel are included as they appear in the listings, e.g., stage carpenter, property ("prop") man, electrician, scenic artist, orchestra leader. The first name listed is that most closely associated with the first date we have of the opera house's existence; subsequent changes in personnel include the date of the change in parentheses. Thus, for an opera house that opened in 1898, we might list "Sam Jones, Fred Smith (1904), stage carpenters." This would indicate that Sam Jones was stage carpenter from 1898–1904, while Fred Smith was stage carpenter from 1904 on.

It is apparent that some of the discrepancies in the guides, both of names of opera houses and of names of individuals, are a result of poor penmanship on the part of the original compiler of the information.

It is inevitable that we have listed the same opera house under two or more different names. New owners or managers invariably renamed the theatre, and because none of the theatrical guides listed dimensions in exactly the same way (and given that contemporary renovation could easily change dimensions in any case), it was often impossible to determine if two or more opera houses in a town were actually different theatres or only the same theatre under different names. To err on the safe side, we listed them all as if they were separate theatres.

We would greatly appreciate receiving further information about any of these opera houses, and we would certainly like to know if we have missed any, whether extant or nonextant.

Ackley (*Franklin*)
> City Hall, ca. 1883 (1883–1889). The stage was 30' wide and 14' deep; capacity was 300. The stage was equipped with one drop curtain. Mgrs. Martin & Faust (1886); F. Perkiewicz (1889).
> **Plaza/Strand**, ca. 1915; 621 Main. Two-story brick, front measures 27'. Operated as a movie theatre until 1969. Now a law office, completely remodeled inside.

Adair (*Guthrie*)

> Adair Opera House, ca. 1912 (1912–1921). By ca. 1914, had a capacity of 450. Mgr. I. J. Swarzman.

Adel (*Dallas*)

> Adel Opera House, ca. 1912 (1912–1921). A ground-floor house, with a 28' wide × 20' high proscenium opening; the stage was 50' wide, 30' deep and 50' high. It had 110 v, 50 amp electrical service. It had two balconies; the auditorium seated 248, the balconies 294; stage boxes seated an additional 32 (total: 574). 4 dressing rooms. By ca. 1914, stage height 30'. Seating capacity 610. Mgr. J. C. Ikenberry (1912–1914), R. O. Roby (1921).
>
> McLaughlin's Opera House, ca. 1886. The stage was 42' wide × 17' deep. It had good scenery. Total capacity was 600. Mgr. D. B. Mclaughlin.

Afton (*Union*)

> Afton Opera House, ca. 1912 (1912–1914) a second-floor house, with a total capacity of 410 (344 on the main floor and 66 in the balcony). The proscenium opening was 22' × 14'; the stage was 44' wide and 17'6" deep, with a 2'6" apron. Gas light. 4 dressing rooms. Mgr. O. B. Emerson (1912), Frank Bolinger (1914–19??)
>
> Johnson's Hall, ca. 1883, had a small stock of scenery and seated 300.

Agency City (*Wapello*)

> Chamberlain's Hall, ca. 1883 (1883–1889), seated 250. "Small stock of scenery."

Ainsworth (*Washington*)

> **Ainsworth Opera House**, 256 N. Railroad. Single-story brick, 36' × 66'; gutted inside.

Akron (*Plymouth*)

> **Akron Opera House**, 1905. Located in a two-story brick building erected in 1905 and opened in 1906 by the American Insurance Company of Des Moines. Offices and businesses were on the first floor and part of the second. The opera house was on the balance of the second floor. The building dimensions are 46' × 90' with a front elevation of 48'. The seating capacity was 600. It had a parquet, balcony and gallery. The stage was 22' deep. The proscenium opening is 22'. The proscenium height is 16'. There was one dressing room on either side of the stage. Scenery was painted by the Flour City Scenic Company of Minneapolis. Vacant for many years it was renovated and is currently being used by the Akron Community Theatre.

Albia (*Monroe*)

> **King's Opera House**, 1903 (1903–1908). Two-story brick, 50' × 100'; rebuilt in 1921, although the side walls are original. Originally the proscenium was 24' wide × 24' high; footlights to back wall, 32'; height to rigging loft, 48'; height to fly gallery, 26'. Seating capacity was 1000.
>
> In 1908, the theatre seated 390 in the orchestra, 158 in the balcony, and 200 in the gallery (total: 748). The proscenium was

30' wide × 24' high; stage was 66' wide × 50' high × 30' deep; 2' apron; 60' between fly girders; 6'6" depth under the stage; 2 traps, center. 24' to fly gallery. 8 dressing rooms. Electric lights. Whitehead, prop man; Hall, stage carpenter, Taylor, orchestra leader—6 in orchestra.

In 1912, seating capacity was 425 on the lower floor, 158 in the balcony, 200 in the gallery and 48 in the boxes (total: 831). The proscenium was 24' wide × 30' high; stage was 66' wide × 50' high × 30' deep; 5' apron; 6'6" under stage. It was 60' between fly girders and 25' to the fly gallery. 8 dressing rooms. Gas and electric light (4 stage pockets).

After alterations, the proscenium now is 27' wide × 16' high; curtain line to back, 16'; 4' apron; 12' wing space; height to rigging loft 22'. It now seats 332 on the main floor and 180 in the balcony (total: 512). Now operating and being restored as Barbary Coast Opera House. The balcony has the original seats. Mgrs: Payton & Swearengen, Elbert Payton (1908), Mr. Hardenbrook.

King Theatre, ca. 1908. (1908–1921). Same as **King's Opera House.** Mgr. Elbus Payton, R. Hanson (1921).

Perry Townsend's Opera House, 1874 (1883–1905), W. side of square on Clinton St. Three-story brick, 54' × 120'. The interior dome is still there, but is virtually inaccessible after extensive interior remodeling. Originally the proscenium was 24' × 24'; the stage was 22' deep × 44' wide. Height to the grooves was 16'. Oil lighting. De Long, scenic artist. Piano in orchestra (organ, 1886). Sonny Williams, of the first-floor Williams Clothing Store, has copies of programs and photo of dome decoration. Also known as Perry's Opera House. Mgrs. J. E. Townsend, S. W. Pennington (1896), Dave A. Martin (1903).

Siefert's Hall, ca. 1883 (1883–1889). Mgr. Chas. E. Griffin.

Alden (*Hardin*)

Alden Opera House, ca. 1870. Two-story brick and limestone building, 18' × 80'. It was a second-floor hall; now remodeled into apartments.

Alexander (*Franklin*)

Community Hall, burned ca. 1942.

Algona (*Kossuth*)

Call Opera House, ca. 1896 (1896–1921). A first floor hall seating 600. Prices $0.25–$1. The proscenium was 21' wide × 20' high; the stage was 46' wide × 27' deep × 31' high, with a 3' apron. 39' between fly girders. It was equipped with four 16' grooves and 4 traps. 11' depth under stage. Illumination was oil. By ca. 1900 it was electric. By ca. 1904, proscenium was 27' wide. By ca. 1908, seating capacity was 650. By ca. 1912, proscenium was 25' wide × 20' high. Stage was 48' wide × 25' deep × 50' high, 5' apron. 6 dressing rooms. By ca. 1914, seating capacity was 600. Stage 46' wide × 39' high × 33' deep. W. E. McMurray, stage carpenter and prop man. W. E. McMurray (1897), Wm. Ward (1904–1905),

Walter Ward (1907–1909), stage carpenters. Tony Little (1897–1899), Edgar Little (1901–1904), prop men. Orchestra leader, D. Walker (1896), Joe Power (1900), O. Johnson (1904–1905), John Scott (1907), Fernly Niconlin (1908–1909); 6–10 in orchestra. Mgrs. C. H. Blossom, Jos. W. Wadsworth (1899), J. L. Donahoo (1900), Jos. W. Wadsworth (1903), Chester C. Call (1904–1905), Roscoe Call (1907), G. A. Brunson (1914–19??), N. C. Rice (1921).

Court House, ca. 1886. Stage ca. 1889, 18′ × 26′, seated 500. Mgr. J. C. Frank.

Wilson's Hall, ca. 1886.

Allerton (*Wayne*)

Trinity Hall, ca. 1889, seated 200. Mgr. J. W. Rankin.

Vest's Hall, ca. 1889, seated 150. Mgr. S. L. Vest.

Allison (*Butler*)

Allison Opera House, No. Main St.

Alpha (*Fayette*)

Alpha Opera House, 1912, Main St. Single-story frame, now serving as a feed storage shed. Building is 30′6″ × 60′6″. The stage was removed ca. 1965, but it is possible to tell that the stage was about 12′ deep. The main floor measures 29′ × 47′. Remnants of stenciled decoration remain on the side walls and ceiling.

Alta (*Buena Vista*)

Alta Theatre, ca. 1908 (1908–1914). A first floor house, the main floor seated 318 and the balcony 167 (total: 485). The proscenium was 22′ × 18′; the stage was 45′ wide × 24′ deep × 36′ high, with a 4′ apron. Lighting was electrical. By ca. 1914, seating capacity was 515. Stage was 59′ wide × 38′ high × 22′ deep. O. Swanson (1908) electrician and prop man. 5 in orchestra; Alf Larson (1908), leader. Mgr. A. L. Denio (1908–1909), L. A. Rader (1914).

Alton (*Sioux*)

Alton Opera House (Hoxmeier), 1891, 203 10th St. Second floor of a two-story brick, 60′ × 45′6″. The main floor is 50′ × 40′9″. The proscenium width is 19′11½″. The proscenium height varies from 7′ to 11′1″ in the center. The curtain line to back wall is 10′6½″. Two dressing rooms are off left. They are 8′4″ × 8′4″ and 9′10″ × 8′. Both are 15′ high. The dressing room off right is 17′ × 8′3″. The stage is 2′11″ higher than the main floor. There are two traps. One is 3′ × 3′. The other was not measurable. There are three sets of ceiling grooves 4′ long on stage left and right, and also pulleys downstage, midstage, and upstage right and left. Currently it is storage for Braun's Hardware below.

Alvord (*Lyon*)

Alvord Opera House, 1908. Financed by selling shares to the public at $10 per share. It is a one-story block building. The block, which comes in 2′ × 1′ sections, was made in near-by Rock Rapids, Iowa. The stage is 3′8″ higher than the main floor. The proscenium opening is 17′½″. The proscenium height is 13′8″ to 14′. The curtain line to the back wall is 15'. Offstage left and right is 10'. Currently it is used as a community hall.

Ames (*Story*)

Ames Armory Theatre, ca. 1912 ("reported closed," 1914), a first floor house with a capacity of 772 (500 on the main floor and 272 in 2 balconies). The proscenium was 24' wide × 16' high; the stage was 48' wide × 24' deep × 26' high, with a 2' apron. It was 42' between fly galleries; 16' to the fly galleries. 7 dressing rooms. Electric light. Mgr. C. E. Bartholomew.

Ames Opera Hall, ca. 1883 (1883–1889), 233 Main. Two-story brick/stucco, 27' × 102'. Stage was 25' wide × 35' deep; seating capacity 500. "Good scenery." Mgrs. Bradley & Reed.

Princess Theatre, ca. 1921, seated 500. The stage was 36' wide × 25' deep × 36' high. Electric light. It was equipped with a 10' × 12' movie screen 85' from the projector. Mgr. J. Gerbrach.

Scenic Theatre, 1893, 121 Main. Two-story brick, 54' × 96'.

Anamosa (*Jones*)

Grand Opera House, ca. 1896 (1896–1921), E. Main St. Now the Evans Theatre, the three-story limestone/brick building measures 40' 6" × 136'. It was remodeled inside after a fire in the 1940s; the proscenium now is 32' wide × 20' high; stage is 20' deep, 36' wide. Originally the proscenium was 24' wide × 24' high; footlights to back wall, 25'; curtain line to footlights, 5', distance between side walls, 50'; 35' between fly girders. Rigging loft, 35', 18' high grooves. 15' depth under stage, 1 trap, center. Grooves could be taken up flush with fly gallery. Seated 850. In 1921 it had a 16'6" × 12' movie screen; 60' throw. Building was further damaged by fire in Jan. 1984. Mgrs. C. R. Howard, Clifford L. Niles (1907).

Holt's Opera Hall, ca. 1883 (1883–1889), seated 400. Stage was 22' wide × 18' deep. It had a "fair amount of scenery."

Lehmkuhl's Hall, ca. 1878 (1878–1889), seated 300. Stage was 12' wide × 16' deep.

Angus (*Boone*)

Bacon's Opera House, ca. 1883. A first floor house with a capacity of 600, equipped with Andrews folding opera chairs. The stage was 44' wide × 32' deep. There were 11 flats, 3 set rocks and a set cottage. Green room and dressing rooms were under the stage.

Thomas Opera House, ca. 1886, had a capacity of 450, and had chairs. The stage was 40' wide × 16' deep and was equipped with 6 scenes. There was an organ. Mgr. L. B. Thomas.

Whitney's Hall, ca. 1883, seated 400. The stage was 23' wide and 20' deep, with 7 scenes and a drop curtain.

Anita (*Cass*)

Anita Opera House, ca. 1886.

Johnson Theatre, ca. 1903 (1903–1909), was a first floor house seating 600. The proscenium was 16' high × 16' wide; the stage was 35' wide and 32' deep, and was equipped with 10 grooves. May be

82

taken up flush with fly gallery. Gas lighting. H. Schaake (1903),
Vern Cochran (1908), stage carpenters. D. Donohue (1903), H.
Millhollin (1908), prop men. 5–8 in orchestra; leader, Professor
Rasmusser (1903), Professor C. Carson (1908). Mgr. H. H. Cate
(1903).

New Majestic Theatre, ca. 1912 (1912–1914), a first floor house seating
450 (400 on the main floor and 50 in the balcony). The proscenium
was 23′ wide × 12′ high; the stage was 35′ wide × 28′ deep with
a 2′ apron. Electric lighting. Mgr. H. H. Cate (1912).

Rink Opera House, ca. 1889, seated 1200. Mgr. C. M. Meyers.

Rood's Opera House, ca. 1889, a brick second-story house, 24′ × 70′.
Seating capacity was 400. By 1896 seating capacity was 250. The
proscenium was 10′ wide. The stage was 24′ wide × 15′ deep, with
a 5′ apron. Oil lighting. Opera house burned down in the teens.
Mgr. J. E. Bruce or J. C. Voorhes (1889), Jas. E. Bruce (1896–
1902).

Unique Theatre, ca. 1921. A first floor house seating 450. Stage was 30′
wide × 35′ deep. Mgr. George Schwenker.

Opera House, ca. 1886.

Anthon (*Woodbury*)

Anthon Opera House, 108 S. 2nd St. One-story brick structure, 24′3″
× 100′4″. Currently the building is a veterinary clinic.

Arlington (*Fayette*)

Arlington Opera House, ca. 1896 (1896–1909), a first-story house
seating 500. The proscenium was 20′ wide × 14′ high; the stage
was 36′ wide × 18′ high × 23′ deep with a 2′ apron. 30′ between
fly girders. 5′ depth under stage. It was equipped with three 12′
grooves and a trapdoor, center. By 1898, stage depth was 33′ deep.
Mgrs. R. N. Hibbard (1896), Frank Hutchinson (1898), R. N.
Hibbard (1903).

Armstrong (*Emmet*)

Armstrong Opera House, ca. 1904 (1904–1913), ground-floor house
seating 550. Proscenium was 20′ wide × 24′ high; stage was 26′
deep with a 4′ apron. Gas lighting. By ca. 1913, proscenium was
20′ wide × 25′ high; stage 35′ wide × 30′ high × 25′ deep, 6′
apron. Six 16′ grooves. 4 dressing rooms. Mgrs. Fleming and
Kingston (1904–1909), F. J. Gibbons (1912–1913).

Gibbons Opera House, ca. 1914, a ground-floor house seating 550. The
stage was 36′ wide × 20′ high × 25′ deep. Mgr. G. J. Gibbons.

Arthur (*Ida*)

Arthur Opera House, 1918. This single-story building had a seating
capacity of 250. It has been extensively remodeled.

Ashton (*Osceola*)

Ashton Opera House.

Aspinwall (*Crawford*)

Aspinwall Opera House. Burned.

Atalissa (*Muscatine*)

Speer's Hall, ca. 1901. Burned.

Good Temperance Temple, ca. 1850, burned ca. 1901.

Atkins (*Benton*)

Atkins Opera House, Main St.

Atlantic (*Cass*)

Academy of Music, ca. 1889, seated 250. Mgr. R. H. Bigler or R. H. Bailey.

(Atlantic) Opera House, ca. 1889. Ground-floor house seating 500 on the main floor and 200 in the balcony; equipped with opera chairs. Proscenium was 21' wide × 18' high; stage was 45' wide × 20' high × 35' deep, with five 13' grooves and 14 sets scenery. There was a piano. Could be the same house as Bacon Opera House.

Bacon Opera House (also called The Opera House or The Atlantic Opera House), 1880. Built by Horace E. Bacon in association with A. A. Hubbard and A. E. Stevens. It was a brick building 47' × 100' with a stage 32' wide × 44' deep; seating capacity 600. Proscenium opening 20', height to grid 13', to loft, 20'. Furnished with Andrews opera chairs. 11 scenes, three set rocks and cottage. It was sold to O. C. Johnson and completely remodeled, no date available. In ca. 1889, the stage was 25' × 35', proscenium opening 18' × 24'; height to grid, 14'; to loft, 20'. Seated 500 on ground floor and 200 in gallery; 14 sets scenery. It burned in 1929 and was remodeled incorporating the remaining side walls. There are conflicting reports as to current usage. Some say it was torn down. Some say it currently is a movie theatre. Mgr. H. E. Bacon (1883–1886).

Atlanta, also known as Atlantic, Opera House, ca. 1896, (1896–1921), ground-floor house seating 500. Proscenium was 23' wide × 18' high; stage was 48' wide × 18' high × 30' deep, with four 14' grooves and a trap. Depth under stage 9'. By ca. 1900, seating capacity 528. By ca. 1903, proscenium 22' wide; stage 44' wide × 22' high × 30' deep. Five 13' grooves. By ca. 1907, seating capacity 600. By ca. 1914, stage was 45' wide × 20' high × 30' deep. Mgr. Lester L. Tilden (1896), C. P. Hubbard (1901–1909), W. P. Frost (1914–19??), Fred Herbert (1921).

Whitney's Hall, ca. 1883. Stage size 20' × 23'. Seven scenes and drop curtain. Mgr. F. H. Whitney.

Auburn (*Sac*)

Auburn Opera House.

Audubon (*Audubon*)

Amusement Hall, ca. 1889, was an old skating rink, seated 200. Mgr. Ed Delahoyde.

Court House Hall, ca. 1889, seated 600 in opera chairs. Has 7 sets scenery.

Russell Opera House, 1888. Built by George B. Russell. It is a three-story brick building with the opera house on the third floor. The building dimensions are 30' × 80'; seating capacity is 600. Currently the lower floor houses retail shops, while the upper story is probably apartments or storage.

Aurelia (*Cherokee*)

    Skating Rink and Hall, ca. 1889. Mgr. E. Daniel.

Avoca (*Pottawattamie*)

    Avoca Opera House, 215 N. Elm. (1883–1889) Two-story brick, 20' × 58'. Currently the lower floor is a True Value Hardware and the upper is empty and gutted. Ca.1883, stage size 18' × 38', seating capacity 450. Mgrs. Coffman and Harlow (1883), A. W. Coffman (1889).

Ayrshire (*Palo Alto*)

    Ayrshire Opera House.

Baldwin (*Jackson*)

    Baldwin Opera House/Griffin Building. Three-story frame, 25' × 54'. Hall was on the second floor. The proscenium is 26'10" wide × 9'3" high; curtain line to back is 10'4". The main floor measures 41'6" × 26'10". A ticket-window is in a door in the hall at the top of the stairs.

Bancroft (*Kossuth*)

    (Bancroft) Opera House, ca. 1912 (1912–1921). Ground-floor hall seating 350. Proscenium was 18' wide × 12' high. Stage was 36' wide × 14' deep with a 4' apron. Gas light. Mgr. P. A. Lourigan (1912).

    Idle Hour Theatre, ca. 1912, So. side of Main St. The 1976 *History of Kossuth County* states that it was a frame building, operating by 1912. It most likely was a movie house as well as a community hall. After going through numerous renovations and name changes it still operates today as a movie house. Could be the same as the Bancroft Opera House.

Barnes City (*Mahaska*)

    Barnes City Opera House, ca. 1920. Two-story brick, 30' × 70'; gutted inside. Was constructed from leftover bricks from building the school in 1920.

Batavia (*Jefferson*)

    Batavia Opera House, on the east side of the street across from the post office. Burned.

Battle Creek (*Ida*)

    Luna Theatre, 1914. It was built by Joe Warnock and Frank Campbell. The building dimensions are 121' × 32'. Extensively remodeled. Currently, storage and apartments.

    Rink Hall, ca. 1886, seated 500. Mgr. A. V. McKown (1889).

Baxter (*Jasper*)

    Klise Opera Hall, 102 N. Main. Lower story remains; upper floor burned in 1956.

    Smith's Hall, ca. 1886 (1886–1889), seated 500.

Bayard (*Guthrie*)

    Bayard Opera House. Burned.

Beaconfield (*Ringgold*)

    Rhoades Opera House. Burned.

Beaman (*Grundy*)

Beaman Opera House, 1909 (1912–1914). Two-story concrete block (made on the site), 36' × 91'. The hall was on the second floor; seating capacity was 300. The proscenium was 18' wide × 19' deep; curtain line to back was 19'. There was 7' offstage R and 9' offstage L, and a 1' apron. Electric lighting. There were four dressing rooms. The main floor measures 34' × 54'. An elevator is backstage. The interior is now completely altered. Three roll drops on the site are now in the Museum of Repertoire Americana, Mt. Pleasant. Mgr. Geo. G. Hotchenk, George A. Hitchcock (1914).

Opera House, ca. 1889, seats 300. Mgr. R. A. Watt.

Bedford (*Taylor*)

Bedford Town Hall, ca. 1889, seated 600.

Clark's, ca. 1914, seated 720. Ground floor. Stage was 64' wide × 59" high × 30' deep. By ca. 1921, seating capacity 600. Stage 66' wide × 48' high × 30' deep. Mgr. John Clark (1914–19??), John Wallen (1921).

Steele Opera House, ca. 1883, seated 600. Stage was 30' wide and 26' deep. Had an organ. By 1889, seated 700. Mgr. Charles Steele.

Belle Plaine (*Benton*)

(Belle Plaine) Opera House, ca. 1903 (1903–1914). Second-story house seating 397 on the main floor, 250 in the balcony and 50 in the boxes (total: 697); prices $0.25, $0.35, $0.50. Proscenium was 22' wide × 24' high; stage was 45' wide × 28' high × 23' deep, with a 3' apron. There were four 14' grooves and 3 traps. 4 dressing rooms. Electric lighting. E. Hunt (1907), J. E. Livings (1908), electricians. J. M. Moore, Ed Froudel (1908), stage carpenters and prop men. Mgrs. J. C. Milner, O. C. Trueblood (1912), W. C. Hippler (1914).

Phoenix Hall, ca. 1883 (1883–1889), seated 600. Stage was 20' wide × 19' deep. Had 9 sets of scenery on flats. Organ in the house. Mgr. Wm. A. Hunter.

Bellevue (*Jackson*)

City Hall, ca. 1889, seated 400. Mgr. C. Kucheman.

Kocheman Hall, ca. 1883 (1883–1886), seated 350. Operated by the German Theatrical Society. Mgr. German Theatrical Society.

Belmond (*Wright*)

Metropolitan Hall, ca. 1889, seated 1000. Mgr. J. C. Butterfield.

Rink Hall, ca. 1886, seated 800.

Bennett (*Cedar*)

Dettman's Hall, ca. 1900, burned in 1928.

Benton (*Ringgold*)

Benton Opera House.

Bettendorf (*Scott*)

Bettendorf Theatre, ca. 1911, West State and 1st St.

Blairsburg (*Hamilton*)

Blairsburg Opera House, ca. 1910. Single-story brick, bank was in front, opera house in back. Measures 58'6" × 140'. Interior remodeled into a bar, but the stage remains; proscenium was 21′6″ wide × 8′6″ high; curtain line to back was 11′. 5′6″ offstage R and L There were footlights immediately before the curtain. Four dressing rooms. Main floor 50′ × 44′.

Blairstown (*Benton*)

Blairstown Opera House, ca. 1914 (1914–1921). Now the American Legion Hall, the 40′ × 120′ aluminum-sided single-story frame building has been completely remodeled inside. It had a seating capacity of 350; the proscenium opening was 32′ wide × 12′ high; the stage was 32′ wide × 12′ high × 16′ deep. Mgrs. W. H. Wood, T. H. Weil (1921).

Brian Opera House, ca. 1904 (1904–1913) seated 600. Ground-floor hall. Proscenium was 20′ wide × 12′ high; stage was 36′ wide × 20′ high × 17′ deep with a 1′ apron. 30′ between fly girders. 3′ depth under stage. Grooves may be taken up flush with fly girders. No scene room. It had seven 10′ grooves. Electric lighting. G. W. Pardey, electrician, stage carpenter, prop man. In 1907, Walter Lee, prop man and stage carpenter, Pardey still electrician. B. F. Paul, orchestra leader; 3–8 in orchestra. Mgr. G. W. Hardey or Pardey (Dr. J. T. Porter, ass't mgr., 1907).

Blakesburg (*Monroe*)

Blakesburg Opera House. Two-story frame, 100′ × 45′.

Blanchard (*Page*)

Blanchard Opera House. Burned.

Blockton (*Taylor*)

(Opera House) on King St. Was used for movies and possibly for stage shows. May be extant.

Blockton Opera House, 1886, on Division St. Second-story of a two-story brick structure, 46′ × 70′. It has a balcony which seated 100. Currently it is occupied by the Blockton Oil Company. There is another building on King Street, now used for storage, where movies were shown and stage entertainments may have taken place there as well.

Bloomfield (*Davis*)

(**Pettit Law Office**), 110 S. Madison. Original name of the theatre unknown, but this two-story brick building, with a front of 36′, is old enough to be Taylor's Opera House, (ca. 1883).

(**Sears Catalog Center**), 110 E. Franklin. This building is also old enough to be Taylor's. It is two-story brick, 36′ × 75′. Entrance to the back of the building through the next-door NAPA Auto Parts store brings one to a storage room with theatrical graffiti on the walls ("Musical Monroes, Sept. 18-19-20 1913"; "Ralph Richards and his Hi-Class Vaudeville Co., 1913"; "George Cole, 1913," etc.).

Idle Hour Theatre, ca. 1914, 107 So. Washington. Two-story brick, now a movie theatre. The stage was originally 18′ deep × 34′ wide × 38′ high. Seating capacity was 700. Mgr. J. Howard Newell.

Taylor's Opera House, ca. 1883 (1883–1889), seated 300. "Good stage and scenery." Mgr. J. A. Taylor (1883); J. H. Taylor & Sons (1889).

Wishard Theatre, ca. 1921, seated 490. Had a 20' wide proscenium; stage was 36' wide × 32' high × 16' deep. 9' × 12' screen, 66' throw. B. Watts, stage carpenter; Helen Wishard, orchestra leader. Mgr. H. A. Wishard.

Blue Grass (*Scott*)

Blue Grass Opera House, ca. 1910, was on the corner of Juanita and Garonne. Stage was 36' wide × 32' high × 16' deep. Torn down in 1919.

Bonaparte (*Van Buren*)

Whiteley Store and Opera House, 1894. Two-story brick with tin facing, 46' × 86'. Theatre was on second floor. Built in 1894–1895 by J. W. Whiteley, a former member of the Queen's Band before coming to the U.S. The theatre has been gutted, but it is possible to tell that the proscenium was 26' wide and the stage was 26' deep. The capacity was reportedly 250 on the main floor and 150 in the gallery. The exterior has been restored to its original appearance; the first-floor interior has been divided into offices and meeting halls. The opera house space on the upper floor remains empty.

Bondurant (*Polk*)

McCleary Hall, 1907. Two-story brick, 44'6" × 80'6". Remodeled inside.

Boone (*Boone*)

(Boone) Opera House, ca. 1886, seated 500. Mgrs. Guzman and Knight. Airdome.

Arie Opera House, 1900 (1900–1914), a ground-floor house, seated 704. The proscenium was 26' wide × 14'6" high; the stage was 47' wide × 22' high × 25' deep, with a 5' apron. There was 1 trap. Electric lighting. The first time Cahn lists Arie is in the 1900–1901 Guide. All Arie statistics are exactly the same as the ones Cahn listed for the Phipps Opera House the year before in the 1889–1900 Guide. According to the September 13, 1965 centennial edition of the *Boone News Republican* newspaper, the Arie burned January 8, 1915. See Phipps' Opera House, Boone. John McClay (1900–1908) prop man. G. H. Bowen (1900), John Duncan (1903–1908), stage carpenters. By ca. 1903, proscenium was 30' × 20'; stage 48' wide × 52' high × 31' deep; 5' apron. Seating capacity 950. Depth under stage 12'. 10 dressing rooms. By ca. 1913, seating capacity was 933. Proscenium was 20' wide × 20' deep; stage was 48' wide × 52' high × 30' deep. By ca. 1914, stage was 48' high, seating capacity 950. Mgrs. Ben B. Wiley (1900), Wiley and Kirby (1903–1905), Ben B. Wiley (1907–1914).

City Hall, ca. 1883 (1883–1889), had a good stage, opera chairs, and a fair stock of scenery. Mgr. H. Sutton. (1883), A. K. Wells (1886), R. Sutton (1889).

Metropolitan Hall, ca. 1878, seated 400. Stage was 16' wide × 20' deep. Mgr. A. K. Wells.

Phipps' Opera House, ca. 1889 (1889–1899), ground-floor house seating
800. Jeffery's (1889) lists the following measurements: stage 26′ ×
37′; proscenium opening 26′; height to grid 14′; to loft, 24′. There
were 12 sets of scenery. House was equipped with opera chairs and
a piano. In ca. 1896, Cahn lists the following measurements:
proscenium 26′ × 14′6″; stage 47′ wide, 22′ high, 25′ deep; height
to loft 22′. 5′ apron. Illumination electric. By ca. 1897, seating
capacity was 704. H. E. Belden (1896), John McClay (1897), prop
men. G. H. Bowen (1897), stage carpenter. E. A. Turner (1898),
electrician. Mgr. Fred L. Shelters (1889), O. B. Phipps (1896),
Wiley, Phipps and Kirby (1898), Ben Wiley (1899). Remodeled and
became Arie's Opera House in 1900.

Sherman's Hall, ca. 1889, in the 15th ward.

Virginia Theatre, ca. 1921, ground-floor hall, seated 500, with 1
balcony. Proscenium was 18′ wide × 30′ high; stage was 40′ wide
× 35′ high × 20′ deep. Electric lighting. Mgr. Geo. B. Flint.

Boonesboro (*Boone*)

Union Hall, ca. 1878, capacity 400. Boonesboro was located 1½ miles
from Boone.

Bouton (*Dallas*)

Bouton Opera House, ca. 1914, burned ca. 1914.

Boxholm (*Boone*)

Boxholm Opera House, 1914. A two-story brick building erected by
John Anderson, Ed Olson, and Elmer Thorngren. First floor used
as theatre. Building stands but extensively remodeled. Current
building dimensions 80′ × 30′. Vacant.

Boyden (*Sioux*)

Boyden Town Hall.

Bradgate (*Humboldt*)

Public Hall, ca. 1878, seated 400. Mgr. A. E. Marchant (1886).

Braman (*unknown*)

Public Hall, ca. 1886. Mgr. M. J. Braman.

Breda (*Carroll*)

Breda Opera House, 1915. Built by the Breda Opera House Association. The building was to be 46′ × 100′; walls 20′ high; basement
22′ × 46′; steel gallery 30′ × 46′. It was two stories high and built
with a pressed brick front. It was erected on the site of an older
building and as much of the old building as possible was incorporat-
ed into the new. Purchased and remodeled by the Breda American
Legion, it is currently used by them.

Brighton (*Washington*)

Carroll Hall, ca. 1886 (1886–1909), second-story hall, seated 200.
Proscenium was 14′ wide × 9′ high; stage was 23′ wide × 16′
deep. Mgrs. E. W. Swisher (1896), S. N. Bice (1898), J. B. Dey
(1900), R. W. Pringle (1903).

Club House, ca. 1912. (1912–1914), ground-floor house. Proscenium
was 20′ wide × 12′ high; stage was 36′ wide × 18′ deep. Gasoline

lighting. By ca. 1914, stage was 34' wide × 18' high × 18' deep. Torn down in 1941. Mgrs. Tracey, Johnson & Day (1912), Johnson, Day and Helmick (1914).

Friend's Hall, ca. 1886, seated 300. Mgr. G. M. Smith.

Nichols' Opera House, ca. 1889, seated 500. Mgrs. D. Nichols & Son.

Swisher's Hall, ca. 1889, seated 300. Same as Carroll Hall. Mgr. E. W. Swisher.

Terry's Opera House, ca. 1889, seated 500.

Bristow (*Butler*)

Bristow Opera House, 719 West St. Two-story brick, measuring 50' × 60'6". Completely remodeled inside, it now houses Barbie's Lounge.

Britt (*Hancock*)

Britt Opera House, ca. 1896 (1896–1909), 22 Main Ave. N. (?). According to *Britt Recollections,* 1978, p. 197, the opera house was on the second floor above the building "now occupied by the Ben Franklin store." Not known if that building is still standing. See *Recollections* for photo of exterior. Cahn (1896) states seating capacity 400; proscenium opening 20' × 12'; stage 40' wide, 18' deep, 2' apron. Depth under stage 3'. Mgrs. Daylor and Stubbins (1896–1905), E. E. Braley (1907).

Daylor's Opera House ca. 1889. Seated 500. Mgr. Thomas Daylor. Possibly the same as Britt Opera House.

Fox Theatre, 95 Main Ave. N. (?). Was operated as a theatre "for several years in the teens." Not known if the building is still standing.

Princess Theatre, ca. 1914 (1914–1921). Renamed the Chief Theatre in 1940s; *Recollections* lists it as "the only movie house now operating in Hancock County." Not known if it is still standing. Seating capacity 400. Stage 25' wide × 24' high × 20' deep. Mgr. F. R. Bandy.

Stubbins D. Daylor's Opera House, ca. 1886, seated 250, and had good scenery.

Brooklyn (*Poweshiek*)

Broadway Theatre, ca. 1921. Same as Brooklyn Opera House. Mgr. Fred Whitehead.

(Brooklyn) Opera House, ca. 1883 (1883–1886), seated 400 and had a fair amount of scenery.

Brooklyn Opera House, 1911 (1914, 1921), 115 Jackson St. Also known as Broadway Theatre. Two-story brick, 40' × 90'6". Opened 2/28/11 with *The Shoemaker's Dream.* The stage has been roofed over at the fly gallery. The proscenium is 22' wide × 16' high; stage is 18' 10" deep × 38' wide; 4' apron. There is a trap, center. Originally the stage measured 23' deep × 42' wide × 33' high. Seating capacity was 400. There are remnants of acetylene apparatus in the grid: photos and history in the library. For some time its fate was uncertain: in 1990 there were plans to restore it. Mgrs. Frank S. Green, Fred Whitehead (1921).

Central Hall, ca. 1889, seated 800. Mgr. O. F. Dorrance.

King's Opera House, ca. 1889, seated 1200. Mgr. Geo. A. King.

Opera House (ca. 1883), seated 400. "Fair amount of scenery."

Stober's Opera House, 1888 (1889), seated 350 in opera chairs, had an organ. Proscenium was 16' wide, stage was 30' wide × 16' deep. Had 4 sets scenery. Mgr. J. C. Stober. Currently houses the *Brooklyn Free Press.*

Burlington (*Des Moines*)

(Burlington) Opera House, 26 December 1881 (1883–1886), cost $200,000. Ground-floor house seating 1400–1600, with 750 of "Andrews elegantly upholstered opera chairs" and a grand piano. Stage was 60' wide × 40' deep, with 16 sets scenery. "Brilliantly lighted and thoroughly heated." There were 24 dressing rooms, 8 at stage level. Mgr. Geo. A. Duncan.

Academy of Music, ca. 1886. Mgrs. Reeder & Edwards.

Grand Opera House, ca. 1889 (1889–1921), seated 404 on the main floor, 878 in 2 balconies, and 52 in boxes (total: 1212–1334); prices $0.25–$1. Proscenium was 30' wide × 33' high; stage was 63' wide × 50' high × 36' deep, with a 4' apron. 46' between fly girders. 9' depth under stage. There were 10 scenes; height to 4 sets of grooves was 24'. Stage had 4 traps and a bridge. 12 dressing rooms. John Agnew (1908), stage carpenter. J. K. Wager (1896), B. Hasselman (1898), Fred Croft (1903), prop men. J. Henri Fisher, orchestra leader (1896); 6–7 in orchestra. Gas light, gas and electric by 1897: Chas. Dummler was the electrician. Mgrs. J. C. Minton; Chamberlain, Barhydt & Co. (1896); F. W. Chamberlain (1897), Chamberlain, Harrington & Co. (1899); Ralph Holmes (1912), Martin Bruhl (1921). Booking agent, 1914; J. Wingfield, Chicago. Same as Grimes Opera House and Union Hall.

Grimes Opera House (1883–1889), seated 1000. Stage was 60' wide × 30' deep. Had folding opera chairs, 10 sets "new and elegant scenery." "Entirely remodeled and refitted., and supplied with all modern appliances." Mgr. R. M. Washburn; Wm. Grimes (1889).

Howard Opera House, 1889, "new."

Mozart Hall, ca. 1886 (1886–1889), seated 1000 (300, 1889). Mgr. Y.M.C.A. (1889).

Peoples' Opera House, ca. 1889, seated 500. Mgrs. Palmer Bros.

Turner Hall, ca. 1878 (1878–1889), seated 700. Had new scenery in 1878. Mgr. John A. Dalldorf; Chris Geyer (1889).

Union Hall, ca. 1878, seated 1000. Mgr. R. W. Washburn. Same as Grand Opera House.

Burr Oak (*Winneshiek*)

Odd Fellows' Hall. Two-story frame, 22' × 68'. First-floor hall (meeting rooms on second floor). Proscenium measures 15' wide × 8'6" high; stage is 21' wide × 10' high × 15' deep. Main floor measures 20' 4" × 47"; there is no balcony. Four roll drops, 15' × 12'; front drop of painted drapery and sailboat scene, others look like landscape drops but won't come down, one has movie screen painted over the middle of it.

Burt (*Kossuth*)

Burt Opera House, 122 Walnut St. On the second story of a two-story
brick building, 24' × 75'. The stage was approximately 20' to 25'
wide. There was no balcony and the seating capacity was 100.
Currently the building is storage and apartments owned by the Burt
Savings Bank.

Bussey (*Marion*)

Kisner's Hall, ca. 1889, seated 300.

Buxton (No longer exists, location unknown)

(Buxton) Opera House, ca. 1921.

Calmar (*Winneshiek*)

(Calmar) Opera House, ca. 1889, seated 350. Mgr. L. O. Moon.

Frana Opera House, 1916, 110 E. Main. Two-story brick, theatre on
second floor. Building has a 70' front; theatre runs parallel with
front. Proscenium is 22' wide × 13' high; stage is 40' wide × 40'
high × 17' deep. Dressing rooms are under the stage. Main floor
seats about 300; balcony about 60—but was more before projection
booth was added. Ad. front drop curtain; painted drapery and sailboat scene. Roll drop standing in corner of stage. Building now
occupied by the Calmar *Courier*.

Landin's Hall, ca. 1883 (1883–1886), seated 200. Mgr. C. W. Gelsen.

Meyer & Dostal's Hall, ca. 1889, seated 250. Mgrs. Meyer & Dostal.

Nichol's Opera House, ca. 1900, W. Main. Second-story hall, above
what is now the Iowa State Bank. Brick building. Proscenium is 15'
wide × 10' high. Main floor measures 54' × 42'. Originally the
theatre ran parallel with the street, but was remodeled to run front-
to-back when original building was separated into two halves.

Calumet (*O'Brien*)

Calumet Town Hall. Used for entertainments. It had flat scenery but no
curtains. Remodeled, it now serves as the fire station.

Camanch (*Clinton*)

Garner Hall, 1913, 311 9th Ave. Now the Camanch Meal Site, this
single-story cement-block building measures 31' × 77'. It has been
completely remodeled into nontheatrical use. There is a 3-seat
section of original seats (perhaps from Brown's Hall) in the
basement.

Cantril (*Van Buren*)

Tulley's Opera House, ca. 1889, seated 300. Mgr. Wm. Tulley.

Carlisle (*Warren*)

Carlisle Opera House, 1898, 125 1st St. Two-story brick, 30'6" × 81'.
Completely remodeled inside—the stage is there but the proscenium
opening is gone and closed in (was at one time converted into a
recording studio). Ralph Bellamy once played here.

Carroll (*Carroll*)

Carroll Opera House, ca. 1904 (1914–1921), seated 750. Proscenium
was 30' wide; stage was 58' wide, 54' high, 38' deep. By ca. 1914,
seating capacity was 600. Stage was 50' wide × 40' high × 30'

deep. Mgr. F. Florencourt (1904–1909), A. McNabb (1914).

Germania Opera House, ca. 1896 (1896–1904), seated 550. Stage was 48' wide, 23' deep. Mgrs. C. H. Hoeft (1896), Wm. Winnike (1898), F. Florencourt (1900–1904).

Music Hall, ca. 1886 (1886–1889), seated 550. Stage was 20' wide and 16' deep. Had good scenery. Mgrs. D. H. Dolls (1886), B. H. Potts (1889).

Carson (*Pottawattamie*)

Briggs Hall, ca. 1889. Mgr. R. W. Briggs.

Carson Opera House, ca. 1896 (1896–1904), 618 Broadway, seating capacity 500. On the lower story of a two-story brick building, 36' × 65'. The proscenium width is 34'. The proscenium height is 10'4½". The curtain line to back wall is 14'6½". The stage height is 35'. The main floor is 46'8" × 33'8". It has been considerably altered. Currently it is McKee Furniture and Gifts. The Masons are upstairs. Mgr. Charles L. Kettlewell (1896), Cassell and West (1903).

Grand Opera House, ca. 1904 (1904–1909), first floor house, seated 500. Electric lighting. Piano. Mgrs. Johnson and West (1904–1905), C. C. Johnson (1907–1909).

Unique Theatre, ca. 1912, ground-floor house, seated 260 on the main floor, 45 in the balcony (total: 305). Proscenium was 18' wide × 9'6" high. Electric lighting. Mgr. S. B. Leoriard.

Cascade (*Dubuque*)

Crawford's Hall, ca. 1883 (1883–1889), 301 1st Ave. W. Seated 500. Also called Cascade Opera House. Razed 1967. Mgrs. Crawford Bros.

Cedar (*Mahaska*)

Cedar Hall, 1916. Two-story concrete block, 30' × 60'.

Cedar Falls (*Black Hawk*)

Cotton Theatre, 1910, 103 Main. Three-story brick, 65' × 133'. Built by Frank Cotton. Now owned by the Cedar Falls Community Theater and undergoing extensive renovation and restoration. The proscenium was 32'6" wide × 22'6" high. The curtain line to the back wall was 36'; there was a 3' apron. There was 15' of wing space stage right and left. There were originally 10 dressing rooms: there were four dressing rooms backstage right and left; additional dressing rooms were located beneath the stage. The house originally seated 505 on the main floor and 290 in the gallery. There were eight boxes. It was the Iris (or Isis) Theatre in 1914, and renamed the Regent Theatre by 1921. Mgrs. Frank Cotton, J. A. Bollentyne (1914). Booking agent, 1914; J. Wingfield, Chicago. See Bibliography.

Isis Theatre, ca. 1914. Mgr. J. A. Bollantyne. Same as Cotton Theatre, Regent Theatre.

Mullarky's Hall, ca. 1886, seated 200. Orchestra available.

Packard's Opera House, ca. 1898 (1898–1909), ground-floor house, seated 800; prices $0.25–$0.50. Proscenium was 30' wide × 18' high; stage was 40' wide, 20' high, 36' deep, with a 4' apron. 4'

[sic] (1898) between fly girders. 20' depth under stage. There were two 14' grooves, a trap, and a bridge. Electric lighting. Champlin, Oliver Racker (or Riker) (1899, 1908), H. Thomas (1900), prop men and stage carpenters. Bicknell, orchestra leader. Mgrs. J. G. Packard, Williams & Bassett (1899), C. W. Champlin (1908).

Pfeiffer's Opera House, ca. 1886 (1886–1889), seated 1000. Proscenium was 24' wide; stage was 44' wide, 14' high, 26' deep. Had a piano and 8 scenes. Orchestra available. Seats at Pfeiffer's Drug Store. Mgr. H. Pfeiffer; Rude & Honeywell (1889).

Phoenix Hall, ca. 1878 (1878–1886), seated 500. Stage was 44' wide, 18' high × 18' deep. There were 2 drop scenes and a curtain. 4 sets of scenery (1883). Mgrs. H. C. Hunt, Wise & Bryant (1883). Seats sold at Wise & Bryant's Drug Store (1883).

Regent Theatre, ca. 1921. Same as Cotton Theatre, Isis Theatre. Acquired in 1991 by the Cedar Falls Community Theatre. Mgr. J. A. Bollantyne.

Cedar Rapids (*Linn*)

Capitol Theatre, 1928, 3rd Ave. and 2nd St. S.E. Now the Paramount Theatre, this six-story brick, 75' × 200' theatre is a beautifully restored example of a 1920s movie/vaudeville palace. The proscenium is 44' wide × 27' high; the stage is 54' wide × 7 stories high × 30' deep; 5' apron. The pinrail is on stage R. There are 4 dressing rooms below the stage as well as the greenroom. The star's dressing room is backstage R. Five more dressing rooms are available on upper levels. The main floor seats 1126 and the balcony 787. An autograph book of all the famous performers is kept in the theatre. There is a Wurlitzer theatre pipe organ that rises up to stage level. Must be seen to be believed, particularly the box office, lobby, and lower-level lounge.

Greene's Opera House, ca. 1883 (1883–1921), ground-floor hall, "one of the handsomest and best arranged theatres in the West. Only house in the city (1889)." Seated 495 on the main floor, 960 in 3 balconies, and 42 in the boxes (total: 1505). A. H. Andrews opera chairs. 21 scenes, piano. In 1896, proscenium was 32' wide × 29' high (30' × 33', 1886); stage was 60' wide × 60' high × 42' deep, with a 1' apron. (in 1886, height to grid was 18'; to loft, 36'). 4 grooves, 5 traps (including star left and vampire right; center traps "in 1," "in 2"), and 3 sinks "in 3," each 42' × 2'. 43' between fly girders. 42 set pieces, calcium lighting, etc. (1883) (electric light by 1912). 11 dressing rooms. L. Powers, Ed Richie (1899, 1901), Will Dayton (1900), Karl Kraft (1903), Albert Rudd (1908), prop men; C. G. Howe (or Houx), Roy C. Dale (1903), C. B. Livingston (1904), Roy E. Pratt (1908), stage carpenters; Jacob Schmidt, orchestra leader. 10 in orchestra. Booking agent, 1914; Klaw & Erlanger, New York: by 1921, A. L. Erlanger and Shuberts. Cedar Rapids Improvement Co., props (1889). Mgrs. C. G. Greene (1883), F. A. Simmons (1889), Geo. B. Peck (1898), Will S. Collier (1903).

Majestic Theatre, ca. 1912, ground-floor house, seated 671 on the main floor, 776 in 2 balconies, and 20 in the boxes (total: 1487). Proscenium was 34' wide × 30' high; stage was 59' wide, 65' high and 29' deep, with a 5' apron. 46' between fly girders; 24' to fly gallery. Electric lighting. Plays vaudeville exclusively. Mgr. "Vic" Hugo.

People's Theatre (ca. 1912), ground-floor house "playing stock and repertoire"; seated 502 on the main floor, 335 in the balcony, and 20 in the boxes (total: 877). Proscenium was 23' wide × 20' high; stage was 40' wide × 25' high × 21'4" deep; 4' apron. 28' between fly girders; 20' to fly gallery. Electric lighting. Mgr. "Vic" Hugo.

Union Opera House, ca. 1878, seated 700. Stage was 20' wide and 18' deep. Mgr. P. Mortel.

Wieler's Hall, ca. 1889, seated 500. Mgr. Wm. Wieler.

Center Point (*Linn*)

Union Hall, ca. 1889, seated 400. Mgr. A. Manaban.

Centerville (*Appanoose*)

Armory Hall, ca. 1889, seated 300.

Armory Theatre, ca. 1903 (1903–1905), a ground-floor hall, seated 850; prices $0.35, $0.50, $0.75. The proscenium was 26' wide × 20' high; the stage was 50' wide × 20' high × 24' deep, with a 6' apron. 35' between fly girders. 10' depth under stage. 1 trap, center. Lighting was electric. Payton, stage carpenter.; Taylor, orchestra leader. 6 in orchestra. Mgrs. Payton & Swearingen.

Drake Ave. Theatre, ca. 1907 (1907–1921), ground-floor hall, seated 583 on the main floor, 518 in 2 balconies, and 40 in the boxes (total: 1141). Prices $0.35, $0.50, $0.75, $1. The proscenium was 30' wide × 24' high; the stage was 50' wide × 50' high × 28' deep, with a 6' apron and one trap. 35' between fly girders; 10' depth under stage. 8 dressing rooms. Electric lighting. Hiatt, electrician; Payton, stage carpenter, Taylor, Whitney (1908), orchestra leaders—6 in orchestra. 55' throw in 1921. Mgrs. Payton & Swearingen (1907, 1912); Chamberlain, Harrington & Kindt (1908); Payton & Dillon (1914), Elbert Payton (1921).

Majestic Theatre, 100 North 13th Street. Three-story brick, 30' × 88'. The interior has been remodeled, although the horseshoe-shaped balcony remains. The backstage area has been gutted. Still operates as the Majestic movie theatre.

Orpheum Theatre, 123 E. Van Buren. Two-story brick, approx. 30' × 100'. Now closed, it was most recently the City Drug Store.

Russell's Opera House, ca. 1883 (1883–1889), a second-floor house, seated 400. The proscenium was 20' wide × 14' high; 10' to rigging loft, 20' deep. There was a fair stock of scenery and 6 grooves. Gas lighting. T. Brooks, prop man. 6 in orchestra. Mgr. H. A. Russell.

Russell Theatre (1897–1902), same as Russell's Opera House. Mgr. H. A. Russell.

Central City (*Linn*)
   Central City Opera House, ca. 1890. Two-story brick, 40' × 60'; hall
      was on the second floor above the hardware store. Nothing now
      remains inside.
Chapin (*Franklin*)
   Chapin Opera House, Main St.; a second-story hall. Burned in 1975.
Chariton (*Lucas*)
   "No theatre at present (1908)."
   Chariton Opera House, 108 N. Grand. Identified as an old opera house;
      two-story brick, 18' × 120'. Now a paint store. Could be Temple
      Theatre (ca. 1912), or The Opera House (ca. 1921).
   Mallory's Opera Hall (Mallory's Opera House), ca. 1883 (1883–1905),
      second-story hall seating 400: equipped with arm chairs and a piano.
      Reed's Orchestra was available. Proscenium was 22' wide × 18'
      high; stage was 40' wide × 14' high × 22' deep with a 4' apron.
      Had 10 sets of scenery, 4 grooves, 3 traps. Scenic artist was Louis
      Syberkrop. Electric light, "Hawkeye system" (1897). C. A.
      Solmon, prop man. Mgrs. S. S. King, W. B. Beem (1897), Dave A.
      Martin (1903).
   Opera House, ca. 1921. Probably the same as Temple Theatre. Mgr. R.
      G. Hatcher.
   Temple Theatre, ca. 1912 (1912–1914), seated 328 on the main floor
      and 175 in the balcony (total: 503). Ground-floor hall. Proscenium
      was 20' wide × 11' high; stage was 60' wide × 20' deep with a 1'
      apron. Had three 9'6" grooves. 3 dressing rooms. Electric lighting.
      Mgr. R. G. Hatcher.
Charles City (*Floyd*)
   Hildreth Opera House, ca. 1896 (1896–1921), ground-floor hall seating
      340 on the main floor, 520 in 2 balconies and 25 in the boxes (total:
      885); prices (1897) $0.25–$0.75. Proscenium was 28' × 28'; stage
      was 50' wide × 46' high × 28' deep with a 2' apron. 42' between
      fly girders. Had five 18' grooves, can be taken up flush with fly
      gallery. (No grooves by 1908.) 10' depth under stage, 1 trap, 1
      bridge. 6 dressing rooms. Electric light; E. Buck, Erving Hering
      (1900), Frank Scott (1903), W. E. Dinkel (1908), electricians. F.
      C. Fisher, Walter M. Alexander (1900), C. M. Roberts (1901),
      Frank Scott (1903), stage carpenters; Erving Hering, Tom Kelly
      (1900), C. M. Roberts (1903), Lou West (1908), prop men; Prof.
      Tover, Prof. Niemock (1900), orchestra leaders; 6 in orchestra.
      Booking agent, 1914; J. Wingfield, Chicago. By 1921 had a 10'6"
      × 13'6" screen; 80' throw. Mgrs. C. H. Shaw, C. F. Dinkel
      (1908), Wm. E. Waterhouse (1921).
   Mahara's Opera Hall, ca. 1886 (1886–1889). Mgr. Frank Mahara.
   Raymond's Hall, ca. 1878 (1878–1884), seated 275. Stage was 20' wide
      × 14' deep (19' × 24', 1883). Mgr. H. C. Raymond.
Charlotte (*Clinton*)
   Colonial Theatre, ca. 1919? Now a house and beauty shop.
   Peterson Theatre, razed ca. 1940.

Charter Oak (*Crawford*)

    Charter Oak Opera House.

    S.A.M. Opera House, ca. 1914, second-story hall seating 450. Stage was 50' wide × 16' high × 16' deep. Mgrs. Snyder and Mair.

Chelsea (*Tama*)

    ZCBJ Hall. Now the Chelsea Community Club. Single-story frame, 65' × 86'6". Stage on long side of hall which measures 42'8" × 84'8"; proscenium measures 21'8" wide × 9'10" high; stage is 20'8" deep. Advertising front drop identical in design and center castle vista to that of Westgate Opera House (now at the Museum of Repertoire Americana, Mt. Pleasant). Interior of hall decorated with original patriotic, scenic and symbolic paintings by a local (?) artist; "Battleship Iowa" (the first one), "Yellowstone Park," "Asia," etc. Worth seeing as examples of primitive folk art.

Cherokee (*Cherokee*)

    Cherokee Opera House, ca. 1889, seated 800. Mgr. John Waters.

    Grand Opera House, ca. 1896 (1896–1921), ground-floor house seating 700. Proscenium was 37' wide × 30' high; stage was 60' wide × 35' high × 22' deep with a 2' apron. There were 3 sets of 16' grooves, 10 traps with bridges under all traps. Gas and electric lighting. Depth under stage 14'. Grooves can be taken up flush with fly gallery. Ruben Gregg (1896–1902), Cal Roye (1907), Geo. Edwards (1908–1909), stage carpenters. Geo. Edwards (1907), Harry Olney (1908–1909), prop men. Scene room. By ca. 1903, seating capacity 600. By ca. 1907, stage depth 20'. 6 in orchestra; leader, H. Cline (1907–1909). By ca. 1914, stage was 64' wide × 45' high × 30' deep. Mgrs. Sanford and Moore, Robertson and Miller (1901), M. E. Robertson (1903–1905), F. Brunson (1907–1909), Ferris Bros. (1914).

    Maple Hall, ca. 1883, seated 250. Stage was 20' wide × 16' deep. Mgr. Robert Buchanan.

Chester (*Howard*)

    Community Building, late 1800s. Single-story brick, 31'4" × 90', it now houses a plumbing supply company. The proscenium measures 19' wide × 10'5" high; stage is 29' wide × 12' high × 16' deep. There is no apron. One trap, stage L There are two dressing rooms backstage. The main floor measures 28'10" × 62'. There is a small balcony. Backstage are seven book flats, plus door flats, wings, etc. A roll drop under the stage is a landscape in poor condition; it measures 15'6" × 11'. The floor of the hall is marked out for basketball.

Cincinnati (*Appanoose*)

    Union Opera House, ca. 1921, seated 300. Mgr. C. W. Best.

Clarence (*Cedar*)

    Clarence Opera House (original name unknown), 611 Lombard. Two-story brick (tin sheathing), 18' × 75'. Now the J & M Antique Shop, it has been completely remodeled inside.

Clarinda (*Page*)

Armory Theatre, ca. 1912 (1912–1921), ground-floor hall seating 874 on the main floor and 326 in the balcony (total: 1200). Proscenium was 32' wide × 20' high; stage was 55' wide × 45' high × 30' deep with a 3' apron. Electric light. 10 dressing rooms. By ca. 1914, seating capacity was 1000. Stage 55' wide × 56' high × 30' deep. By ca. 1921, seating capacity was 900. Stage was 55' wide × 56' high × 30' deep. Mgr. George Landers (1912–1914), S. O'Hare (1921).

Clarinda Opera House.

Hawley Opera House, ca. 1883 (1883–1909), 100 N. 16th St. The second story of a two-story brick building, 46'2" × 85'. The auditorium is 44' × 81'6". There is a small balcony. Currently it is empty. Downstairs is a Hardware Hank. Ca. 1883, stage size 20' × 60'. Seating capacity 500. Fair amount of scenery. By ca. 1889 stage was 20' × 50'; proscenium opening, 20'; height to grid 18'. Seated 650, piano, 6 scenes. By ca. 1897, proscenium opening was 20' × 18'; stage was 17' deep × 50' wide with a 3' apron; 8 grooves 15' high; illumination electric; 2 traps. Scene room. Depth under stage 5'. Seating capacity 700. By ca. 1904, no grooves. F. Whitman (1897), Wm. Couts (1899–1905), E. Howard (1907–1909), electricians. Wm. Stirk (1897), Charles Simmington (1900), Frank Trousdale (1901), Harry Harmon (1903–1905), E. Howard (1907–1909), prop men. F. La Fevre (1897), Robt. Ward (1903), Frank Trousdale (1904–1905), Dee Stonebreaker (1907–1909), stage carpenters. W. C. Fisher (1897), E. T. Farrens (1901), Dr. Sellards (1903–1905), Dr. Killingsworth (1907–1909), physicians. Mgr. F. W.Parrish (1883–1886), J. D. Hawley (1889).

Clarion (*Wright*)

Lake View Opera (Hall) House, ca. 1889, seated 600 in chairs. Had an organ. Proscenium was 20' wide; stage was 40' wide × 15' high × 20' deep. Had 8 sets scenery. "Only house in town." Mgr. C. W. Smith.

Clarksville (*Butler*)

Auditorium, ca. 1907 (1907–1909), brick two-story building with the opera house on the second floor. Seated 41 in the orchestra, 100 in the balcony, 210 in the parquet (total: 351); prices orchestra, $0.25; balcony, $0.50; parquet, $0.35; dress circle, $0.50. Proscenium was 24' wide × 14' high; stage was 41' wide × 23' deep with a 6' apron. 4' depth under stage. Grooves could not be taken up flush with fly gallery. 1 trap, center. No scene room. Jesse Cox, scenic artist; W. J. Sutcliff, electrician; C. S. Ford, prop man and stage carpenter; Miss Ruea Root, orchestra leader—5 in orchestra. Electric light. Stage was equipped with grooves. Side entrances to stage and backstage were covered with theatrical posters, bills, and graffiti. Potbellied stove backstage. Many pigeon corpses and droppings. Mgr. J. L. Hesse. Burned 1984.

Opera Hall, ca. 1886 (1886–1889), seated 550. "Good scenery." Mgr.

D. C. Harrison.

Clayton (*Clayton*)

Opera House, ca. 1889.

Clear Lake (*Cerro Gordo*)

Electric Theatre, ca. 1921. Mgr. C. E. Carrigar.

Halvorson Opera House, ca. 1899 (1899–1909), seated 500. Proscenium was 20' wide; stage was 44' wide × 22' deep. "Closed indefinitely" in 1899; "reopened" in 1903. Mgr. H. N. Halvorson. Same as New Opera House.

New Opera House, ca. 1896 (1896–1898), second-story hall, seated 500. Proscenium was 22' wide × 12' high; stage was 44' wide × 22' deep. Mgrs. Halvorson & Clausen.

Opera House, ca, 1886 (1886–1889).

Pavilion, ca. 1899 (1899–1909), had a 24' wide proscenium; the stage was 20' deep. Seated 2500. Mgr. Western Lakes Resort Co.

Sprague Music Hall, ca. 1899 (1899–1905), seated 225. Proscenium was 16' wide; stage was 24' wide and 12' high.

Whittaker's Covered Dock Theatre, ca. 1904 (1907–1909) seated 800. Proscenium was 26' wide; stage was 50' wide and 30' deep. Mgr. I. Whitaker.

Clearfield (*Taylor*)

Clearfield Opera House, 1891. According to the 1982 *Clearfield Community Centennial,* it was located on the second story of a two-story building constructed in 1891. Hartman's Hardware store occupied the first floor. Sources conflict as to the building's present disposition. One says it was torn down in 1957. The other says that in the early 1960s the top half was declared unsafe and was torn off leaving a one-story building which housed the Bailey Seed Company.

Clermont (*Fayette*)

Clermont Opera House, 1915, Mill St. Two-story blonde brick, with fire department in basement. Building is 52' × 78'. The proscenium is 21'8" wide × 13'6" high; curtain line to back wall is 18'6". There is a 6' apron; offstage right and left measure 9'6", and the grid is 15' high. There is one trap (sealed), center. The flat main floor measures 39'8" × 50'; the balcony measures 39'8" × 20'3". There is a 16'6" × 24' front drop, painted with a country river scene (perhaps by Sosman & Landis). As of 1990 there were plans for some restoration.

Cleveland (*Lucas*)

Opera House, ca. 1889.

Clinton (*Clinton*)

Academy of Music, ca. 1889. Mgr. L. F. Benton.

(Clinton) Opera House, ca. 1878 (1878–1886), seated 2000. Stage was 36' wide × 32' deep. "Full set of scenery with fine stage appointments." Mgr. E. M. Davis. Probably the same as Davis Opera House.

Clinton Theatre, ca. 1904 (1904–1921), ground-floor house seating 1258;

prices $0.25–$2. Proscenium was 32' wide × 30' high; stage was 58' wide × 55' high × 41' deep with a 4' apron. 45' between fly girders. 10' depth under stage. There was 1 trap, center; no grooves. Gas and electric lighting. Ed Buckley, B. F. Tate (1907), prop men; Chas. Stone, electrician and stage carpenter; Edward Lorenzen, stage carpenter (1921); F. F. Blocker, J. V. Barborka, orchestra leaders. The same as Economic Theatre. Booking agent, 1914; Klaw & Erlanger, New York. Mgrs. Clinton Theatre Co., C. E. Dixon (Klaw & Erlanger) (1907). By 1921, booking agents were A. L. Erlanger and Shuberts.

Davis Opera House, ca. 1889 (1889–1898) seated 1200. Stage was 36' wide × 32' deep. Mgr. E. M. Davis. Same as (Clinton) Opera House, "Dove's" Opera House.

"Dove's" Opera House, ca. 1896 (Davis Opera House by 1898). third-floor hall seating 1200. Proscenium was 35' wide × 18' high; stage was 16'6" high × 28' deep. 4 grooves, 16'6" high. Depth under stage, 3'. 2 traps. 6 in orchestra. Frank Stone, stage carpenter. Gas lighting. Same as Davis Opera House: "Dove's" was apparently a misprint for "Davis" in the guide, although there seems to have been some remodeling done when the management changed. Mgr. W. McMillan.

Economic Theatre, ca. 1898 (1899–1904), seated 1200; prices $0.25–$1. Proscenium was 30' wide × 26' high; stage was 58' wide × 55' high × 45' deep with a 5' apron. 45' between fly girders. 10' depth under stage. 4 traps. Gas and electric lighting. William Redden (1901), scenic artist; F. Stone, William Redden (1901), Charles Stone (1903), stage carpenters; T. H. Hansen, Frank Stone (1900), electricians; Blair Tate (1903), prop man; F. Blocker, orchestra leader. Mgrs. Busby Bros. Same as Clinton Theatre.

New Music Hall, ca. 1883 (1886–1889), seated 800. Stage was 34' wide × 26' deep. "Good scenery." Gas lighting. Mgrs. Markee & C. E. Fenlon; C. E. Fenlon (1886).

Orpheum Theatre, ca. 1910, 218 6th Ave. S. Two-story brick, the theatre measures 50' × 130'. The proscenium measures 28' wide × 30' high; the stage is 21' deep × 40' high × 48' wide, plus a 4' apron containing a footlight trough. A pinrail is off right. The original balcony has been converted into a small movie theatre (the building now houses the Capri I, II, & III movie theatres). There is a drop rolled and hanging backstage behind the movie screen box.

Rialto, ca. 1910, 216 6th Ave. S. The 42' × 130' brick building has been completely remodeled into a modern movie complex.

Smith's Opera House, ca. 1889, seated 1000. Mgr. Milo Smith.

Clutier (*Tama*)

ZCBJ Hall. Two-story frame with scalloped false front; main floor is 46' × 54'. Proscenium measures 19'1" wide × 11' high; stage is 11'7" deep × 13' high; apron is 1'6". One trap, center. Footlights, one set single groove. Amateur ad. front drop is 19'8" × 13'; landscape drop (Universal Scenic Studio, St. Paul) is 18'6" × 13".

Clutier Community Hall, 1926. Two-story frame; interior has painted movie screen with surrounding drapery (painted); footlights.

Coggon (*Linn*)

Coggon Opera House, 1915 (1921), 209 E. Main St. Single-story brick, 44′ × 91′. Proscenium is 26′ high × 14′ wide; stage is 30′ wide × 18′ deep. Has original flats from Twin Cities Scenic Studio, Minneapolis; the stage is enclosed with a "cyc" made of Twin Cities flats repainted white. Mgr. T. F. Donnelly (1921).

Coin (*Page*)

Coin Opera House.

Colesburg (*Delaware*)

Bush Opera House, ca. 1912, second-story hall, seated 300. "Reach by stage from Osterdock." Proscenium was 14′ high × 10′ wide. Gas lighting. Mgr. John V. Bush.

Colfax (*Jasper*)

Colfax Opera House, ca. 1860, 1½ Howard St. Two-story brick/stucco, now remodeled into Cross Apartments. Measures 36′ × 72′. Royal E. Cross has an acetate sheet on which he transcribed the graffiti.

Collins (*Story*)

Collins Opera House, was in the Lingenfelter Building. May be extant. New Vasey Opera House, 1912, burned in 1917.

Colo (*Story*)

Legion Hall.

Columbus Junction (*Louisa*)

Columbus Theatre, 1876 (1883–1889), 232 Main St. Three-story brick, 36′ × 66′, now remodeled into apartments and businesses. The opera house originally seated 1000. An orchestra available. Mgr. J. L. Collins.

Conrad (*Grundy*)

Phoenix Opera House, 1894, N.E. corner Main and Center. Two-story brick, hall was on second floor. Building measures 51′ × 69′6″. The interior has been completely remodeled.

Town Hall, ca. 1886, seated 250.

Conroy (*Iowa*)

Opera House, second-floor hall. Shows were put on by an "Indian Doctor."

Coon Rapids (*Carroll*)

Coon Rapids Opera House. On the second story of a two-story brick building. The bottom story was used for business. Badly burned in 1934, only half of the upper story was rebuilt. Currently it is a Coast-to-Coast store.

Corning (*Adams*)

Corning Opera House, 1900 (1903–1921), 800 Davis Avenue. It was built by a company headed by Fred Reese. It is a two-story brick building with the opera house on second floor. There has been some remodeling. An apartment is in the rear of auditorium. The proscenium width is 22′. The proscenium height is 13′ at sides and 15′7″ at center. The curtain line to back wall is 18′10″. The auditorium dimensions are: main floor 38' × 36'; horseshoe balcony not measurable—much floor damage. There are 12 sets of pulleys for drops. There are two proscenium doors stage right, one stage left. Cahn first lists statistics in the 1903–1904 guide as follows: Seating capacity 724. Electric illumination. Proscenium 22' wide × 16' high. Stage; 45' wide × 24' deep, 4' apron. Ten 16' grooves. May be taken up flush with fly gallery. No scene room. Sosman and Landis of Chicago, scenic artists. By ca. 1914, seating capacity was 800. Stage was 44' wide × 16' high × 24' deep. By ca. 1921, proscenium was 24' wide × 16' high. Stage 44' wide × 18' high × 28' deep. Wm. Hines (1903–1905), C. K. Muns (1907–1908), electricians. Mgr. F. C. Reese. Current function: storage for *Adams County Free Press,* Dan Field, editor.

Corning Opera House, ca. 1889. Seated 500. Mgr. G. C. Calkins.

Palace Rink Opera House (ca. 1889), seated 500. Mgr. F. M. Smith.

Correctionville (*Woodbury*)

Columbia Opera House 1888 (1904–1909), N. side of 5th St. Built by Ely Laub; second story of a two-story brick, 80' × 50'. The stage was 50' wide × 20' deep. The seating capacity was 500. There were opera chairs for the front seats and common seats for the back. The scene painter was J. F. Briggs of Waterloo. Allegedly the building still stands with the opera house portion empty and a grocery below but the investigator was denied access, therefore a positive identification remains tenuous. First appears in Cahn (1904–1905) with following statistics: Seating capacity 400. Proscenium 27'6" wide × 12' high; stage 50' wide × 13' high × 15' deep, 5' apron. 19 grooves 13' high. Scene room, bridge. Grooves may not be taken up flush with fly gallery. J. Freeman (1904–1908), prop man. L. Rogers (1904–1908), electrician. E. S. Mowan (1904–1908), stage carpenter. Gas and electricity. Mgr. I. L. Hardenbrook.

Idle Hour Theatre, ca. 1912 (1912–1914), second-floor hall, seated 450. Proscenium was 27' wide × 15' high; stage was 40' wide × 15' high × 15' deep, 3' apron. Had 4 grooves. Electric light. Mgr. W. M. Wright.

Laub Opera House. Burned.

Corwith (*Hancock*)

Opera House.

Corydon (*Wayne*)

Auditorium, 1907 (1912–1921), three-story brick, opera house on second floor. Seated 650 on main floor, 250 in balcony. Proscenium was 35' wide × 20' high; stage was 60' wide × 40' high × 21' deep, 4' apron. 3 dressing rooms. Electric light. In 1921 had a 10' × 12' screen; 60' throw. H. E. Hook, stage carpenter; Mrs. F. H. Morrison, orchestra leader. Building may still be standing. Mgrs. M. C. Lugar, John Morrison (1914), F. H. Morrison (1921).

New Opera Hall, ca. 1886 (1886–1889), seated 400. Stage was 60' wide × 16' deep. Had 7 scenes. Mgr. W. Hughes.

Princess, ca. 1914. Mgr. John Morrison.

Wayne Theatre, corner W. Jackson & N. Franklin. Single-story concrete block, 35' × 100'.

Council Bluffs (*Pottawattamie*)

Bloom & Nixon Opera House, ca. 1883. Stage was 60' wide × 40' deep. Had 15 sets scenery. Seated 1000. Mgr. John W. Kilgore.

Dohaney's Opera House, ca. 1883. Size of stage 31' × 44'. Seating capacity 800. Six sliding and eight rolling scenes. Mgr. John Dohaney.

Dohaney's New Opera House, ca. 1886 (1886–1914), also called Dohaney's Theatre. Ground-floor house, seating capacity 1069. The proscenium was 30' × 30'; stage was 60' × 38'. Height to grid, 18'; to loft, 43'. 10 scenes. By 1889, stage 40' × 60'; height to loft 47'; seating capacity 1100. By 1896, called Dohaney's Theatre; seating capacity 1226. Stage depth 33'6", width 60', apron 6'6". W. C. Dalby, scenic artist; gas and electric light; 1 trap. Six 18' grooves. Depth under stage 3'. Orchestra 7–10. By ca. 1900 proscenium 30' × 44'; stage depth 38'6", width 60', height 44', apron 6'6". Four 18' grooves. Depth under stage 6', 4 traps. 6 in orchestra. By ca. 1913, seating capacity 750; ground 378, balcony 290, gallery 50, boxes 32. Proscenium 30' wide × 30' deep. Stage 66' wide × 40' high × 35' deep, 4' apron. Mgrs. John Dohaney, Geo. N. Bowen (1897), Stroman and Kennedy (1900), Geo. Stevenson (1901–1902), Paul C. Mooney (1912–1913), Wm. Cassel (1914).

Dohaney's Opera Hall, ca. 1878, seated 800. Stage was 44' wide × 31' deep. Had 6 sliding and 8 rolling scenes.

New Opera House, ca. 1883.

New Theatre, ca. 1903, ground-floor house, seated 1226. Proscenium was 30' × 30'; stage was 65' wide × 45' high × 30' deep, with 3' apron. Had 4 traps. Depth under stage 7'. Electric light. By ca. 1904, stage depth 26' with 4' apron. No grooves, no scene room. Depth under stage 8'. 6 in orchestra, Art Smith (1903–1909), leader. By ca. 1907, stage was 66' wide × 48' high × 31' deep with 4' apron. Mgr. A. B. Beall (1903–1909).

Crawfordsville (*Washington*)

Crawfordsville Town Hall, ca. 1889. Two-story brick, 30' × 50'. Now cafe on first floor, Masonic Lodge on second. Stage, etc. gone. In 1926 it was referred to as "the old opera house." (c.f. 25th Anniversary edition of the *Evening Journal,* 3 April 1926, p. 21.) Mgrs. Manners Bros.

Cresco (*Howard*)

Cresco Opera House, 1914, 115 2nd Ave W. Three-story brick grand opera house, 50' × 100'. Proscenium is 28' wide × 24' high. Curtain line to back, 20'. 4 foot apron; 10' wing space on each side. Rigging loft is 46' high. There is a fly gallery, seven dressing rooms, and footlights. The main floor seats 228, the balcony 235, and there are 4 boxes. The basement holds a renovated dance-hall.

There is an orchestra pit—pit entrance from the dressing rooms. Originally modeled after a Chicago theatre (unidentified). Theatre has been renovated; original decorations include a multitude of bas-relief gilded cherubs above proscenium arch and stage boxes.

Cresco Opera House, ca. 1896 (1896–1921), second-story hall, seated 700. Proscenium was 21' wide × 14' high; stage was 12' high × 19' deep; 4'9" apron. Had 4 grooves, 2 traps. Mgrs. F. B. Lomar or Lomas, L. Morrissey (1921).

Lyric Hall, ca. 1883 (1883–1889), seated 800, 512 in chairs. Proscenium was 18' wide; stage was 20' wide, 14' high, 18' deep. Had 5 sets scenery, 1 drop curtain. Mgrs. Lomas Bros. & Weaver; Lomas Bros. (1889).

Creston (*Union*)

Creston Opera House, 1883 (1883–1909), by ca. 1896 called Creston Theatre. See Patt Opera House. Seated 1000 in Andrews opera chairs. Stage 35' × 60'. 30 sets of scenery on flats. By ca. 1889, stage 37' × 60'; seated 900. By ca. 1896, proscenium was 22' wide × 15' high; stage was 60' wide × 17' high × 30 deep; 7' apron. Depth under stage 12'. Had five 15' high grooves, 3 traps; seating capacity 850. Louis Syberkrop (1883), scenic artist. By ca. 1897 gas and electric lighting. By ca. 1903, proscenium 28' wide × 25' high; stage was 60' wide × 27' high × 30' deep; 7' apron. Five 25' high grooves. Depth under stage 9'. By ca. 1904, stage height 45', grooves 40' high, depth under stage 8'. Mgrs. T. H. B. Beach and Louis Syberkrop.(1883), J. H. Patt (1889).

Patt Opera House (probably also Creston Theatre and Creston Opera House), 1882, Adams St. According to researcher Nancy Jo Egly, it was on the first floor of a three-story brick building erected by J. H. Patt and the Creston Opera House Company. It had a gallery. The seating capacity of the house was 1000. The stage was 35' × 60'. There were four large dressing rooms and 30 complete sets of scenes. The scenic artist was Louis Syberkrop. It has been extensively altered. Currently it is a movie house and retail stores.

Temple Grand Opera House, 1902 (1904–1921), southwest corner Montgomery and Oak. Also according to Egly, it was built by the Masons; located on the first floor of a three-story brick building. Lodge rooms occupied the second and third floors. The seating capacity was 1000. The interior was destroyed by fire in 1920. The exterior shell remained and the structure was rebuilt. It has been used for a variety of purposes over the years. First appears in Cahn (1904–1905) with following statistics: Seating capacity 884. Electric illumination. Proscenium 29'6" wide × 23'6" high: stage 53' wide × 53'6" high × 40' deep, 3' apron. No grooves. Depth under stage 12', 1 trap. Scene room, 3 bridges. By ca. 1907, seating capacity was 907: 554 in orchestra, 203 in balcony, 118 in gallery, 32 in boxes. Proscenium 29'6" wide × 24' high; stage 55' wide × 40' high × 40' deep, 3' apron. By ca. 1908, seating capacity 875: 555 in orchestra, 203 in balcony, 117 in gallery. Proscenium 30' wide

× 24' deep. Stage 53' wide × 53' high × 40 deep, 3' apron. By ca. 1914, seating capacity 850, stage "ample." By ca. 1921, seating capacity 850, stage still "ample." Howard Tuttle (1908), scenic artist. Donald Bain (1907), Roy Jolly (1908), prop men. Teller (1907), Frymier (1908), electricians. Gas and electric light. Roy Jolly (1907), stage carpenter. 5 in orchestra; leader T. E. Agnew (1907). Mgrs. Weiser and Bear (1904–1905), Busby Bros. (1907–1909), Emerson and Davenport (1914–19??), Hall Kelly (1921).

Cumberland (*Cass*)

Cumberland Opera House.

Cushing (*Woodbury*)

Cushing Opera House, Main St. Second floor of a two-story building, 50'2" × 75'5". The proscenium is 20'6" × 11'3". The curtain line to back wall is 10'1". The main floor is 62'2" × 27'1". There have been considerable alterations. Currently it is empty. A Clover Farm Store and the Holstein State Bank are below.

Dakota City (*Humboldt*)

Snook's Hall, ca. 1886, seated 300. Mgr. Ed. Snook.

Humbolt Hall, ca. 1886, seated 500. Mgr. B. H. Harkness.

Dallas Center (*Dallas*)

Dallas Center Opera House. Burned.

Danbury (*Woodbury*)

Danbury Opera House, ca. 1913, 220 Main. Second story of a two-story brick building, 40' × 100'. Considerably altered, it currently is used by the Masons.

Danville (*Des Moines*)

Grange Hall, ca. 1889, seated 200.

Davenport (*Scott*)

American Theatre, ca. 1911, ground-floor house, 324 W. 3rd St., seating 500 on the main floor, 700 in 2 balconies, 10 in the boxes (total: 1210). Proscenium was 28' wide × 25' high; stage was 50' wide × 45' high × 30' deep, 1' apron. 35' between fly girders, 24' to fly gallery. Electric light, 4 stage pockets. Mgr. Charles Berkell.

Burtis Opera House, ca. 1878 (1878–1921), ground-floor house, 415 Perry St., seating 504 on the main floor, 754 in 2 balconies, and 40 in the boxes (total: 1298); prices (1896) $0.25–$1 ($0.50–$2.50 by 1921). In 1896 proscenium was 33' × 60'; stage was 72' wide × 62' high × 36' deep; 4' apron. Grooves were 18' high. 12' depth under stage. 3 traps, center, right, left; 1 bridge, back. Grooves can be taken up flush with fly gallery. 46' between fly girders. Gas and electric lighting (1896). 15 dressing rooms. "Entirely new and refitted (1907)." Proscenium 33' wide × 33' high (other dimensions as in 1896). No grooves. Still gas and electric light. Louis Kindt (1896), scenic artist; Michael Lamb (1896), Matt Lamb (1900), Charles Hutchinson (1903), electricians and stage carpenters; Matt Lamb (1907), electrician; Henry Raap (1907), stage carpenter; Hugh Conwell (1896), Eugene Bateman (1900), B. F. Maddox (1903), P. Struve (1904), Chester Taylor (1907), prop men; Ernest

Otto (1896, 1907), Otto Eckhardt (1900), Al Peterson (1903), orchestra leaders; 6-10 in orchestra. Mgrs. Burtis Skeels; W. K. Fluke (1889); Chamberlain, Kindt & Co. (1896); Charles T. Kindt (Chamberlain, Kindt & Co.) (1904).

In 1907, "entirely new and refitted," proscenium was 33' wide × 33' high; stage was 72' wide × 62' high × 36' deep; 4' apron. 46' between fly girders, 12' depth under stage, no grooves. 3 traps. Gas and electric light. Matt Lamb, electrician, Henry Raap, stage carpenter, Chester Taylor, prop man; E. Otto, Ceno Peterson (1921), orchestra leaders. Booking agent, 1914; John Cort, New York. By 1921, A.L. Erlanger & Shuberts. Mgrs. Frank J. Jervis (1907), Ed V. Giroux (Ben M. Giroux, local mgr.) (1912), M. S. Scovill (1914), Chas. T. Kindt (1921).

Casino Theatre, ca. 1911, 213 W. 3rd.

Claus Groth Hall, 1900, 1224-28 W. 3rd St. Later called Thomas St. Martin.

Columbia Theatre, ca. 1911, 406 W. 3rd.

Crystal Theatre, pre-1911, 328 Harrison.

Davenport Theatre, pre-1911, 1129 W. 3rd.

Eagle Theatre (Northwest Theatre), pre-1911, 1518 Washington.

East Davenport Theatre, pre-1911, 2115 E. 11th St.

Elite Theatre, ca. 1911, 311 W. 2nd.

Family Theatre, ca. 1911, 215 W. 3rd.

Gem Theatre, ca. 1911, 118 W. 2nd.

German Theatre, 1878, 3rd and Scott. Same as Turner Opera House, Grand Opera House.

Grand Opera House, ca. 1889, 3rd and Scott, seated 1500, in opera chairs throughout. Proscenium was 34' wide, stage was 70' wide × 45' high × 32' deep; 4' apron. Stage to fly gallery floor, 24'; 45' between fly girders. 8' depth under stage. 3 traps, 1 center, 1 each side. Electric light. (Measurements as of 1907). Same as German Theatre, Stadt Theatre, Turner Opera House. Mgr. Wm. Bowman (1908). Razed 1960s.

Har-Cen-Art, pre-1911, 1814 Harrison.

Hobson Vaudeville Theatre. ca. 1900, 217-19 Perry St. Later called Princess, Liberty.

Jewel Theatre, ca. 1911, 1718 W. 4th.

Iowa Theatre, ca. 1911, 324 W. 2nd.

Lahrman's Hall, 1868, 2nd and Ripley. Also called German Theatre.

Library Hall, ca. 1883 (1883-1886), 6th and Brady, seated 500. Mgr. Library Rooms.

Liberty Theatre, ca. 1900, 217-19 Perry St.; same as Hobson Vaudeville Theatre, Princess Theatre.

Majestic Theatre, ca. 1911, 329 Brady.

Mirror Theatre, ca. 1911, 129 E. 3rd.

New German Theatre, ca. 1889, seated 1200. Mgr. J. Hill.

New Grand Opera House, ca. 1896 (1896-1913), ground-floor house seating 1000. Proscenium was 35' wide; stage was 80' wide × 60' high × 45' deep; 3' apron. 50' between fly girders. 5 sets of 18' high grooves. 12' under stage; 4 traps located center and 2 sides. 1 bridge on back wall. Gas and electric lighting. John Dunlap, prop man. Mgrs. Otto H. Lahrmann, Fred Kuehl (1899).

Olympia Theatre, ca. 1911, 1832 W. 3rd.

Olympic Opera House, ca. 1889, seated 1000. Mgr. W. B. Wiley.

Palace Theatre, pre–1911, 1504 Harrison.

Palm Theatre, ca. 1911, 428 Brady.

Princess Theatre, ca. 1912. Same as Hobson Vaudeville Theatre, Liberty Theatre.

Royal Theatre, ca. 1911, 127. E. 3rd.

Star Theatre, pre–1911, 224 Harrison.

Summer Theatre, pre–1911, 501 W. 4th.

Thomas St. Martin, 1224–28 W. 3rd St. Originally Claus Groth Hall.

Turner Opera House, ca. 1889. Same as German Theatre, Grand Opera House. Mgr. Chas. Kindt.

Victor Theatre, ca. 1911, 1406 Harrison.

Davis City (*Decatur*)

Opera House, ca. 1914, ground-floor house, seated 350. Stage was 29' wide × 12' high × 19' deep. Mgr. J. Lymon McLain.

Dawson (*Dallas*)

Dawson Opera House.

Dayton (*Webster*)

Brundein's Hall, ca. 1886.

Bumquist's Opera House, (ca. 1896–1909), second-floor house, seated 300. Proscenium was 10' wide; stage was 24' wide × 10' high × 29' deep; 1' apron. 18' between fly girders. Had four 9' grooves. 3' depth under stage, 1 trap. Oil lighting. By ca. 1899 seating capacity 200. Probably the same structure as Burnquist's Opera House. Mgr. Omar Richardson (1896), A. C. Lindberg (1899–1905), S. A. Burnquist (1907).

Burnquist's Opera House, ca. 1896, 39 S. Main. Called Bumquist's Opera House in Cahn's Official Theatrical Guide until the 1899–1900 edition when it was called the Burnquist Opera House. On the second story of a two-story building erected by the Swenson Brothers. It had two stages, one on the west and one on the east side of the building. Only one is left now. The building dimensions are 42' × 100'7". The proscenium width is 19'8". The proscenium height is 9'8". The curtain line to back wall is 16'4". Offstage right is 9'10" × 16'2". Offstage left is 8'2" × 9'2". The stage height is 3'2" above the main floor. The main floor is 51' × 39'8". There is a large elevator off left which goes to the first floor. However, these measurements may not be for either the Burnquist or Bumquist Opera House but for a structure now known as the Dayton Opera House, which was constructed in 1898, and is in the process of being remodeled by local residents, Christine and D. W. Hanson. See Bumquist's Opera House, above.

Dayton Opera House, ca. 1889, 27 Main St. Was situated over the

Anderson & Co. Store; was 24' × 80', had "fine scenery," and seated about 700, according to the *Dayton Centennial Book*, 1956. Now the site of Manco Industries. This structure may or may not still be standing.

IOOF Hall, ca. 1889, seated 150.

Nelson Hall, ca. 1889, seated 300. Mgr. John Nelson.

Johnson and Swenson Brothers Hall, ca. 1902.

Decatur City (*Decatur*)

Decatur City Opera House. On the second story of a two-story brick building measuring 40' × 80'. The proscenium height is 12'; curtain line to back wall 20'; stage height above the main floor is 2'6". Currently it is storage for M and M Welding, located on the first floor.

Decorah (*Winneshiek*)

Grand Opera House, ca. 1897, first-story house seating 350 on the main floor, 530 in 2 balconies, and 24 in the boxes (total: 904); prices (1896) $0.35–$1. In 1896, proscenium was 30' wide; stage was 46' wide × 42' high × 32' deep; 2'6" apron. 40' between fly girders. There were three 16' high grooves, could be taken up flush with fly gallery. 10' under stage, 3 traps, right, left, center. Gas and electric lighting. 12 dressing rooms. O. Korsrud (1897), Jno. Praper (1898), M. Sherry (1899), Chas. Lambert (1908), electricians; H. Amblie (1897), stage carpenter and prop man; Geo. Thayer (1898), R. Donaldson (1899), stage carpenters; C. Webster (1898), W. Jorgenson (1901), Chas. Bromley (1907), prop men; B. O. Marsh, stage manager (1900); J. J. Kovarik, orchestra leader; 9 in orchestra. Booking agent, 1914; Shuberts, New York. Mgrs. C. J. Weiser & B. B. Morse; B. B. Morse (1898); Weiser & Bear (1899).

New Grand Opera House, ca. 1899, first-story house seating 900. Proscenium was 30' wide; stage was 48' wide × 65' high × 29'6" deep; 2'6" apron. 5 traps, electric light. Probably the same as the Grand Opera House.

Rudolph's Hall, ca. 1889. Mgr. Chas. Rudolph.

Steyer's Opera House, 1870 (1883), 102½ W. Water St. Three-story brick, 44' front. Theatre on 3rd floor. Built by Joseph B. Steyer; remodeled in 1875 to present configuration. In 1883 stage was 15' × 22'. Stage is on long side of room, (running front to back). Today, proscenium measures 28'6" wide × 12'7" high; stage is 19' deep; apron, 4'; 17' offstage R, 12' offstage L. Stage ceiling about 15' high. One trap, 2' × 2' center. Footlights in covered trough. Four full sets grooves. Winch off L; overhead blocks. Storage loft backstage L; dressing rooms/offices off L and R. Central chandelier; proscenium doors. Fancy embossed tin decoration on walls and ceiling. Balcony on three sides. Main front curtain rolled up against wall (had been torn down—some 18" remained attached to proscenium arch, but the curtain has now been restored). Three strips of muslin with *Uncle Tom's Cabin* show posters glued to them to make a show banner. Full set of wing and groove scenery, most painted in 1875 by Harry Dressler of Chicago, and signed by him. Scenes include a water mill, woods, double-sided plain interior/prison, town, country, moor (with concealed doors), fancy interior, stone exterior. Mgr. J. Steyer. See Bibliography.

Dedham (*Carroll*)

Stangel Hall. Two-story brick building located at 514 Second Street. Its dimensions are 44' × 80' and it is currently used as storage for an oil company.

Deep River (*Poweshiek*)

Memorial Hall 1927. Two-story brick, theatre on second floor. Building measures 30' × 69'.

Defiance (*Shelby*)

Tilton Auditorium 1916. One-story frame, constructed by W. R. Tilton; 100' × 35'5½". According to Neil Tilton, son of the builder, it had a 20' stage and balconies were located around two-thirds of the building. It also had wings and drops. It has been remodeled and used for various purposes. Currently it is a tractor and auto repair shop.

Delaware (*Delaware*)

Stone Hall, ca. 1883, seated 400. Mgr. R. Boone.

Stour Hall, ca. 1889, seated 200. Same as Stone Hall? Mgr. C. B. Lont.

Delhi (*Delaware*)

Heath's Hall, ca. 1883 (1883–1889), seated 350. Stage was 30' wide × 14' deep. "No scenery." Mgr. M. T. Heath.

Delmar (*Clinton*)

Westover Hall, ca. 1886 (1886–1889), seated 150. Stage was 19' wide × 12' deep. Mgr. O. C. Tomlinson.

Delta (*Keokuk*)

Princess, 1st. St., east of bank.

Denison (*Crawford*)

Denison Opera House, ca. 1921, 1st Ave. N., two-story brick, 44'6" × 74'10". Proscenium was 30' wide × 25' high; stage was 60' wide × 52' high × 27' deep. Electric light. Seating capacity 800. Possibly now the Masonic Temple. Mgr. Peter Krauth.

Germania Hall, ca. 1886, seated 600. Proscenium was 25' wide × 14' high; stage was 52' wide × 16' high × 30' deep; 2' apron. Had fair scenery. Mgr. R. Huard.

Germania Opera House, ca. 1904 (1904–1909), ground-floor house seating 700. Proscenium was 25' wide × 14' high; stage was 44' wide × 16' high × 22' deep; 2' apron. Depth under stage 10'. No scene room. P. Kranich (1905–1906), P. Krauth (1907–1909), prop men. Gas and electric lighting. By ca. 1907, electric only. W. P. Hover (1904), electrician. Mgrs. B. J. Sibbert (1904–1905; 1908), P. J. Klinker (1907). May be the same as Germania Hall.

McHenry's Hall, ca. 1883, seated 300. Stage was 22' wide × 17' deep; had 7 sets of scenery and a drop curtain. Seating capacity, 300. Mgr. W. A. McHenry.

Derby (*Lucas*)
  Derby Opera House, 1900. Single-story brick. 34'6" × 66". Stage is
    still inside.
Des Moines (*Polk*)
  Academy of Music, ca. 1878, seated 684. Stage was 45' wide × 23'
    deep. A "new house" in 1878; 13 changes of scenery. Mgr. Wm.
    Foster.
  Auditorium, ca. 1901 (1901–1909). "Devoted to repertoire attractions."
    Mgrs. Earl P. Adams, Wm. Foster (1909).
  Berchel Theatre, ca. 1912 (1912–1921), ground-floor house seating 563
    on the main floor, 638 in 2 balconies, and 32 in the boxes (total:
    1233). Proscenium was 35'3" wide × 34' high; stage was 64'6"
    wide × 52' high × 39' deep; 3' apron. 44' between fly girders,
    23'6" to fly gallery. Electric light. 12 dressing rooms. Mgrs. Elbert
    & Getchell (E. H. Hayes, local mgr.). Booking agents (1914), Klaw
    & Erlanger, S. & H. (Shubert & Harris?), New York; A.L.
    Erlanger (1921).
  Capitol City Opera House, ca. 1889, seated 1000. Mgr. W. C. Ross.
  Foster's Opera House, ca. 1883 (1883–1909). "This elegant place of
    amusement is on the principal business street," Walnut St. Ground-
    floor house seating 1300 (2 balconies), folding chairs throughout,
    "including gallery"; piano; prices (1896) $0.25–$1. Had "all
    modern appliances, and is complete in every respect." In 1896,
    proscenium was 33'6" wide × 32' high; stage was 82' wide × 56'
    high × 46' deep; 4' apron. 42' between fly girders. Four 18' high
    grooves; can be taken up flush with fly gallery. 3 traps, center and
    2 sides. Electric light by 1896. J. C. Wallace, O. Sundes (1908),
    electricians; Sam Ward (1896), G. Macklin (1898), prop men; R.
    L. Hess (1904), C. Fairleys (1907), A. G. Hyland (1908), stage
    carpenters and prop men; Fred Schneider, orchestra leader (1896);
    7 in orchestra. Mgr. Wm. Foster.
  Grand Opera House, ca. 1897, ground-floor theatre, seated 1400; prices
    $0.15–$0.75. Proscenium 33' wide × 58' high; stage was 63' wide
    × 54' high × 42' deep; 4' apron. 40' between fly girders. 4
    grooves, 18' high; could be taken up flush with fly gallery. 8' depth
    under stage. 3 traps, center and 2 sides. 1 bridge, center, "back of
    3." Clyde Fowler, prop man; D. E. Bradish, stage carpenter; Fred
    Schneider, orchestra leader; 3–5 in orchestra. Gas light: gas and
    electricity by 1907. Mgr. Wm. Foster.
  Lewis Opera House, ca. 1883 (1883–1889), the only opera house in East
    Des Moines, "the place where the legislature meets." Seated 1600.
    "A wide and commodious stage. . . . Well stocked with scenery."
    Mgrs. Brandt & Wilcox, E. Des Moines; Frank Wilcox (1889).
  Majestic Theatre, ca. 1912, ground-floor house seated 598 on the main
    floor, 256 in the balcony, 32 in the boxes (total: 886). Proscenium
    was 22' wide × 18' high; stage was 42' wide × 26' high × 25'
    deep. 8 dressing rooms. Plays Sullivan & Considine Vaudeville.
    Mgrs. Elbert & Getchell (E. H. Hayes, local mgr.).

Moore's Opera House, ca. 1878 (1878–1886), 4th and Walnut. Seated 1200. Stage was 65' wide × 35' deep. Gas lighting, steam heat. Mgr. W. W. Moor.

New Grand Opera House, ca. 1883 (1883–1889), ground-floor house seating 1400 in plush upholstered opera chairs. "No low-priced plays admitted. Only theatre that has never played at 10c., 20c., and 30c. prices. This house has the best location in the city, between two principal business streets, adjacent to five of the leading hotels, and two street car lines run directly in front of its doors [1889]." Piano. Proscenium was 33' wide × 58' high; stage was 63' wide × 54' high × 38' deep; 4' apron; 40' between fly girders. 8' depth under stage. Four 18' high grooves, could be taken up flush with fly gallery. 20 sets scenery, 3 traps, center & both sides. 1 bridge, center. Gas light. Jno. Steele, orchestra leader; 3–5 in orchestra. Mgr. W. W. Moore, Wm. Foster (1889).

Orpheum Theatre, ca. 1912.

Princess Theatre, ca. 1912, ground-floor house seating 620 on the main floor, 671 in 2 balconies, and 62 in the boxes (total: 1353). Proscenium was 34' wide × 32' high; stage was 62' wide × 35' deep; 2'6" apron. 48' between fly girders. Electric light. Mgrs. Elbert & Getchell.

Unique Theatre, ca. 1912.

De Witt (*Clinton*)

De Witt Opera House, 1876 (1883–1909). Two-story brick/stucco theatre, measuring 44'6" × 86'. There was originally a cupola above the entrance which has been removed. The stage has undergone numerous revisions, but now has a 32' wide × 13' high proscenium. Was 42' wide × 26' deep in 1883. Curtain line to back wall is 32'; stage is 40' wide. There is one trap, center. Originally there were eight full scenes and two drop curtains. Seating capacity originally was 700; now the main floor seats 186 and the balcony 39. Photographs in the theatre office show the original exterior, and a shot of the stage shows some scenery and a portion of the ad. front drop. Mgr. Geo. K. Ryder.

Dexter (*Dallas*)

Dexter Community Hall, 1916. An unusual one-story circular building of glazed hollow tile block, 263'10" in circumference. The stage height is 3'9" above the main floor; proscenium width 28'7"; proscenium height 12'9"; curtain line to back wall 22'. There is one trap center 5'8" × 1'8". Dressing room is below the stage. The main floor is 47'2" side to side.

Dexter Normal Hall, ca. 1889, seated 400. Piano. Proscenium was 18' wide; stage was 45' wide × 18' deep or 45' wide by 42' deep. Mgr. W. H. Monroe.

Swihart's Hall, ca. 1883, seated 250. Stage was 22' wide × 14' deep. No scenery. Mgr. Simon Swihart.

Diagonal (*Ringgold*)

Diagonal Opera House.

Dike (*Grundy*)
> Dike Opera House, ca. 1914, 400 block of Main St. Ground-floor house seating 400. Stage was 18' wide × 19' high × 16' deep. Mgrs. Dreher & Reisinger.

Dixon (*Scott*)
> **Dixon Opera House.** Single-story wood-frame. Now just a shed—nothing left inside (if there ever was).

Donahue (*Scott*)
> Goettsch Hall, ca. 1930. Burned in 1979.

Donnellson (*Lee*)
> **Krebill Building,** 1911. 2 blocks south of 600 Main. Single-story brick, 42' × 45'. Now an auto parts store.
> **Orpheum Theatre,** 1911. 600 Main. Also called the Dickey Building, this two-story brick is 32' × 72', and had the theatre on the second floor. Nothing now remains of the theatre.

Doon (*Lyon*)
> Woodman Hall. Burned.

Dubuque (*Dubuque*)
> City Hall, ca. 1886 (1886–1989), seated 600.
> (Dubuque) Opera House, ca. 1878 (1878–1889), seated 900. Stage was 64' wide × 36' deep; 24' × 35' (1883). In 1889 proscenium was 32' wide × 23' high; stage was 64' wide × 28' high × 35' deep; 18' to grid. Complete stock of scenery. 24 scenes (1889). An orchestra is available. Mgrs. Stewart & Scott, Duncan & Waller (1883).
> **Grand Opera House,** 1889 (1896–1914), 135 8th Street. Four-story (plus two attics) grand opera house, constructed of redstone, brick and limestone; measures 70' × 129'. The front has been faced with modern steel panelling. Seating capacity in 1896 was 1350; prices (1897) $0.25–$1. The proscenium opening was 35' wide × 35' high—by 1909 (and today) the height was reduced to 25'. The stage is 67' wide × 70' high × 31' deep (36' in 1897); 3' apron (has footlights). The distance between fly girders was 38'; height of the grooves from the stage was 20', with four sets of grooves. 16 dressing rooms. When visited recently the stage was ceilinged off at proscenium height. There was one bridge, and the grooves could be taken up flush with the fly gallery. Depth under the stage was 10'; there were four traps. The theatre had its own scene room. It was lighted by gas (by 1897 illumination was gas and electric). Jack Brode (1896), James Coffee (1899), Elmer Volz (or Voels) (1907), stage carpenters. Joe Strinskey (1896, 1901), F. R. Houps (1900), Harry Cleaver (1907), electricians. There were seven in the orchestra, C. M. Thomas, leader (1896). By 1983, with the second balcony made into a projection room, the seating capacity was 445 on the main floor and 236 in the first balcony (total: 681). The gallery is closed off. There is a ballroom and a rehearsal hall on the fourth floor. In 1987 a restoration project was under way. Booking agents (1914) Klaw & Erlanger, New York. Mgrs. Wm. T. Roehl,

John H. Maclay (1912).

Majestic Theatre, 1910, corner of 4th and Main. Now part of the Five Flags entertainment complex, the six-story brick grand opera house measures 65' × 113'. Original seating capacity, 1400. The proscenium opening was originally 35' wide × 25' high—it is now 31'10" wide (boxcar width). Stage was originally 70' wide × 70' high × 37' deep; 7' apron; 40' between fly girders; 22' to fly gallery. 16 dressing rooms. Today, the curtain line to the back wall is 28', there is an 11' apron. Offstage right measures 11'; offstage left is 7'; 56' to the grid. The stage is now quipped with 5 traps. Today, with the gallery closed off, and after thorough restoration and remodeling ($10,000 in gold leaf) the main floor seats 322, the balcony 357, and the boxes 38 (total: 717). There has been a theatre on this site since 1840. Booking agent (1921) A.L. Erlanger, New York. Mgr. Jake Rosenthal (1921). See Bibliography for the Rosenthal Collection.

Turner's Hall, ca. 1886 (1886–1889), seated 800.

Dumont (*Butler*)

Dumont Theatre, 2nd St.

Dundee (*Delaware*)

Schroeder Hall, second-story hall next to the post office.

Dunlap (*Harrison*)

Opera House, ca. 1886 (1886–1909), ground-floor house seating 500. Stage 24' × 48'. By 1889, proscenium opening 20', height to grid 16', to loft 16', seating capacity 700. By 1896, seating capacity 600. Proscenium was 24' wide × 14' high; stage was 48' wide × 20' high × 22' deep; 3' apron. Four 14' high grooves. Height to loft 20'. Depth under stage 7'. By ca. 1904 proscenium 28' wide × 24' high. Stage: 50' wide × 41' high × 39'6" deep, apron 2'6". Depth under stage 12'. No scene room. No grooves. Gas lighting. By ca. 1907, seating capacity 650. Thomas (1904–1909), scenic artist. Ed Young (1904–1905), John Lehan (1907–1909), prop men. Aldridge (1904–1909), stage carpenter. 6 in orchestra; A. Emge (1904–1905), leader. Mgrs. S. J. Patterson (1886), T. A. Dean (1900), J. C. Clyde (1901), D. T. Child (1903), Moore and Roberts (1904–1905), L. K. Moore (1907).

Lehan's Hall, ca. 1886.

Dyersville (*Dubuque*)

City Hall, ca. 1889.

Dyersville Opera House, ca. 1914. Second-story hall seating 400. Stage was 25' wide × 16' high × 20' deep. Mgr. Chas. P. Roth.

Plaza Theatre, 1915, 319 1st Ave. S.E. The two-story brick building measures 34' × 114'; in 1955 the stage house was removed and a hotel was built on the second floor. Originally the proscenium opening was 24' wide × 15' high; Stage was 40' high × 30' deep. Seating capacity was 450—it is now 400. Mgr. A. V. Lippert.

Dysart (*Tama*)

Dysart Opera House, ca. 1898 (1898–1914), seated 500. Proscenium was

22' wide × 15' high; stage was 41' wide × 14' high × 24' deep; 3' apron. 14' high grooves. Mgr. E. F. Douglas.

Town Hall, ca. 1889, seated 300. Mgrs. Pierce & Browne.

Eagle Grove (*Wright*)

Armory Opera House, ca. 1912. Burned ca. 1914.

Cosmo Theatre, ca. 1908 (1908–1909), ground-floor house seating 200. Proscenium was 14' wide × 12' high; stage was 23' wide × 13' deep; 3' apron. Electric light. Mgr. E. W. Groesbech.

Eagle Grove Opera House, ca. 1889 (1889–1921), ground-floor house 40' × 90', seated 400 in chairs on the main floor, 200 on benches in the balcony. "Handsomely papered and painted." Piano. Proscenium was 20' wide × 22' high; stage was 40' wide × 30' high × 22' deep. 8 scenes by Sosman & Landis, Chicago. "Built for the business." By ca. 1904, proscenium was 32' wide × 25' high; stage 50' wide × 38' high × 25' deep, apron 5'. Electric lighting. Depth under stage 12', 1 trap center. Seating capacity 600. By ca. 1921, seating capacity was 537. Stage was 49' wide × 25' high × 27' deep. Mgr. G. Hutchings (1889), W. F. Insell (1904–1905), W. Stewart (1921).

Princess, ca. 1914, ground-floor hall seating 537. Stage was 49' wide × 25' high × 27' deep. Mgr. John J. Nanert.

Ryder's Hall, ca. 1886; stage was "temporary" in 1886.

Earlham (*Madison*)

Earlham Opera House, 1900. Located on the second story of a two-story brick building erected by Fred Biderback. There were business firms on the lower floor. Sources conflict as to building dimensions. Either they were 43'6½" × 98'5" or 45' × 70'. The building may have been enlarged later. The main floor now is 41' × 81'6"; proscenium height 9'6"; curtain line to back wall 16'; offstage right 9'6"; offstage left 9'7"; stage height from the main floor is 2'9½". Currently it is used for storage.

Earlville (*Delaware*)

Earlville Town Hall. Seated 300. Located where Ken Demoss has his body shop. Reportedly, part of Mr. Demoss's home was part of the opera house.

Early (*Sac*)

Early Opera House. Burned.

Eddyville (*Mahaska*)

Eddyville Opera House, 107 Walnut. Two-story brick, 24' × 78'. Interior was "filled in—floor levelled."

GAR Hall, ca. 1889, seated 200. Mgr. GAR Post.

Legett's Opera House, ca. 1883 (1883–1921), ground-floor hall seating 450. Proscenium was 22' wide × 14' high; stage was 42' wide × 20' deep; 2' apron; ten 12' high grooves. Electric light. 5 dressing rooms. Mgrs. E. Leggett, John Legett (1889), L. A. Rowe (1912), Mrs. L. A. Rowe (1914).

Edgewood (*Delaware*)

Charles & Hubert Hesner Theatre, Union and Washington streets.

Also, variously, the McCallum Theatre, Orlando Sheffert Theatre, Lyle Eastman Theatre and the Charles Moorman Theatre. The current function is the Edgewood Legion Club. The Dick Ripley Players (a Toby show) operated out of Edgewood.

Elberon (*Tama*)

Kaloupek's Hall.

Eldon (*Wapello*)

GAR Hall, ca. 1889, seated 400. Mgr. W. G. Crow.

McHaffey's Opera House, 1891, Elm St. Three-story brick, 45' × 90'. Second-third story hall; proscenium is 19'6" wide × 12' high; stage is 30'6" wide × 16' high × 15' deep; 4'6" apron. Dressing rooms off R and L. Original capacity was 500. in 1914, stage was listed as 44' wide × 16' high × 20' deep. Original seats are in the building; some posters, playbills, old flats, many pigeon corpses. Mgr. David McHaffey (1914).

Eldora (*Hardin*)

Excelsior Rink Hall, ca. 1889, seated 400. Mgr. D. C. Clark.

Porter & Moir's Hall, ca. 1878 (1878–1889), seated 800. Stage was 32' wide × 18' deep; 16' × 44' (1883). Mgrs. Porter & Moir, W. J. Moir (1889).

Wisner Opera House, ca. 1883 (1896–1921). Second-floor hall seating 340 on the main floor, 224 in 2 balconies, 40 in the boxes (total: 604); prices (1896) $0.25–$0.75. In 1896, proscenium was 30'6" wide × 28' high; stage was 62' wide × 42' high × 24' deep; 4' apron. 41' between fly girders. 3'6" depth under stage. Had three 18' high grooves, could be taken up flush with fly gallery. 1 trap, center; 1 bridge. Electric light (1896). 6 dressing rooms. Kirt Ellsworth (1896), Chas. Kenoyer (1898), stage carpenters; Charles McConnelong (1896), prop man. Burned 1921. Mgrs. J. H. Bales, John C. Crockett (1898), Gilman & Kenoyer (1903), G. E. Gilman (1908), H. W. Emeny (1912), E. A. Bloomgast (1921).

Eldridge (*Scott*)

Eldridge Turner Hall, 102. W. LeClaire Rd. Not known if plays were performed here, but a roll drop with the Turner emblem used to be in the building.

Elgin (*Fayette*)

Elgin Opera House, east end of Center St.

Elkader (*Clayton*)

Boller's Hall, ca. 1883 (1883–1889), seated 400. Mgr. V. Boller.

New Elkader Theatre (Elkader Opera House), 1903 (1904–1921), 207 N. Main. Three-story brick. The building measures 50' × 87'. The proscenium is 27' wide × 18' high; curtain line to the back is 23'. There currently is no apron (the stage was being rebuilt). Originally the proscenium was 27' wide × 18' high; the stage was 48' wide × 34' high × 24' deep; 3' apron. Height to the fly gallery was 20'. The depth under the stage was 7'; there were two traps, center 3 & center 1. No scene room. 6 dressing rooms. Electric light. Fred Seebrock, C. Gleason (1907), electricians; Frank Hofer, C. Quinn

(1907) stage carpenters and prop men; Max R. Melin, Dean Prouty (1907), orchestra leaders. The main floor seats 325; the gallery seats 277 (total: 602); the seats are original. Seating capacity in 1904 was 683; prices were $0.35–$0.50. There are dressing rooms under the stage; the building has the original front curtain. In 1921 there was a 18′ × 18′ screen; 85′ throw. Doug Prouty, stage carpenter; P. N. Wilke, orchestra leader. George M. Cohan was the opening act. Mgrs. Louis J. Kramer (1904), F. L. Wolf (1907), Wm. F. Reinecke (1908), Gus H. Wilke (1912).

Turner Opera House, ca. 1896 (1896–1902), ground-floor house seating 300. Proscenium was 18′ wide × 11′ high; stage was 35′ wide × 11′ high × 16′ deep; 2′ apron. 18′ between fly girders. 5′ depth under stage. Had 4 grooves, 1 trap. Mgrs. Reinecke & Falkenhaines; B. F. Falkenhaines (1899). Burned 2 Feb. 1903.

Elkport (*Clayton*)

Elkport Town Hall. Single-story frame, 40′ × 100′. A room has been built on the stage, but it is still possible to determine dimensions: the proscenium opening is 15′9″ wide × 12′ high; stage is 40′ wide × 16′ deep. The main floor measures 39′ × 72′.

Elliott (*Montgomery*)

Elliott Opera House, 1897, Main St. According to resident Gale Eshelman, it was the second story of a two-story brick structure. The stage was about 25′ × 25′. There were no dressing rooms and no balcony . The seating capacity was about 200 and the facility was heated by two coal stoves. It was converted into a one-story building and is currently Milner's Garage.

Wood's Opera House, ca. 1912, second-story hall seating 250. Proscenium was 18′ wide × 10′ high. Stage was 30′ wide × 18′ deep, 2′ apron. 2 dressing rooms. By ca. 1914, stage was 24′ wide × 16′ high × 16′ deep. Mgr. W. J. Wood.

Ellston (*Ringgold*)

Ellston Opera House. The opera house has been remodeled into stores and businesses.

Elma (*Howard*)

Elma Opera House, 1903. Single-story brick, 44′ × 80′. Now houses the Elma locker. Some tin panels and molding are only remnants of the theatre.

Emerson (*Mills*)

Emerson Opera House.

Emmetsburg (*Palo Alto*)

Iowa Theatre, ca. 1907 (1907–1914), ground-floor house seating 342 on the main floor and 358 in 2 balconies (total: 700). Proscenium was 30′ wide × 20′ high; stage was 60′ wide × 43′ high × 24′ deep; 6′ apron. No grooves, 2 traps. Depth under stage 12′. L. J. Hoggerty, F. E. Ellis (1908–1909), stage carpenters. 6 in orchestra: leader, Miss M. O'Connor, (1907–1909). By ca. 1913, seating capacity was 688. Proscenium opening was 20′ × 20′. Stage was 29′ deep, 6′ apron. 6 dressing rooms. By ca. 1914, seating capacity was 700. Mgr. A. N. Keller (1907), Robert Laughlin (1908–1913).

Ormsby's Music Hall, ca. 1883 (1883–1905), seated 500 in Andrews folding opera chairs. Piano. Size of stage 20' × 43'. 6 sets of scenery. By 1896 called simply Music Hall. Seating capacity 400. Proscenium was 20' wide × 18' high; stage was 24' high × 24' deep. 1 trap. Depth under stage 3'. Gas light. Electricity ca. 1901. Theatre second floor. Grooves can be taken up flush with fly gallery. Mgrs. Ormsby Brothers (1883–ca. 1886), Smith and Keller (ca. 1896).

English River Township (*Washington*)—See Richmond.

Essex (*Page*)

Essex Opera House, 1877/1894, Main and Denison. According to the *Essex Centennial,* it was originally the Baptist Church, built in 1877 at a cost of $3,000. It moved to its present location in 1894. It is a frame building 40'2" × 65'. Its seating capacity was about 200. It had folding chairs and an ad. curtain. Originally the stage used kerosene lamps. It was extensively remodeled and is currently the American Legion Hall.

Estherville (*Emmet*)

Armory Theatre, ca. 1912, ground-floor hall seating 600 on the main floor and 300 on the balcony (total: 900). Proscenium was 26' wide × 16' high; stage was 66' wide × 22' high × 24' deep. Electric light. 4 dressing rooms. Mgr. Spencer R. Cox.

Court House Hall, ca. 1889.

Grand Theatre, ca. 1921, seated 1000. Proscenium was 24' wide × 30' high; stage was 50' wide × 75' high × 30' deep; 5' apron. Mgr. F. H. Graaf.

Graves Hall, ca. 1889.

Lough Opera House, ca. 1896 (1896–1909), second-story house seating 700. Proscenium was 28' wide × 18' high; stage was 44' wide × 19' high × 23' deep; 5' apron. 1 trap. Depth under stage 4'. Grooves can be taken up flush with fly gallery. By ca. 1903, stage height 48', no grooves. Mgr. James Cox (1896), (1900); F. H. Rhodes (1898), J. S. Cox and Jesse Cox (1903), J. J. Klopp (1904–1905), James S. Cox and Co. (1907).

Exira (*Audubon*)

Whited Hall, ca. 1889, seated 200. Mgr. J. C. Whited.

Fairbank (*Buchanan*)

Opera House.

Fairfield (*Jefferson*)

New Grand Opera House, ca. 1896 (Grand Opera House in 1897). Ground-floor theatre seating 800; prices (1896) $0.25–$0.75. Proscenium 25' wide × 20' high (14' in 1897); stage was 56' wide × 24' high × 35' deep; 6' apron. 30' between fly girders. Five 16' high grooves, could be taken up flush with fly gallery. 8' depth under stage. 2 traps, R and L of center. 2 bridges, "located up and down." "All drops" by 1899. Bob Angstead (1896, 1904), Ed Trowbridge (1903), stage carpenters; Nute Aldrich, Orville Wilson

(1903), Butch Moore (1904), Oscar Ragus (1907), prop men. Gas and electric lighting. Mgrs. M. F. Black (1896), Lou Thoma (1897, 1904), D. F. Drake (1903). Burned ca. 1914.

Orpheum Theatre, 119 W. Broadway. Two-story brick, 60' × 120'. Completely altered inside to modern dual-movie theatre complex.

Seaman's Opera House, ca. 1883 (1883–1889), seated 500. Was "Semon [sic] Opera House" in 1889. Stage was 44' wide × 20' deep. Mgrs. H. Seaman, R. H. Moore (1889).

Victory Theatre, 114 E. Broadway. Two-story brick, 18' frontage.

Well's Hall, ca. 1878, seated 400. Stage was 40' wide, 8' deep. Had a drop curtain and limited scenery.

Farley (*Dubuque*)

Public Hall, ca. 1883 (1883–1886), seated 400. Mgrs. O'Connell Bros.

Rink Hall, ca. 1889, seated 400. Mgr. Geo. McGee & Co.

Farmersburg (*Clayton*)

Farmersburg Opera House, three-story frame, 36'6" × 120'. Auditorium measured 35' wide × 89'6" long, with a narrow balcony along the three sides. Proscenium was 17' wide × 12' high; stage was 19' deep × 35' wide. Harlem Globetrotters once played here. Razed July 1983.

Farmington (*Van Buren*)

Miller Opera House, ca. 1890. Brick two-story, hall was on the second floor. Was remodeled from a pants factory.

New Opera House, ca. 1889 (1889–1921), seated 300. Had "good stage, no scenery." In 1912 the proscenium was 30' wide × 15' high; stage was 75' wide × 12' high × 25' deep; 5' apron. 4 dressing rooms. In 1921 stage was 22' wide × 12' high × 24' deep. Mgrs. W. D. Carr, J. E. Carr (1912), T. C. Jansen (1914).

Opera House, ca. 1889. second-story house, seated 500. Proscenium was 30' wide × 15' high; stage was 75' wide × 12' high × 20' deep; 5' apron. Electric light. Mgr. T. B. Boler.

Farnhamville (*Calhoun*)

Farnhamville Opera House, 1912, Garfield Ave.

Fayette (*Fayette*)

Duncan Hall, ca. 1883 (1883–1886), seated 500. Mgr. H. G. Pest.

Fayette Opera House, ca. 1914 (1914–1921), 300 block of S. Main. Now the Masonic Hall, the single-story frame building measures 36' × 92'. The interior was remodeled and the stage removed after a fire in 1980. Originally the proscenium was 34' wide and 16' high; curtain line to the back wall was 22'. Seating capacity was 550. Mgrs. Otto E. Noble, Albert Stegall (1921).

Fenton (*Kossuth*)

Fenton Opera House, ca. 1912. First-story house seating 350 on the main floor and 150 in the balcony (total: 500). The proscenium was 28' wide × 14' high; stage was 36' wide × 12' high × 16' deep; 4' apron. 2 dressing rooms. Gas light. Mgr. R. S. Blossom.

Floris (*Davis*)

IOOF Hall, ca. 1908, north side of Main St. Second-story hall.

Fonda (*Pocahontas*)

McKee's Opera House, ca. 1889, seated 500 (see Mullin Opera House).

Mullin Opera House, ca. 1889 (originally McKee's Opera Hall). According to Grace Mullin and the 1970 *Fonda Centennial,* it was located on Main Street. It was purchased by J. P. and Owen Mullin in 1908. In 1912 that building and the one next to it were combined to form a two-story brick structure with the opera house on the second floor and businesses on the lower. The building dimensions were then 50′ × 100′. The stage and dressing rooms were on the east side and a small balcony was on the west. The proscenium is 22′7″ wide × 7′9″ high on both sides and 10′½″ high in the middle. The curtain line to back wall is 17′9″; offstage right space is 12′7″ × 18′; offstage left is 18′4″—the other dimension is not measurable. The balcony is 16′ × 27′3″ and rises 2′ from front to back. Currently empty but being restored. First listed in Cahn/ Leighton 1912–1913. Statistics from Gus Hill (1914) as follows: Stage 34′ wide × 12′ high × 20′ deep. Mgr. Mullen Bros.

Fontanelle (*Adair*)

Opera Hall, ca. 1886. Seated 500. Mgr. C. W. Kundiff (1889).

Forest City (*Hancock*)

(Forest City) Opera House, 1866.

Forest Theatre, ca. 1921, seated 500. Stage was 42′ wide × 32′ deep. Screen was 12′ × 12′; 82′ throw. See New Opera House (1914). Mgr. J. P. Weist.

New Opera House, ca. 1889, seated 500.

New Opera House (1914). Became the Forest Theatre. Burned 1950.

Fort Atkinson (*Winneshiek*)

Opera House.

Fort Dodge (*Webster*)

(Fort Dodge) Opera Hall, ca. 1889, seated 1000.

Berry's Hall, ca. 1878, seated 600. Stage was 45′ wide × 13′6″ deep. Mgr. J. M. Berry.

Fessler's Opera House, ca. 1883 (1883–1900), also called Tessler Opera House. Size of stage 20′ × 30′. Seating capacity 1000. Piano supplied and complete line of scenery. By ca. 1896, seating capacity was 1350. Proscenium was 21′ wide × 18′ high; stage was 23′ deep; 4′ apron. Grooves could be taken up flush with the fly gallery. Scene room. Gas light. Theatre second floor. Mgrs. D. Fessler, Guy Rankin, Proprietor D. Fessler (1889), Rankin and Smith (1896), Clarence H. Smith (1899).

Midland Theatre, ca. 1900 (1900–1909), ground-floor theatre seating 406 on the main floor, 523 in 2 balconies, 64 in the boxes (total: 993). Proscenium was 34′ wide × 30′ high; stage was 67′ wide × 75′ high × 36′ deep; 2′ apron; 2 traps. Gas and electric lighting. Depth under stage 8′. P. V. Jones, E. R. Cunningham (1901), Andrew Belt (1903–1904), electricians. John Campbell (1900), Ray Mansfield (1901), Frank Schaffner (1903–1905), prop men. J. N. Stine (1900), Harry Thursh (1901), H. T. Kelley (1903–1905), stage carpenters. Professor Rogers (1900), Professor Carl Quist (1903), orchestra leaders. 8 in orchestra. By ca. 1903, 10 in orchestra. Mgr. S. T. Meservey (1900), Beth M. Meservey (1903), A. B. Beall (1904–1905), W. P. Dermer (1907), Tom Arthur (1908).

Princess, ca. 1914 (1914–1921), ground-floor hall seating 800. Stage was 57' wide × 70' high × 32' deep. By ca. 1921, seating capacity 780. Stage 57'6" wide. Mgr. Carl Hepler (1914–19??), P. F. Nuget (1921).

Fort Madison (*Lee*)

Concordia Hall, 1866 (1878–1886), Ave. H. Two-story brick, 60' × 126', now houses the Elks Club, overlooking the Mississippi. Originally the stage was 20' × 22'; seating capacity was 400, and there were "seven good scenes." Mgr. Chas. Doerr (1886).

Ebinger Grand, ca. 1896 (1896–1914), ground-floor hall seating 506 on the main floor, 728 in 2 balconies, 30 in the boxes (total: 1264); prices (1896) $0.25–$1. In 1896, proscenium was 30' wide × 44' high; stage was 64' wide × 45' high × 35' deep; 5' apron. 42' between fly girders. 8' depth under stage. Four 18' grooves, 1 trap, center. Gas light (gas and electric by 1903). 16 dressing rooms. Chas. Emerick (1896), Peter Penrod (1904), Fred Podeyn (1908), stage carpenters; Guy Hunt (1896), Charles Huffman (1904), Fred Hall (1908), prop men; Billy Schutzheimer (1896), John Stein (1904), orchestra leaders—12 in orchestra. Booking agent, Klaw & Erlanger (1914), New York. Mgrs. Chas. H. Salisbury, E. Ebinger (1907), W. Ebinger (1912), George Shaffner (1914).

Grand Theatre, ca. 1921, seated 1000. Stage was 55' wide × 70' high × 45' deep; 40' between fly galleries. 16' × 20' screen; 75' throw. Fred Podyne, stage carpenter; Bryd Zwald, orchestra leader. Booking agents, A. L. Erlanger, Shuberts, & Gus Hill, New York. Mgr. L. V. Murphy.

New Bennett Opera House, ca. 1889, seated 1000; opera chairs, piano. Stage was 36' wide × 38' high × 35' deep; 16' to grooves. 22 sets scenery. "Fireproof." "Only opera house in the city" (1889). Prop. S. R. Bennett. Mgr. J. W. Campbell (1889).

Fremont (*Mahaska*)

Strand, south side of Main St. Burned in 1928. Fremont also had 2 other small theatres that burned.

Galt (*Wright*)

Galt Opera House, west side of Main St. Burned, 1922.

Galva (*Ida*)

Loeb Theatre, Main St. A one-story brick building 26'2" × 100'2". Extensively remodeled it is now the American Legion Hall.

Garden Grove (*Decatur*)

Dilsaver Opera House, 1917. Two-story brick building located on Main Street. The theatre was located on the ground floor. It has a balcony. The building is 38' × 81'. The main floor is 35' × 60'; stage height from main floor is 3'; curtain to back wall 15'7½"; footlight trough 2' wide and 13'1" long; balcony 11'5" × 35'. It has been extensively remodeled and currently is the American Legion and Community Building.

Opera House, ca. 1883 (1883–1889), seated 500. Stage was 24' wide × 24' deep. Had a good stock of scenery. Mgr. A. B. Stearns.

Garnavillo (*Clayton*)

Garnavillo Turner Hall.

Garner (*Hancock*)

"Theatre at this point, but no information available (1912)."

Fell's, ca. 1914. See Garner Opera House. Stage was 24' wide × 10' high × 14' deep. Seating capacity 300. Mgrs. Fell Bros.

Garner Opera House, ca. 1896, 3rd and State. Two-story brick, same as Fell's. 66' × 75', now completely altered inside. Was second-floor house. Mgr. Fell Bros.

Moak's Hall, ca. 1889, seated 500. Mgr. W. C. Moak.

Garwin (*Tama*)

Savoy Theatre, 1914, Main St. Single-story brick, with a striking double-arch front, with the name of the theatre above in contrasting brick: 23'4" × 91'6". The stage is gone, but it measured 14' wide × 12' high × 10-12' deep. A dilapidated landscape drop hangs on the back wall.

Geneva (*Franklin*)

Geneva Opera House. Second-story hall above grocery store. Two-story frame, 44'8" × 72'. Owner wouldn't let investigator upstairs, but assures us that the stage is removed and "nothing is left."

See also the entry for Maysville.

George (*Lyon*)

George Opera House.

Gilman (*Marshall*)

Masonic Opera House, ca. 1889, E. Main and Highway 146. Seated 450.

Gilmore City (*Pocahontas*)

Gilmore City Opera House. Burned.

Gladbrook (*Tama*)

(Gladbrook) Opera House, ca. 1907 (1907–1921), seated 450. Ground-floor house. Proscenium was 20' wide × 12' high; stage was 36' wide × 14' high × 16' deep; 2' apron; six 12' high grooves; could be taken up flush to fly gallery. 10' depth under stage. Scene room. 4 dressing rooms. Gas and gasoline lighting. In 1921, George Poland was stage carpenter, Louise Barton, orchestra leader. Mgrs. T. E. Mann, Cato F. Mann (1921).

Mann's Hall, ca. 1886 (1886–1889), seated 590. Mgr. T. E. Mann.

Mann's Opera House, ca. 1889, seated 400, chairs. Proscenium was 16' wide × 12' high; stage was 26' wide × 14' high × 16' deep; 2' apron. 12' to grooves; limited scenery, drop curtain. "This is the only house here" (1889). Mgr. T. E. Mann. Probably the same as Mann's Hall.

Music Hall, ca. 1889, ground-floor hall seating 450; prices $0.35 and $0.50. Proscenium was 20' wide × 12' high; stage was 36' wide × 17' deep; 4 grooves, could be taken up flush with fly gallery. Scene room. Gas light. Mgr. T. E. Mann.

Uptown Theatre, 1893. Could be the original Music Hall or Opera House. Two-story concrete block, 24' × 80'.

Glenwood (*Mills*)

Cilley's Opera House, ca. 1889, seated 350. Mgr. H. G. Cilley.

Glenwood Opera House, ca. 1878, seated 400. Stage was 38' wide × 23' high × 23' deep. Had 6 scenes, drops & flats. Mgr. H. G. Cilley.

Rex Theatre, ca. 1912 (1912–1921), ground-floor house seating 350 on the main floor and 150 in the balcony; 2 boxes (total: 500+). Proscenium was 24' wide × 14' high; stage was 44' wide × 24' high × 18' deep; 2' apron; six 12' grooves. 2 dressing rooms. Electric light. Also known as Glenwood Opera House. Mgrs. Seymore and Fair, Fair Bros. (1914).

Glidden (*Carroll*)

Armstrong Hall. Burned.

Glidden Opera House. Glidden had a second-story opera house by 1893. It burned in 1904. The structure was rebuilt and renamed the Armstrong Building. It burned in 1905 and became a one-story building, went through numerous changes, and is currently the home of the Glidden *Graphic*.

Goodell (*Hancock*)

Goodell Opera House/Town Hall, one-story frame, 18' × 36'. Now the post office.

Gowrie (*Webster*)

Gowrie Opera House.

Hoyt's Hall, ca. 1886, seated 200. Mgr. Hoyt.

Tower Opera House, ca. 1914 (1914–1921), first-story hall seating 400. Stage was 30' wide × 16' high × 16' deep. Mgr. E. M. Wing (1914–19??), David Lennerson (1921).

Graettinger (*Palo Alto*)

Hawkeye Theatre, ca. 1912 (1912–1921), first-story hall seating 320 on the main floor and 130 in the balcony (total: 450). Proscenium was 20' wide × 11'6" high; stage was 38' wide × 23' high × 18' deep; 2' apron. Gas light. 3 dressing rooms. By ca. 1914, stage was 38' wide × 24' high × 18' deep. By ca. 1921, seating capacity was 400. Mgr. C. S. George (1912–1914), John Olson (1921).

Grafton (*Worth*)

Grafton Opera House, ca. 1900.

Grand Junction (*Greene*)

Grand Junction Opera House.

Harvey's Hall, ca. 1886, seated 250. Mgr. J. Harvey.

Grand Mound (*Clinton*)

Jones and Jansen's Hall, ca. 1886, seated 500. Grand Mound was listed in the 1886 Jeffrey's as "Green Mound."

Stiers Opera House, Main St. 1898. A two-story brick/concrete block building, 46' × 90'6". The exterior has been altered, and a fire inside plus extensive remodeling have left nothing of the theatre. The front curtain is reportedly still in town.

Grand River (*Decatur*)

Grand River Opera House. Two-story brick building with the opera house on the second floor. The building is 26' × 61' and was built by Jacob Switzer around 1880. It was extensively remodeled; became a hotel and later was sold to the Masons. There are apartments downstairs and storage upstairs.

Gravity (*Taylor*)

Dionne Opera House, ca. 1890, 302 Main St. Second story of a two-story building erected between 1890 and 1900; 32'2" × 75'. The main floor is 31' × 44'. Stage is 16" above the main floor. The proscenium is 15'9" wide × 8'4" high. The stage is 12' deep. Offstage right and left are 7' wide × 9'6" high. Currently it is storage.

Greeley (*Delaware*)

Opera House.

Greene (*Butler*)

Crystal Theatre, 1913, 104 E. Traer. Single-story brick, 48' × 115'. Now completely remodeled into Family Medical Practice and apartments.

Green Opera House, ca. 1889, seated 600. Proscenium was 20' wide; stage was 23' wide × 14' high × 20' deep. "One scene (new)." Mgr. S. A. van Saun.

Ingalls' Opera House, ca. 1914 (1914–1921), 205 N. 2nd St. Single-story brick. The stage was 44' wide × 30' deep × 32' high. Seating capacity was 600. Now completely remodeled inside into a candle factory. Mgr. A. Ingalls.

Greenfield (*Adair*)

Opera House, ca. 1886, seated 500. Stage was 20' wide × 14' deep. Had fair scenery. By 1889 seated 450 to 500. Mgr. J. Hetherington.

Warren Opera House, 1896 (1896–1914), 156 Public Square. Built by E. Warren, according to Don E. Prichard (*Iowa State Historical Department Buildings Survey Inventory,* 1970). In the 1920s the building was declared unsafe for large crowds. Upper stories which housed the opera house were later used as a basketball court and apartment house. They are now vacant. The lower story houses retail establishments. Sources conflict as to total building size, either two and a half or three stories. Auditorium area is 82' × 44'. Prosenium 20' × 14'; stage 42' wide × 16' high × 18' deep with a 3' apron. Three 12' grooves. Second floor theatre with electric illumination. Seating capacity 550. By ca. 1898, loft height was 20', seating capacity 600. By ca. 1912, seating capacity 525. Proscenium opening 20' wide × 13' high. Stage 42' wide × 18' high × 19' deep, 3' apron. Three 11' grooves. 4 dressing rooms. By ca. 1914, stage width 44'. Entered in *National Register of Historic Places* on October 18, 1979 as a well-preserved example of Iowa's small town opera house and late nineteenth-century commercial architecture. J. H. Brown (1896–1909) prop man. Mgr. E. E. Warren (1896).

Greenville (*Clay*)

Greenville Opera House. The second story of a two-story frame building located on Main Street. The building dimensions are 23'3" × 65'2". Currently the upper story is vacant/storage and the lower is a grocery/post office.

Grinnell (*Poweshiek*)

College Hall, ca. 1889, seated 700. Mgr. S. J. Buck.

Colonial Theatre, 1902 (1907–1921), brick three-story block at 935 Broad St. Ground-floor house seated 343 on the main floor, 450 in 2 balconies, and 32 in the boxes (total: 825). Proscenium was 32' wide × 30' high; stage was 53' wide × 45' high × 35' deep; 3' apron. Scene room. 6 dressing rooms. Electric light. W. H. Mart, stage manager and electrician; L. N. Bailey (1908), electrician; W. H. Mart (1908), stage carpenter and prop man. Torn down April, 1974. Booking agent (1914) Klaw & Erlanger, New York. Mgrs. Chamberlain, Busby & Co.; Busby Bros. (1908); Yeager & Stoakes (1912); W. H. Mart (1914); H. W. Spaulding (1921).

Grand Army Hall, ca. 1889, seated 400. Mgr. T. N. Bray, Quartermaster.

Preston's Opera House, ca. 1886 (1886–1905), three-story building on Main St. Opera house was on the second floor and seated 700. Piano. Proscenium was 20' wide × 11' high; stage was 28' wide × 20' deep; 3' apron. Had fair scenery, 1 trap, center. Scene room. Electric light. Fred Rinefort, electrician. Most recently was a Coast-to-Coast store; may still be standing. Mgrs. Preston & Proctor, J. S. Preston (1889), F. O. Proctor (1897), H. F. Preston (1903).

Stewart's Hall, ca. 1879 (1879–1886), seated 350. Stage was 16' wide × 12' deep. No scenery.

Griswold (*Cass*)

Griswold Opera House, ca. 1888. Two-story brick, built on the north side of Main St. It had a large stage, two sets of drops, two sets of folding curtains, an orchestra pit, a balcony, and a seating capacity of 700. It was enlarged ca. 1900. It has been extensively remodeled.

Rink Hall, ca. 1889, seated 300. Mgr. H. K. Forsyth or Capt. C. P. Chisley.

Grundy Center (*Grundy*)

Geer's Hall, ca. 1883. "American Express."

Opera House, 602 7th St. Supposedly originally a livery stable, converted to a theatre, then to a movie theatre. Single-story brick, 27' × 100'.

Orchestra Hall, 1883 (1886–1889), 7th St. and F Ave., seated 500. Stage was 30' wide × 16' deep. Had a full set of scenery. Remodeled in 1883 as Robinson's Hall. Mgr. Orchestra Hall Co. (1886), C. C. Shuler (1889). See Shafer Opera House.

Robinson's Hall, 1883. See Orchestra Hall, Shafer Opera House.

Shafer Opera House, ca. 1914 (1914–1921), seated 500. Ground-floor hall. Stage was 50' wide × 16' high × 24' deep. In 1921, height of stage was 36'. 60' throw in 1921. Formerly Robinson's Hall,

Orchestra Hall. Mgr. A. C. Schafer.

Guernsey (*Poweshiek*)

Opera House, Main St. Burned.

Guthrie Center (*Guthrie*)

McLuen Theatre, ca. 1912 (1912–1914), ground-floor house seating 450 on the main floor, 200 in the balcony, 24 in the boxes (total: 674). Proscenium was 26′ wide × 16′ high; stage was 40′ wide × 22′ high × 19′ deep; 3′ apron. Electric light. 4 dressing rooms. By ca. 1914, seating capacity was 600. Stage was 40′ wide × 20′ high × 20′ deep. Mgr. Powd McLuen.

Motz Opera House, 1881 (?) , 216–218 State St. The second story of a two-story brick structure built by John E. Motz. The entire building cost $20,000. Its dimensions are 86′ × 60′. The stage was 22′ deep × 60′ wide. It had a drop curtain and other scenery. Its seating capacity was 500. Mgr. J. W. Motz (1889). It currently is Feilmeyer's Furniture Store.

Guttenberg (*Clayton*)

Turner Hall, ca. 1883 (1883–1914), seated 800. Mgrs. Robert Horsh, Carl Ihm (1914).

Hamburg (*Fremont*)

Opera House, ca. 1883 (1883–1889), seated 500. Stage was 40′ wide × 22′ deep. Mgr. C. W. Boulton (1886), A. D. Hunter (1889).

Opera House, ca. 1889, seated 500. Stage was 44′ wide × 20′ deep.

McKunch Hall, ca. 1886, seated 600. Stage was 44′ wide × 24′ deep.

Hamburg Opera House, ca. 1914. Upstairs theatre seating 450. Stage was 44′ wide × 14′ high × 18′ deep. Could be either McKunch Hall or the 1889 Opera House. Mgr. Mrs. M. F. Cooley.

Hamilton (*Marion*)

Hamilton Opera House, Main St.

Hampton (*Franklin*)

Harriman's Opera House, ca. 1879 (1879–1909), second-story house seating 600. Stage was 15′ × 40′ (1883). In 1897, proscenium was 18′ wide × 10′ high; stage was 40′ wide × 10′ high × 20′ deep; 1′6″ apron. Had 4 grooves, 1 trap, 4 scenes and a drop curtain. 3′6″ depth under stage. Electric light (by 1897). H. B. Day (1897), J. J. Roe (1907), electricians; E. J. Stonebraker, J. Costello (1908), prop men. Mgrs. O. B. Harriman, O. B. Harriman & Son (1903), Ed Harriman (1907), E. J. Stonebraker (1908).

Olympic Theatre, ca. 1903 (1904–1909), seated 550; prices $0.25, $0.35, $0.50, $0.75. Electric light. Fred Tyler, electrician. Mgr. L. L. (or I. L.) Stuart.

Windsor Theatre, 1913 (1914–1921), 103 Federal North. Two-story brick, 66′ × 127′. The proscenium is 32′ wide × 20′ high; stage is 64′ wide × 55′ high × 23′ deep. There are dressing rooms offstage R and L, and in the basement. A front drop hangs above the movie screen box. The apron is still equipped with footlights; lighting control board offstage R. The orchestra pit has been filled in. Built originally by the Knights of Pythias. Original architect's drawings in the theatre; architect was James S. Cox, Estherville, IA. In 1921, stage was 60' wide × 55' high × 32' deep; 20' between fly galleries. Had a 12' × 16' screen; 90' throw. Geo. Hamilton, stage carpenter; Walter Peterson, orchestra leader. Mgrs. Bert Stover, Chas. Peterson (1921).

Hancock (*Pottawattamie*)

Hancock Opera House.

Harlan (*Shelby*)

Harlan Opera House, ca. 1889, seated 700, opera chairs, piano. Proscenium was 25' wide; stage was 42' wide × 12' high × 26' deep. Had 8 sets of scenery, 14 wings, ocean view set, set waters, set rocks, set balustrades. Probably same as Lay's Opera House, Long's Opera House. Mgr. S. K. Pratt (1889).

(Harlan) Opera House, ca. 1903 (1903–1921), second-story hall, seated 700. Proscenium was 21' wide × 11' high; stage was 26' wide × 23' high × 33' deep; 8' apron. Had twenty-one 11' high grooves, 2 traps. Grooves may not be taken up flush with fly gallery. Geo. W. Cox (1903–1908), electrician. By ca. 1904, stage was 41' wide × 23' high × 16' deep, 8' apron. By ca. 1914, stage was 42' wide × 20' high × 26' deep. Mgr. D. M. Wayland (1903–1909), B. Wayland (1914).

Lay's Opera House, ca. 1883, seated 700. Stage was 42' wide × 26' deep. Had a complete stock of scenery. Probably the same as Harlan Opera House. Mgr. B. P. Hunt.

Long's Opera House (Harlan Opera House), 1882. On the second and third stories of a three-story brick building erected by J. M. Long. Building is 44' × 120'. The main floor of the auditorium was 44' × 66'. The gallery was 44' × 42'. The stage was 26' deep × 42' wide. It was originally illuminated with gas. A complete stock of scenery was painted by Sosman and Landis of Chicago. Seating capacity 750. Mgr. B. P. Hunt (1883). Currently it is a movie house and retail shops.

Harris (*Osceola*)

Harris Opera House.

Hartley (*O'Brien*)

Hartley Opera House.

Hastings (*Fremont*)

Hastings Opera House.

Hawarden, also spelled Harwarden, (*Sioux*)

Auditorium Theatre, ca. 1921, seated 600. Mgr. S. Van Sickle.

Brunskill's Theatre, ca. 1904 (1904–1914), seated 450. Proscenium was 20' wide × 12' high; stage was 18' deep. Depth under stage 2', 1 trap. Gas and electric light. Bishop (1904–1905), John Doctor (1907–1909), electricians. By ca. 1914, seating capacity was 350. Stage was 24' wide × 10' high × 16' deep. Mgr. D. Brunskill (1904–1914).

Deek Hall, ca. 1889, seated 500. Mgr. T. J. Deek (1889).

Rink Hall, ca. 1886, seated 400.

Hawkeye (*Fayette*)

Opera House. Second-story hall over the hardware store.

Hazleton (*Buchanan*)

Opera House, ca. 1886.

Hedrick (*Keokuk*)

Baldwin's Hall, ca. 1889, seated 530. Mgr. A. M. Baldwin.

Henderson (*Mills*)

Henderson Opera House, seated 100. May be extant.

Hillsboro (*Henry*)

Hillsboro Opera House, 1901. Now functioning as the Masonic Hall, this two-story brick building measures 33' × 51'. Opera house was on the second floor; city hall was on the first floor. The stage has been removed.

Holstein (*Ida*)

Turner Hall, ca. 1914. Ground-floor hall, seated 600. Stage was 56' wide × 20' high × 20' deep. Mgr. C. J. Wohlenberg.

Hopkinton (*Delaware*)

Hopkinton Opera House, ca. 1866. Two-story brick building, measures 30' × 70'. It has been totally remodeled inside (an interior second floor was added in 1922), and now houses the Old Brick Inn.

Hornick (*Woodbury*)

Hornick Opera House.

Hospers (*Sioux*)

Hospers Opera House. Located on the second story of a two-story building erected by the Richter Brothers who were bankers. The building dimensions are 25' × 60'. Currently it is apartments.

Hubbard (*Hardin*)

Dean's Hall, ca. 1886 (1886–1889), seated 100.

Hadley & Ray's Hall, ca. 1886 (1886–1889), seated 200.

Hudson (*Black Hawk*)

Opera House. Second-story hall over the Hudson State Bank. Now a tavern.

Hull (*Sioux*)

Davidson Theatre, ca. 1912 (1912–1921), seated 192 on the main floor and 225 in 2 balconies (total: 417). Ground-floor theatre. Proscenium was 26' wide × 18' high; stage was 50' wide × 36' high × 17'6" deep; 4'6" apron. Gas light. 3 dressing rooms. By ca. 1914, seating capacity was 425. Mgr. C. L. Beach.

Humboldt (*Humboldt*)

Harkness Hall, ca. 1889, seated 300. Mgr. B. H. Harkness.

Humboldt Hall, ca. 1886, seated 500.

Russell Opera House, ca. 1904 (1904–1921). Ground-floor house seating 600. Proscenium was 22' wide × 14' high; stage was 44' wide × 36' deep. Electric light. By ca. 1907, proscenium was 22' wide × 16' high; stage was 40' wide × 36' deep. By ca. 1912, proscenium was again 22' wide × 14' high. Stage 40' wide × 28' deep. 4 dressing rooms. By ca. 1914, stage was 16' high. Mgr. H. H. Russell.

Humeston (*Wayne*)

Middlebrook Hall, ca. 1889, seated 400. Mgr. Robert Middlebrook.

Princess Theatre, ca. 1912 (1912–1921). Ground-floor house seating 350 on the main floor and 300 in the balcony. Proscenium was 20' wide × 15' high; stage was 44' wide × 16' high × 20' deep. Had seven 11' high grooves. 4 dressing rooms. Electric light. Booking agent (1914) J. Wingfield, Chicago. Mgr. A. L. Barker.

Huxley (*Story*)

Princess Theatre.

Ida Grove (*Ida*)

Grand Opera House, So. Main St. Prior to the 1890s the Unitarians built a second-story opera house called the Grand by remodeling an existing structure. All that remains is the ground floor and basement. Its current dimensions are 48'4" × 102'. It is now Iverson Radio and TV and apartments. See Grand Theatre.

Grand Theatre, ca. 1904 (1904–1921), ground-floor hall seated 515. Proscenium was 24' wide × 13' high; stage was 48' wide × 22' deep; 2' apron. Had four 12'2" high grooves, 1 trap. Grooves may be taken up flush with fly gallery. Depth under stage 4'10". By ca. 1912, called the Grand Opera House. Proscenium 23' wide × 13' high. Stage 48' wide × 23' deep, 3' apron. 2 dressing rooms. By ca. 1914 called New Grand. Stage was 50' wide × 18' high × 30' deep. Seating capacity was 500. Mgr. J. E. Easton (1904), W. L. Hester (1914–19??), Harry Lowder (1921).

Williams' Opera House, ca. 1896 (1896–1908), ground-floor hall. Proscenium opening 20' × 30'; stage 22' deep, 42' wide, 50' high; 2' apron. Two 24' high grooves, 1 trap. Depth under stage 8'. Grooves can be taken up flush with fly gallery. Seating capacity 800. Mgr. Geo. T. Williams.

Opera House, ca.1886. Seated 700. Good stage scenery. Possibly the same as Williams' or Grand Opera House. Mgrs. Hallam Brothers.

Independence (*Buchanan*)

Gedney Opera House, ca. 1896 (1896–1921), ground-floor hall, seated 350 on the main floor, 586 in 2 balconies, and 28 in the boxes (total: 850–964); prices $0.25–$0.75 ($0.25–$1 by 1907). Proscenium was 28' wide × 30' high; stage was 57' wide × 55' high × 34' deep; 7' apron. 42' between fly girders. 8' depth under stage. Had six 20' high grooves (no grooves by 1907), 3 traps between curtain line and tormentors, and 1 center, between 2nd and 3rd entrance. 1 bridge, between 3 and 4. Scene room. 6 dressing rooms. Electric light. J. F. Van Vors (1896), Jas. Pepper (1907), electricians and stage carpenters; Noxon & Toomey, scenic artists; Prof. Fritz Hasshold (1896), Prof. C. W. Hansen (1904), Prof. E. W. Raymond (1907), orchestra leaders. Booking agent (1914) J. Wingfield, Chicago. Mgrs. R. M. Campbell (1896), C. E. Ransier (1904), J. S. Bassett (1907, 1914), Clyde H. Wilson (1912).

Gedney Theatre, ca. 1921. Seated 800. Prices $0.50–$1. The proscenium was 35' wide; the stage was 50' wide × 20' high × 35' deep; 40' between fly girders. There was a 12' × 15' screen; 55' throw. Bob Young was stage carpenter; E. W. Raymond was orchestra leader. Mgr. J. S. Bassett.

King's Opera House, 1875 (1883–1889), 330 First St. E. Two-story brick. The building measures 56'6" × 120'6". In 1889 it had a stage which measured 24' deep × 52' wide, with five scenes, and seated 1000. Mgr. Chas. King. The theatre has been totally remodeled inside, and now houses the Midwest Refrigerated Equipment Company. See Bibliography.

Leytze Hall, ca. 1878 (1878–1886), seated 350. Stage was 16' wide × 6' deep, "with extension." No scenery. Mgr. A. Leytze.

Indianola (*Warren*)

Empress Theatre, ca. 1921, seated 400. Mgr. A. Keeney.

Opera Hall, ca. 1879 (1879–1889), "one of the best of its size in the state," seated 500. Stage was 42' wide × 20' deep. Had 4 scenes and a drop curtain. In 1883 it was refurbished, with 500 "office" chairs with 6 chairs "always reserved for families." Stage was 20' × 42'. Had 6 sets of "elegant new scenery, all on rollers." Mgrs. J. W. Campbell (1883), Campbell & Spray (1889).

Inwood (*Lyon*)

Inwood Opera House, ca. 1914, (1914–1921), ground-floor house seated 600. Stage was 40' wide × 16' high × 20' deep. Mgr. S. J. Mak (1914–19??), Hugo Rennis (1921).

Ionia (*Chickasaw*)

Ionia Opera House, Hoffman Building, Main Street. A second-story hall, destroyed by the tornado of 1948.

Iowa City (*Johnson*)

Clark & Hill's Opera House, 1877 (1878–1889), Clinton and College streets. Became Coldren's Opera House in 1897. Three-story brick, theatre on second floor. Originally had a 30' × 60' stage, a seating capacity of 1000, six full sets of scenery and extra set pieces. Later had eight full sets of scenery; heated by steam and lighted by gas. In 1897 it was described as having a proscenium 22' wide × 18' high; footlights to back wall, 34'; curtain line to footlights, 4'; distance between side walls, 60'; four grooves 16' from stage; 4'6" depth under stage, three traps, center and each side. Was on the second floor. Mgr. J. N. Coldren.

Coldren Opera House, 1897. Seated 314 on the main floor, 531 in 2 balconies (total: 845). Proscenium was 25'6" wide × 48' high; stage was 60' wide × 55' high × 27' deep; 3' apron. 45' between fly galleries, 27' to fly gallery. 11 dressing rooms. 3 traps. In 1904 it was still lighted by gas; by 1907 it had switched to electric light. Mgrs. Perry Clark (1897), J. N. Coldren (1903), C. C. Rowley (1907), Will S. Collier (1908) (H. W. Fairall, local mgr., 1912).

Englert Theatre, 1913 (1914–1921), 221 E. Washington. Three-story brick, 63' × 150'. Still a movie theatre, it was completely rebuilt after a fire in 1926. In 1914 the stage was 32' deep × 62' wide × 58' high. The proscenium opening was 30'. The stage to the fly gallery was 40'; footlights to back wall, 40'. Height to the rigging loft was 60'. In 1921 the stage was 60' wide × 60' high × 40' deep; 40' to the fly gallery. Screen was 15' × 20'—100' throw. Sherm Casebolt was stage carpenter. Booking agents were Shuberts, Erlanger (New York) and Wingfield (Chicago). Mgrs. W. H. Englert, W. M. McKenzie (1921).

Ham's Hall, ca. 1878, seated 800. Stage was 36' wide × 15' deep. Had 8 scenes and a drop curtain. Mgr. Daniel Ham.

Iowa Falls (*Hardin*)

Anderson Opera House, ca. 1883, seated 500. Stage was 40' wide × 16' deep. Mgr. J. D. Steere.

Leonard & Chesboro Opera Hall, ca. 1878 (1878–1886), seated 500. Stage was 24' wide × 18' deep. No scenery, no orchestra available.

Leonard's Opera House, ca. 1889. Same as Leonard & Chesboro Opera Hall. Mgr. W. W. Leonard.

Metropolitan Opera House, 1899 (1900–1921), 515 Washington Ave. Three-story brick grand opera house, 66'6" wide by half a block long. The proscenium measures 30' × 21'; curtain line to back 26', with a 3' apron (original measurements gave 34' from footlights to back wall). Stage is 62' wide. The stage now has a movie screen box installed. Originally there was 50' between fly girders, and the rigging loft was 45' high. There was 9' under the stage, one trap, one bridge between 3 and 4, but no grooves. Electric light. Frank Weldon (1903), electrician; William Allison (1903), E. V. Collins (1904), M. M. Kickels (1907), stage carpenters; Art Woodward (1903), Clifford Carpenter (1907), prop men; A. Munroy (1903), orchestra leader—9 in orchestra. There are dressing rooms backstage and in the basement: in 1912 there were 9. Originally the seating capacity was 450 in the orchestra, 258 in the balcony and 100 in the gallery; prices were orchestra $1 and $0.75, balcony $0.35 and $0.50, gallery $0.25. Today the main floor seats 300 and the balcony 200. The gallery has been made over into a projection booth. There is a roll drop above the stage, but the movie screen renders it inaccessible. There are now some grooves—resembling a huge hay-rake—that hinge up to the fly gallery. There are old posters, photos, and playbills; there is a mural of the Muses (?) painted over the proscenium arch. The lobby has some nice art deco decorations. Some of the original seats are in storage. Booking agent, A. L. Erlanger, New York. Mgr. E. O. Ellsworth.

Opera House, ca. 1883 (1883–1886), seated 500. No piano. Stage was 40' wide × 16' high. Fair amount of scenery. Mgr. R. A. Casleton.

Smith's Hall, ca. 1889, seated 200.

Ireton (*Sioux*)

Ireton Opera House, 1908. According to *Ireton—A Proud Heritage,* it was built in 1908 or 1909 by Roy Mitchell. A one-story frame building, 40' × 100': located in the middle of the block on the north side of 4th St. between Main and Oak. Its current dimensions are 32'4" × 44'8". Currently it is a blacksmith shop. First appears in

Hill (1914) with following statistics: Seating capacity 450. Stage 32' wide × 20' high × 18' deep. Mgr. M. L. Mitchell.

Wing's Hall, ca. 1886, seated 300. Mgr. Dr. D. E. Wing.

Jamaica (*Guthrie*)

Jewell Opera House, ca. 1900, Main St. A two-story brick building with opera house on the second floor, it was built by George W. Heater and, according to *Bricks on the Chimney,* by Bruce F. Towne, it was named "Jewell" in honor of his only daughter. The building dimensions are 50' × 70'4". There was a large balcony. Currently it is used by the Masons. First appears in Cahn/Hill in 1921 with the following notations: Seating capacity 250. "Plays traveling companies." Mgr. George Herter.

Janesville (*Bremer*)

Janesville Opera House, 1899, 304 Main St. Two-story brick, 44' × 70'. Opera house on the second floor. Proscenium measures 21' wide × 13' high; stage is 42' wide × 9'3" deep.

Opera House, 3rd and Main. Razed 1976.

Jefferson (*Greene*)

Head's Opera House, ca. 1889 (1880–1909), seated 1000. First-story hall. By ca. 1896, seating capacity was 600. Proscenium was 24' wide × 14' high; stage was 42' wide × 18' high × 30' deep; 4' apron. Had six 12' high grooves, 2 traps. By ca. 1897 proscenium was 30' × 14'; stage was 42' wide × 18' high × 14' deep. Depth under stage 20'. By ca. 1904, proscenium was 20' high × 16' wide; stage 40' wide × 18' high × 21' deep; 4' apron. Mgrs. Louis Cline (1896), J. F. Hassett (1897), A. M. Head (1899), E. C. Margus (1904), C. E. Margus (1907), Haag and Taylor (1908). See Jefferson Opera House.

Jefferson Opera House, 1884 (1884–1921), (also known as Head's Opera House) 212 Main St. Three-story brick structure built by the Masonic Lodges of Jefferson. It is 42'4" × 120'7". Sources conflict as to seating capacity. One says it had a raked balcony which sat about 100 and a main floor which sat around 350. The other says its capacity was 700. It had a proscenium opening about 25' and roll drops and flats. Currently it is the Sierra Movie House. By ca. 1886 (Jeffrey's), the stage was 15' × 42', with A. H. Andrews opera chairs, 5 scenes. Noted in Cahn/Hill 1921, no statistics. Mgrs. Gallaher and Thompson (1886–18??), Wood and Gottlieb (1921).

Thompson & Gallaher's Opera House, ca. 1883. Mgr. Frank Thompson.

Jessup (*Buchanan*)

Bank Opera House, ca. 1883 (1883–1889), seated 400. Stage was 25' wide × 15' deep. 4 sets of scenery. Organ in hall. Orchestra available.

Grand Opera House, ca. 1856, 7th and Young streets. Second-third story brick. Building is 50' × 65'. Seated 512. The second and third stories have been converted to apartments; the ground floor houses the Black Stallion Bar.

Grand Theatre, ca. 1921, seated 512. Probably the same as the Grand

Opera House. Mgr. J. A. Miller.

Colonial Theatre. Supposedly located on second floor above present library/city hall, on corner of 6th and Young streets.

Jewell (*Hamilton*)

Jewell Junction Town Hall, ca. 1889, seated 175.

Jolley (*Calhoun*)

Woodman Hall.

Kalona (*Washington*)

Kalona Theatre, B Ave. and 6th St.

Kanawha (*Hancock*)

Opera House. Second-story hall above a restaurant/bowling alley. Now apartments.

Kellogg (*Jasper*)

Cravens Opera House. Single-story brick, 27' × 57', now houses the Kellogg Men's Club.

Kensett (*Worth*)

Opera House. Second-story hall, but second floor has been removed from the building.

Keokuk (*Lee*)

Baker's Hall, ca. 1886 (1886–1889), seated 600.

Gibbon's Opera House, 1870 (1878–1886), 627–629 Main. Three-story brick, 45' × 126'. Opera house was on the third floor. Now houses the Knights of Columbus and a Sears store on the ground floor. Originally the stage was 24' × 50', and it seated 1000. Had a "good set of scenery." Mgr. F. Sirvers.

Grand Opera House, ca. 1912 (1908–1921), first-story hall, seated 344 on the main floor, 630 in 2 balconies, 40 in boxes (total: 1014). Proscenium was 32' wide × 40' high; stage was 60' wide × 40' high × 24' deep; 24' to fly gallery; 6' apron. 11 dressing rooms. Electric light. In 1921 size of screen was 16' × 20'; 65' throw. Tom Buey, stage carpenter; Arthur Miller, orchestra leader. Mgrs. D. L. Hughes, Leonard C. Worley (1912), C. H. Dodge (1914), Baker-Dodge Theatres, Inc. (1921). Booking agent Klaw & Erlanger (1914), New York. A. L. Erlanger & Shuberts, 1921. Remodeled from Keokuk Opera House.

Grand Theatre, 1924, 26 N. 6th St. Modern brick theatre, 66' × 90'. Restored, operates as stage house and movie house.

Keokuk Opera House, 1883 (1883–1908), "new, elegant and complete, and supplied with all modern appliances," seated 964. Ground-floor house. Piano. Stage was 60' wide × 40' deep. Had 16 sets scenery, "ample" set pieces. Gas light. Steam heat. Mgr. D. L. Hughes.

By 1886 it seated 1064; prices $0.25–$1. Piano. Proscenium was 30' × 30'; stage was 60' wide × 40' high × 40' deep, 6' apron. 40' between fly girders. 18' depth under stage. 4 sets of grooves were 18' high; had 16 scenes, 4 traps (2 center, 1 L front, 1 R front), 1 bridge, rear. Electric light. By 1907, stage was 60' wide × 46' high × 36' deep; 6' apron. 46' between fly girders. A. Gregory (1897), C. M. Hood (1899), Henry McCutchen (1901), C.

S: Abel (1903), electricians; William Buey, scenic artist and stage
carpenter; John Thalberg (1897), A. Whalen (1897, 1899), Harry
McCutcheon (1898), Clarence Kicks (1900), John Sellberg (1901),
Murray Teeten (1907), prop men. 6–10 in orchestra. J. C.
Hubinger, owner (1898). Mgrs. D. L. Hughes; D. R. Craig (1889);
J. C. Hubinger (1898); Chamberlain, Harrington & Co.—C. A.
Laubach (1899), Edmund Yaeger, Jr. (1900), resident managers; D.
L. Hughes (1907). Same as Grand Opera House.

Keosauqua (*Van Buren*)

Union Opera House, ca. 1883, 402 Cass St. Seated 250 with chairs.
Stage was 18' wide × 15' deep. Had 5 sets scenery. Mgr. J. B.
Bleakmore.

K Opera House, ca. 1921. Seated 325. Mgrs. Price & Sommerville.

Keota (*Keokuk*)

Keota Opera House, ca. 1889, seated 400. Mgr. H. Henkle.

Keystone (*Benton*)

Schuett's Hall, 1893. Two-story frame. Opera house was part of
Keystone House Hotel; was on the first floor.

Kingsley (*Plymouth*)

Kingsley Opera House, ca. 1904 (1904–1908). Ground-floor hall seated
300. Proscenium was 24' wide × 10' high; stage was 16' deep; 4'
apron. Oil light. No scene room. Mgr. J. H. Conrady.

Kingsley Opera House, ca. 1912 (1912–1914). Was located over the
present drugstore. Seated 400. Proscenium was 25' wide × 13'
high; stage was 45' wide × 16' high × 21'6" deep; 3'6" apron.
Gas light. Could have become the Casino Theatre ca. 1921. It is
currently apartments. It could have been called the Kingsley New
Theatre as well. Mgr. J. E. Cathcart.

Kingsley New Theatre, ca. 1908. Seating capacity 400. Proscenium was
30' wide × 12' high. Stage was 45' wide × 22' deep, 3' apron.
Theatre on second floor. Gas light, steam heat. Could be either of
the Kingsley Opera Houses listed. Mgrs. F. S. Cathcart and Sons.

Rink Hall, ca. 1889, seated 400.

Casino, ca. 1921. Seating capacity 400. Stage 45' wide × 16' high ×
25' deep. Mgr. J. E. Cahill.

Klemme (*Hancock*)

Opera House. Burned.

Knierim (*Marion*)

Knierim Opera House. Burned.

Knoxville (*Marion*)

Grand Theatre, ca. 1912 (1912–1921), ground-floor house. Seated 527
on the main floor, 358 in 2 balconies, 48 in the boxes (total: 933).
Proscenium was 30' wide × 24' high; stage was 60' wide × 52'
high × 39' deep; 55' between fly galleries; 24' to the fly gallery.
8 dressing rooms. Electric light. Mgrs. Elbert Payton (1912) (P.
Little, local mgr., 1912), Clarence H. Smith (1914), C. Young
(1921). Same as the Knoxville Opera House.

Knoxville Opera House, ca. 1878 (1878–1909), ground-floor house, seated 500. Proscenium was 25' wide × 12' high; stage was 40' wide × 14' high × 30' deep; 3' apron. Had 7 scenes in 1883, six 14' high grooves. 1 trap, center. 3' depth under stage. By 1897 was lighted electrically (Edison system). Fred Nichols (1897), Frank Carter (1908), prop men; C. Gaston (1897), electrician. Mgrs. J. B. Ruffner, R. H. Law (1883), W. I. Collins (1889), Gibson & Gibson (1897), W. P. Gibson (1898), T. G. Gibson (or Gilson) (1903), D. Mullholland (1908).

Reaver Opera House, 1918, 100 E. Main St.(?). Location unclear. May not be extant.

Lacona (*Warren*)

Opera House, Main St.

Ladora (*Iowa*)

Ladora Opera House, Pacific St.

Lake City (*Calhoun*)

Church Building, ca. 1886.

Lake City Opera House. See Townsend Grand Opera House.

Smith's Opera Hall, ca. 1889, seated 300 in opera and common chairs. Piano. Proscenium was 24' wide; stage was 40' wide × 9' high × 13' deep. Had 5 sets—Sosman & Landis (Chicago) scenery. Mgr. C. W. Smith.

Townsend Grand Opera House, ca. 1903 (1903–1921). Built by Billy Townsend and located on the second story of a three-story brick building on the corner of Illinois and Main streets. First appears in Cahn 1903–1904 guide. Seated 400. Proscenium was 21' wide × 10' high; stage was 42' wide × 15' deep; 3' apron. No grooves. Depth under stage 2'6". Electric light. By ca. 1912, stage was 44' wide × 10' high × 13'6" deep, apron 2'6". Grooves 10' from stage. 2 dressing rooms. By ca. 1914, stage was 42' wide × 11' high × 16' deep. By ca. 1921, seating capacity was 600. C. Halford (1903–1905), O. E. Brownell (1907–1909), electricians. Mgr. E. W. Townsend. Also known as Lake City Opera House. Current condition is not known.

Lake Mills (*Winnebago*)

New Opera House, ca. 1901 (1901–1914), seated 600 in opera chairs. Proscenium was 24' wide × 15' high; stage was 30' deep. Electric light. By ca. 1907 only 500 sat in opera chairs. Presumably, the others were not so comfortably seated. By ca. 1914, stage was 45' wide × 12' high × 25' deep. Probably became the Rialto Theatre in 1921. Mgr. A. G. Anderson, Anderson and Parker (1903–1905), Glietz and Son (1907–1909), Emil Glietz (1914).

Opera House, ca. 1889 (1889–1901). Ground-floor house seating 400. By ca. 1896, seating capacity was 300. Proscenium was 18' wide × 10' high; stage was 35' wide and 20' deep. Depth under stage 3'. Electric light. Wallace Wadsworth, orchestra leader (1896–1900). 4 in orchestra. Mgr. J. B. Lloyd (1889), H. M. Martinson (1896).

Rialto Theatre, ca. 1921, seated 600. Stage was 45' wide × 12' high × 25' deep. Mgr. James Nisti. See New Opera House.

Lake Park (*Dickinson*)

    BEH Opera House.

Lake View (*Sac*)

    Lake View Opera House.

Lamoni (*Decatur*)

    Coliseum, 1911, N. Maple St. Three stories plus a grid. The building is 61' × 117'; main floor 41' × 48'; balcony 18' × 48'. Proscenium is 28' wide × 21' high; stage is 21' deep. Three dressing rooms; control electric; extensively remodeled and used as movie house. Currently it is empty and owned by Graceland College.

Lamont (*Buchanan*)

    Wheeler Opera House, ca. 1912. Second-floor house. Proscenium 16' wide × 10' high; stage was 44' wide × 11' high × 10' deep; 2' apron. Gas light. 2 dressing rooms. By ca. 1914, stage was 30' wide × 14' high × 16' deep. Mgrs. Goldsmith and Abbott (1912–1913), Goldsmith and Gladwin (1914).

Lanesboro (*Carroll*)

    Lanesboro Opera House. Burned.

Lansing (*Allamakee*)

    Germania Hall, ca. 1878 (1883–1914), ground-floor hall seating 400 on the main floor and 100 in the balcony. In 1896, proscenium was 23' wide × 12' high; stage was 38' wide × 15' high × 24' deep; 5' apron. Had 15' high grooves, "good stage and scenery." 2 dressing rooms. Electric light in 1912. Mgrs. M. Kerndt, Herman Boeckh (1896), Moritz Kerndt Jr. (1900), H. C. Nielander (1903), J. Boeckh (1912).

    Parish Auditorium, ca. 1921. "Used by Roman Catholic Parish, . . . also plays high class censored films for industrial and educational purposes." Interior, wall-to-wall, was 40' × 60'. Proscenium was 20' wide × 10' high; stage was 22' deep. Screen was "standard"; throw was 60'.

La Porte City (*Black Hawk*)

    Allen's Opera House, ca. 1889, ground-floor house, seated 600. Proscenium was 24' wide × 12' high; stage was 40' wide × 12' high × 20' deep. Had 8 scenes. Mgr. M. S. Allen.

    Opera House, ca. 1886. Probably the same as Allen's. Mgr. Jas. Hasman.

    Salmon Opera House, ca. 1914, seated 500. Stage was 42' wide × 16' high × 22' deep. Mgr. E. E. Salmon.

Larrabee (*Cherokee*)

    Town Hall.

Latimer (*Franklin*)

    DBS Hall, ca. 1882. Single-story frame, 27' × 48', built by the Danish Brotherhood Society. Interior completely remodeled. It's the second oldest building in Latimer, which held its centennial in 1982.

Laurel (*Marshall*)

    Opera House. Burned.

Laurens (*Pocahontas*)

Elite Theatre, ca. 1921, seated 500. Stage was 40′ wide × 14′ high × 18′ deep.

Kreul's Hall.

Noble Opera House, ca. 1904 (1904–1912), seated 500. Second-floor hall. Proscenium was 28′ wide × 14′ high; stage was 24′ deep. Gas light. By ca. 1912, called the Laurens Opera House. Seating capacity 475. Stage 50′ wide. 4 dressing rooms. By ca. 1914, seating capacity was 460. Stage was 40′ wide × 14′ high × 18′ deep. Prop man, stage carpenter and Mgr. V. A. Noble (1904). Prop man, carpenter and Mgr. M. T. Nilsson (1908–1909), C. A. Carlson (1912).

Elite Theatre, ca. 1921. Seating capacity 500. Stage 40′ wide × 14′ high × 18′ deep. Probably the renamed Noble Opera House. Mgr. V. A. Noble.

Lawler (*Chickasaw*)

Lawler Opera House. Main St.

Noble Opera House. Main St.

Le Mars (*Plymouth*)

Van Sickle's Hall, ca. 1876.

Apollo Hall, Remodeled in 1883. (1883–1889). Stage 16′ × 48′. Seating capacity 430. Chairs, 5 sets of scenery. By ca. 1889, seating capacity was 450. Mgr. George E. Pew (1883).

Dalton's Grand Opera House, ca. 1889. Mgr. T. J. Andrews.

Hoyt's Opera House, 1883 (1883–1889), seated 900. Stage was 32′ wide × 26′ deep. Had 10 sets scenery. Seating capacity 900. By ca. 1889, stage was 65′ × 28′, with 9 scenes. Mgr. H. L. Hoyt (1883).

Opera House, ca. 1896 (1896–1909), seated 500. Second-floor hall. Proscenium was 25′ wide × 20′ high; stage was 64′ wide × 24′ deep × 22′ high. Had three 16′ high grooves, 2 traps center and back. Gas light. Depth under stage 4′. By 1898, seating capacity 850. W. Kynoch (1900), H. Butler (1903–1908), stage carpenters. By ca. 1907 proscenium was 26′ wide × 18′ high; stage 64′ wide × 24′ deep × 32′ high, 6′ apron. 3 traps, no scene room. Grooves can be taken up flush with fly gallery. Seating capacity 800. Electricity and gas light. Mgr. E. A. Dalton, R. B. Dalton (1900).

Royal Theatre, ca. 1921. "Plays Traveling Companies." Mgr. C. A. Honnold.

Ledyard (*Kossuth*)

Ledyard Opera House.

Lennox (*Taylor*)

Child's Opera House, 1912. See Lennox Opera House.

Lennox Opera House, ca. 1885 (1896–1914), 111–113 N. Main. On the second floor of a two-story building erected between 1885 and 1890. First mentioned in Cahn in 1896. Seated 600. It was used for a skating rink. Proscenium was 24′ wide × 12′ high; stage was 42′ wide × 16′ deep; 2′ apron. Depth under stage 3′. Had six 10′ grooves, 1 trap center. Grooves can be taken up flush with fly gallery. Was Child's Opera House by 1912 and seated 500. Proscenium 30' wide. Stage, 44' wide × 12' high × 14' deep, 4' apron. 2 dressing rooms. By ca. 1914 called Lenox Opera House. Stage was 42' wide × 16' high × 16' deep. Currently it is empty and the Bunn Jewelry Store is on the first floor. Mgr. H. A. Childs (1896–1909), Maharry Bros. (1912), Colman and Rankin (1914).

Olympia Theatre, ca. 1921, seated 500. Stage was 42' wide × 16' high × 16' deep. Probably the same as the Lenox Opera House. Mgr. H. H. Hobert.

Leon (*Decatur*)

Hildreth's Opera House, ca. 1883 (1883–1886), seated 600. Proscenium was 18' wide; stage was 22' wide × 18' high × 18' deep. Seating capacity 600, 7 scenes, organ. Mgr. J. Hildreth (1886).

Leon Opera House, ca. 1914, 1 block south of the square; seated 600. Second-story hall. Stage was 44' wide × 38' high × 26' deep. Mgr. L. P. Van Werden.

Lewis (*Cass*)

Rink Opera House, ca. 1889, seated 500. Mgr. Henry Barton.

Linden (*Dallas*)

Linden Opera House. Burned.

Lineville (*Wayne*)

Auditorium, ca. 1907 (1907–1913). Mgr. R. J. Phillips. See Lineville Opera House.

Isabella, ca. 1914, seated 300. Second-story house. Stage was 35' wide × 15' high × 25' deep. Mgr. C. E. Glessman.

Lineville Opera House, ca. 1896 (1896–1905), seated 450. Proscenium was 28' wide; stage was 12' high, 17' deep; 3' apron. Had 1 trap. Became the Auditorium in 1907. Mgr. P. A. Raktrock [sic, should be Rockhold] (1897–1905).

Lisbon (*Linn*)

Lisbon Opera House, 1892 (1896–1914). 122 Main St. Three-story brick, 40' × 90', now houses the Lloyd Table Company. Ground-floor house seated 600. Originally the proscenium was 19'6" wide × 14'3" high; footlights to back wall was 19'10"; curtain line to footlights 3'. Distance between side walls was 37'6". Distance between fly girders, 22'. There were three grooves, 12' from the stage; stage to ceiling was 16'8". There was 12' under the stage, which had one trap, center. 4 dressing rooms. Electric light, steam heat. Basketball was played on the second floor, and a dance hall was on the third floor. Mgrs. J. T. Williamson, Albert M. Floyd (1897), T. L. Wolfe (1903), D. Bates (1907), A. M. Floyd (1914).

Liscomb (*Marshall*)

Had 2 small unnamed halls, ca. 1889. Mgrs. R. O. Tripp, D. T. Parnell.

Little Sioux (*Harrison*)

Kerr Opera House, ca. 1912 (1912–1921), ground-floor house, seated 400. Proscenium was 21' wide × 11'6" high; stage was 36' wide × 11'6" high × 12'6" deep; 2' apron. Acetylene gas lighting. 2 dressing rooms. By ca. 1914, seating capacity was 425. Stage was 31' wide × 12' high × 14' deep. By ca. 1921, seating capacity was

240. Proscenium opening 9'6" wide × 14' high. Stage 30' wide × 10' high × 14' deep. Mgr. H. W. Kerr.

Littleport (*Clayton*)

Littleport Hall, razed ca. 1940.

Livermore (*Humboldt*)

Idle Hour, ca. 1921, seated 400. "Plays Traveling Companies." Mgr. F. Coolings.

Miller Opera House, ca. 1896 (1896–1908), seated 350. Ground-floor house. Proscenium was 25' wide × 8' high; stage was 35' wide × 20' deep. Electricity. Depth under stage 3' Had scenery by Sosman & Landis (Chicago). Mgr. W. F. Miller (1896–1905), Perry Davis (1907).

Opera House, ca. 1908, seated 300. Ground-floor hall. Proscenium was 20' wide × 10' high; stage was 29' wide × 15' deep. Gasoline lighting. Depth under stage 3'; 2 dressing rooms. Mgr. J. E. McManus (1908).

Skating Rink Hall, ca. 1889. Seated 300. Mgr. George McCaully.

Logan (*Harrison*)

Logan Opera House, ca. 1912 (1912–1914), ground-floor house seating 224 on the main floor and 200 in the balcony (total: 424). Proscenium was 18' wide × 16' high; stage was 18' wide × 19' deep; 1' apron. 3 dressing rooms. Electric light. By ca. 1914, seating capacity was 450. Stage was 25' wide × 35' high × 30' deep. Mgrs. Moses Smith (1912), C. W. Plummer (1914).

Public Hall, ca. 1886, seated 600. Stage was 39' wide × 16' deep. Had 3 scenes. By ca. 1889, stage 16' × 30'. Mgr. J. M. C. Logan.

Lohrville (*Calhoun*)

Bowen Opera House. Burned.

Lone Rock (*Kossuth*)

Lone Rock Opera House. Burned.

Lone Tree (*Johnson*)

Lone Tree Opera House. Burned.

Fisher Opera House. Burned.

Lorimor (*Union*)

Lorimor Opera House.

Lovilla (*Monroe*)

Lovilla Opera House.

Low Moor (*Clinton*)

Odd Fellows' Hall, 1907, Main St. Two-story brick, 24' × 54'. Completely remodeled inside.

Lowden (*Cedar*)

Germania Hall, 1878. Became Liberty Hall ca. 1920. Razed 1956.

Liberty Hall, ca. 1920. See Germania Hall.

Lowden Opera House, 1895. Two-story frame sheathed in tin panels, on the corner of Main and McKinley streets. The building measures 36' × 61'6", and houses the Reliance Tap on the ground floor. The opera house was on the second floor, now sealed off, the stage is reportedly gone.

Lu Verne (*Kossuth*)
>Academy of Music, ca. 1886.
>Lu Verne Opera House. Burned.
>McNally Hall, ca. 1886.

Luana (*Clayton*)
>**Luana Town Hall**, ca. 1929. Located on second floor above Luana Tavern. Building is frame, 48' × 89'. The ceiling in the hall has been lowered; the proscenium measures 16'3" wide; curtain line to back is 12'. There is a 3'10" apron. Offstage space is 8' on each side. The main floor measures 55' × 45'. The stage is still equipped with footlights.

Lucas (*Lucas*)
>Knott's Opera House, ca. 1889, seated 800. Stage was 60' wide × 20' deep. Had 8 sets scenery. Mgr. W. H. Snedaker.

Lynville (*Jasper*)
>**Lynville Opera House,** may have been housed in tin-covered building now the Lynville Seed Co.

Lyons (*Clinton*)
>Hopkins' New Opera House, ca. 1889, seated 800. Proscenium was 30' wide; stage was 60' wide × 26' high × 28' deep. Had 12 sets new scenery, drop curtain, and the stage was lighted by 24 electric lamps. Mgr. J. O. Hopkins.
>Le Grande Theatre, ca. 1889, seated 900. Mgr. G. W. Ashton.
>Masonic Temple, ca. 1886, seated 400.
>Murphy's Hall, ca. 1886, seated 350.
>Odeon Hall, ca. 1878 (1878–1889), seated 500. Had 10 scenes. Stage size was 22' × 35'. By 1883, stage size was 25' × 50', 12 scenes. Mgr. Justus Lund.

Lytton (*Sac*)
>**Lytton Opera House/IOOF Hall,** 1919. According to resident T. E. Denise, it was located on the west side of Main Street with a more elaborate theatre than a previous hall again placed on the lower floor. The building has been remodeled several times and currently is a Golden Sun Feed and Pioneer Seed Corn business.

McCausland (*Scott*)
>Swan's Hall, Main St. Burned ca. 1980.

McGregor (*Clayton*)
>Atheneum, ca. 1878 (1878–1889), seated 600. Stage was 40' wide × 20' deep. Had a full set of scenery. Mgr. Thomas Arnold.
>Sullivan Opera House, ca. 1914 (1914–1921), second-story house seating 425. Stage was 50' wide × 11' high × 24' deep. Mgr. T. J. Sullivan.

Macedonia (*Pottawattamie*)
>Macedonia Opera House. Burned.

Madrid (*Boone*)
>**Woodman Opera House,** ca. 1889. Built on Second Street as a two-story brick building with opera house on the second floor. Current building dimensions are 68'6" × 78'9". Current occupant is

Lawrence Hardware and Appliance.

Magnolia (*Harrison*)

Opera House, pre–1921. Was "not running" in 1921 according to Cahn-Hill guide; town also mistakenly listed as "Magnokita."

Malcom (*Poweshiek*)

Malcom Auditorium, 1899. Single-story frame, 36′ × 72′.

Opera House, ca. 1883 (1883–1889), seated 350. Had fair amount of scenery.

Mallard (*Poweshiek*)

Mallard Opera House.

Malvern (*Mills*)

Malvern Opera House.

Manchester (*Delaware*)

Central Opera House, ca. 1896 (1896–1914), seated 900 (accommodate 2200); prices (1896) $0.25–$0.50. Ground-floor house with 8 exits. Proscenium was 27′ wide × 17′ high; stage was 50′ wide × 20′ high × 30′ deep. 4′ depth under stage. Had 4 grooves, 2 traps. Oil lighting. Electric light by 1908. Booking agent (1914) J. Wingfield, Chicago. Mgrs. E. J. Conger, Ralph W. Conger (1908).

City Hall, ca. 1883 (1883–1889), seated 600. Stage was 22′ wide × 12′ deep. Had a fair stock of scenery. Mgr. C. H. Day.

Ford's Hall, 1883 (1883–1886), "new and first-class," seated 400; had 144 "settees" and the rest were chairs. Stage was 25′ wide × 18′ deep. Had 7 sets scenery, 2 drop curtains. Mgrs. Ford Bros.

Opera House, ca. 1889. Seats 1200. Mgr. Congar & Smith.

Plaza, 120 N. Franklin. Old, two-story brick; 23′3″ × 112′10″: completely remodeled inside.

Manilla (*Crawford*)

Germania Opera House. Burned.

Manly (*Worth*)

Manly Opera House, 113. E. Elmore. Two-story brick, 66′ × 80′. Completely altered inside.

Manning (*Carroll*)

Manning Opera House, ca. 1921, seated 500. Proscenium was 16′ wide; stage was 40′ wide × 25′ deep. Electric light. Mgr. Robert Kuhl.

Manson (*Calhoun*)

Manson Opera House.

Richards Opera House, ca. 1912 (1912–1914), ground-floor hall seating 800. Proscenium was 25′ wide × 15′ high; stage was 48′ wide × 15′ high × 24′ deep; 2′ apron. 6 grooves 12′. 4 dressing rooms. Electric light. Mgr. Chas. E. Bale.

Mapleton (*Monona*)

Chamberlain's Hall, ca. 1886, seated 500.

Opera House, ca. 1921, seated 400. Mgrs. Lamb and Gardet.

Maquoketa (*Jackson*)

Centennial Opera House, ca. 1889, seated 600. Proscenium was 20′ wide; stage was 25′ wide × 20′ high × 20′ deep. Was 18′ to grooves. 7 sets scenery. Piano. Mgr. A. C. Edson.

Grand Opera House, ca. 1889, seated 1000, with chairs on a raised platform. Proscenium was 40' wide; stage was 60' wide × 20' high × 35' deep. Had 13 sets scenery with set rocks, house, cottage, bar, etc. Piano. Mgrs. Thompson & Butterworth. Could be the same as Rice's Grand Opera House.

Grand Opera House, ca. 1907 (1907–1909). The same as Rice's Grand Opera House, but renamed during these two years. Mgrs. Frank J. Pain (1907), M. Rice (1908).

Harris Opera House, ca. 1878 (1878–1884), seated 800. Had a full set of scenery. Mgr. J. C. Harris.

Odeon Hall, ca. 1889 (1889–1897), seated 800. Mgr. Fred Tinker.

Opera House, ca. 1886 (1886–1889), seated 700. Piano. Proscenium was 20' wide × 12' high; stage was 46' wide × 15' high × 29' deep. Mgrs. Wm. Current, Wm. Stephens (1889).

Rice's Grand Opera House, ca. 1896 (1896–1914), second-floor hall, seated 420 on the main floor and 400 in the balcony. Proscenium was 30' wide × 16' high; stage was 62' wide × 20' high × 31' deep; 4' apron. 50' between fly girders, 30' to fly gallery. 4' depth under stage. Had 4 sets 12' high grooves, could be taken up flush with fly gallery. 1 trap, center. 4 dressing rooms. Electric light in 1898. Booking agent (1914) J. Wingfield, Chicago. Mgrs. M. Rice, Weber & Sanders (1914).

Marathon (*Buena Vista*)

Marathon Opera House. Burned.

Marble Rock (*Floyd*)

Old Opera House.

Marcus (*Cherokee*)

Marcus Opera House. Burned.

Marengo (*Iowa*)

Stover's Opera House, ca. 1879 (1879–1921), "complete and first-class in all respects," seated 600 in chairs. Second-floor house. Proscenium was 18' wide × 14' high; stage was 40' wide × 20' high × 20' deep. 32' between fly girders. 3'6" depth under stage. Had 4 sets 14' high grooves, 5 scenes, 2 traps, center. and back. Had electric light by 1897. Mgrs. M. W. Stover, Bert Stover (1904), Otto Panknen (1921).

Marion (*Linn*)

"No theatre at present," 1907–1913.

Daniel's Opera Hall (Daniel's Opera House), 1881 (1889–1905), 7th Ave. and 11th St. Two-story brick, theatre was on the second floor, seated 700; price $0.25–$0.50. Originally the proscenium was 22' wide × 12' high; distance between side walls was 45'; height of grooves was 11'6"; 4' depth under stage. Electric light by 1897. Mgr. A. J. Daniels.

Garden Theatre, 1914 (1921), 752 10th St. Two-story brick, 40'6" × 118'; proscenium measures 25' wide × 14' high; curtain line to back is 18'; apron is 2'; wing space is 6' on each side. The grid is closed off at about 16' up. The main floor seats 297; the balcony has been converted into a projection booth. Originally the proscenium was 22' wide × 20' high; in 1921 stage was 22' wide × 20' high × 20' deep. Seating capacity was 879. Screen was 11' × 14'— throw was 96': Powers Projecting Machine, R. Kirk, operator. Theatre belonged to the Adams Circuit. Mgr. A. Dumbolton.

Marion Opera Hall/Mentzer's Hall. Two buildings identified as former opera houses are a two-story brick at 1138–1144 7th Ave. (39' × 102') and a two-story brick at 710 10th St. (21' × 69'). Each is apparently old enough to have been the **Marion Opera Hall** or **Mentzer's Hall.**

Marion Opera Hall, ca. 1879 (1879–1886), seated 1000; stage was 20' wide × 14' deep (20' × 30' in 1883). Had 4 scenes (7, 1883). Mgr. J. I. Berryhill.

Mentzer's Hall, ca. 1889, seated 500. Mgr. B. F. Mentzer.

Orpheum, ca. 1914, ground-floor hall seating 370. Stage was 22' wide × 12' high × 12' deep. Mgr. B. W. Umbreit.

Marshalltown (*Marshall*)

Guild Hall, ca. 1889, seated 300.

Odeon Theatre, 1889 (1889–1921), ground-floor house seating 407 on the main floor, 612 in 2 balconies, 48 in boxes (total: 1067–1508); Andrews opera chairs; prices (1896) $0.25–$1. Piano. Proscenium was 33' wide × 32' high; stage was 75' wide × 50' high × 40' deep; 2' apron. 38' between fly girders. 12' depth under stage. It was 18' to the 6 grooves; 21 sets scenery, 3 traps (center, right, left), 1 bridge, 4E. Grooves could be taken up flush with the fly gallery. By 1907 the stage was 68' wide × 50' high × 36' deep; 50' between fly girders, 22' to fly gallery: no grooves. Had orchestra (8), leaders were F. A. Fitzgerald, Julius Holm (1899, 1904), B. S. Barborka (1900), and Julius Holms (1908). Had own prop shop; William Hayes (1896), C. W. Johnson (1898), Herman Palmer (1903), Harle (or Hade) Hilman (1904), Charles Gossard (1908), prop men. Fred Tate (1896), William Hayes (1898), stage carpenters. Gas and electric lighting. Mr. Bowman (1908), electrician. Booking agents (1914), Klaw & Erlanger, New York; A.L. Erlanger (1914). Mgrs. Marshalltown Opera House Co., I. C. Speers (1896), Busby Bros. (1903).

Opera House, ca. 1886, seated 800 in Andrews folding opera chairs. Stage was 30' wide × 22' deep. Supplied ushers and stagehands. Gas light. Mgr. L. C. Goodwin.

Orpheum Theatre, 209 E. Main. Now converted into shops, etc. Two-story brick, 44' × 179'.

Woodbury Hall, ca. 1878 (1878–1884), seated 800. Stage was 30' wide × 22' deep. In 1878 had been "recently refitted and lit with gas." Had 7 scenes and a drop curtain. In 1883 ushers, a janitor and stagehands were furnished. Mgrs. C. F. Fraker, L. C. Goodwin (1883).

Martell (*Jones*)

Ellison Hall, 120 Marion St. Two-story building; second floor was removed after 1974 fire.

Martinsburg (*Keokuk*)

Alexander's Hall, ca. 1889, seated 250. Mgr. J. C. Alexander.

Mason City (*Cerro Gordo*)

Lloyd and Tuttle's Hall, ca. 1879 (1879–1889), seated 350 in chairs. Stage was 26' wide × 16' deep (16' × 28', 1883). Had 4 scenes. Mgrs. Lloyd & Tuttle.

Parker Opera House, 1883 (1883–1905), 21 N. Federal. Built by H. G. and A. T. Parker (designed by William Foster of Des Moines), three-story limestone. The opera house was on the ground floor. The building is 40' × 117' and originally seated 700 in folding chairs; prices (1897) $0.25–$1. Proscenium was 26' wide × 18' high; stage was 48' wide × 18' high × 26' deep; 3' apron. 40' between fly girders. 10' depth under stage. Stage had 4 grooves, could be taken up flush with fly gallery. 3 traps, 2 bridges. Gas and electric lighting by 1897. H. E. Dyer, electrician; Jno. M. Smith, Fred Jorn (1900), Lyle Hartwell (1903), prop men and stage carpenters. C. T. Schnehall, J. S. Emery (1903), orchestra leaders. Mgrs. A. T. Parker; H. G. and A. T. Parker (1886), A. T. Parker (1898). In 1967 the interior was completely remodeled into offices and apartments. For additional information, see *Mason City, Iowa: An Architectural Heritage,* p. 14.

Princess Theatre, ca. 1912 (1912–1914). Ground-floor house seating 485 on the main floor and 229 in the balcony (total: 714). Proscenium was 22' wide × 18' high; stage was 44' wide × 40' high × 14' deep; 1' apron. 36' between fly girders; 18' to fly gallery. Electric light. Mgrs. Arthur & Howland.

Wilson Opera House, 1898 (1903–1909), 16 N. Washington. Three-story brick, built by Charles Wilson; rebuilt and renamed after a fire in 1912; currently functioning as the Park 70 Movie Theatre. The building is 60' × 165'. The proscenium is 31' wide and 30' tall, with 37' from the curtain line to the back, plus a 3' apron. Offstage wing space measures 13' on each side. The grid is 51' high, with a fly gallery on stage right. Also on stage right is the original electric board. There are two backstage dressing rooms on each side of the stage, plus eight more in the basement. The main floor and the first balcony seat 648; there is also a second gallery. In 1912 the main floor seated 595, with an additional 770 in 2 balconies plus 36 in the boxes (total: 1401); prices $0.25–$1. Proscenium was 32' wide × 26' high; stage was 61' wide × 50' high × 44' deep; 24' to fly gallery. 4' apron. 50' between fly girders. 8' depth under stage. No grooves. Scene room. Ray Coe (1903), electrician; C. Seeley (1903), prop man; J. Emery (1903), orchestra leader—7 in orchestra. Electric light. Was also known as Wilson's Theatre from 1903–1909; Cecil Theatre from 1912–1964. In 1921 Wm. T. Smith was stage carpenter; John Kopecky, orchestra leader. Booking agents (1914), Klaw & Erlanger, New York. Mgrs. Cleve Wilson (1903), Tom Arthur (1907, 1914), Arthur & Howland (1912). For additional information see *Mason City, Iowa: An Architectural Heritage,* 18.

Massena (*Cass*)

IOOF Opera House, ca. 1912 (1912–1914) seated 350. Ground-floor house: proscenium was 20' wide × 10' high; stage was 28' wide × 10' high × 22'6" deep; 1'6" apron. 4 grooves 10' from stage. 4 dressing rooms. Gas lighting. By ca. 1914, seating capacity was 400. Stage was 30' wide × 8' deep. Mgr. P. D. Griffith.

Maurice (*Sioux*)

Maurice Opera House. Sources conflict as to whether the building which housed the opera house still stands. According to one source it was a two-story brick building which burned and is now a vacant lot. According to another it still stands and is the upholstery shop of John Vanderstelt.

Maxwell (*Story*)

Maxwell Opera House, 1894. Two-story brick, 45' × 80'; theatre was on the second floor. The ad front curtain hangs at the Maxwell Museum; it is 23' × 12'. The grand opening was 12 January 1894. See *Maxwell, Iowa 1883–1983* for floor plan. Museum has photos, and memorabilia.

Maynard (*Fayette*)

Opera House, Main St.

Maysville/Geneva (*Franklin*)

Maysville School/Opera House, 1865. Maysville is a ghost town. Originally started by returning Civil War veterans, the only building now standing is the two-story, hand-hewed limestone school house, measuring 30' × 50'. The theatre is on the second floor. The proscenium measures 27' wide × 12' high; stage is 27' wide × 11'2" deep. The hall measures 27' × 26'9". Ad. front drop, 18'6" × 10'.

Mechanicsville (*Cedar*)

Huryer's Opera House, ca. 1921, seated 400. Stage was 40' wide × 12' high × 20' deep. Mgr. John Thimnes.

Opera House, ca. 1886 (1886–1889), seated 300. Stage was 18' wide × 13' deep. Had "fair scenery." Mgr. W. H. Sturges.

Sturges Theatre, ca. 1912 (1912–1914), second-story house seating 400. Proscenium was 22' wide × 12' high; stage was 40' wide × 14' high × 18' deep; 24' between fly girders; 3' apron. 3 dressing rooms. Gas and electric lighting. Mgr. Fred Sturges.

Mediapolis (*Des Moines*)

Mediapolis Hall, ca. 1889. May be the two-story brick building with a double-archway entrance at 620 Main, although dimensions in 1889 were 22' × 50'. The front of 620 Main measures 18'. It now houses apartments on the second floor and a barber shop on the ground floor. Mgr. J. N. Hall.

Melcher (*Marion*)

Casino Theatre.

Rink Theatre.

Melrose (*Monroe*)

Melrose Opera House.

Melvin (*Osceola*)

Melvin Opera House.

Merrill (*Plymouth*)

Merrill Opera House.

Messervey (*Cerro Gordo*)

Opera House.

Miles (*Jackson*)

Opera House/Agricultural Hall.

Millersburg (*Iowa*)

Opera House.

Milo (*Warren*)

Milo Opera House, 1899. Two-story brick; opera house was on the second floor. Had winter and summer scenes. Burned 15 September 1938.

Squire's Hall (1880), east end of Main St. Seated 250.

Milton (*Van Buren*)

Waller's Hall, ca. 1889. Mgr. J. K. Waller.

Minburn (*Dallas*)

Minburn Opera House.

Mineola (*Mills*)

Mineola Opera House, ca. 1915. According to *Then and Now,* by Viola N. Bichel, there were two opera houses. The first, a two-story frame, was owned by Louis Bichel. The opera house was on the first floor. It had moveable chairs and drop curtains. Upstairs were doctor's offices and club rooms of the Sons of Herman. It was destroyed by fire in 1915. It was rebuilt by Louis Bichel and enlarged by Roy Wasserman, who added a dance hall. Currently it is used as a community building.

Missouri Valley Junction also known as Missouri Valley (*Harrison*)

Majestic Theatre, ca. 1921, seated 1000. "Plays Traveling Companies." Mgr. K. Moreland.

Town Hall, ca. 1883 (1883–1889). Size of stage 12' × 18'. Seating capacity 220. Three sets of scenery. By ca. 1889, seating capacity increased to 350. Mgr. A. L. Tamisied.

New Theatre, ca. 1896 (1896–1909), seated 804. Ground-floor house: proscenium was 20' wide × 18' high; stage was 60' wide × 35' high × 25' deep; 5' apron. Had four 16' high grooves, 3 traps (2 star traps), 1 bridge. Electric light. By ca. 1899 seated 700. Stage 50' wide. Depth under stage 8'. By ca. 1907 stage was 33' high. Beto York, R. B. Harmon (1899–1905), Leo Hiller (1907–1908), B. Obanion (1908), electricians. W. D. McKenney, A. McTuiggen (1899–1904), Leo Hillar (1907), B. Obanion (1908), stage carpenters. Scenic artist, W. Grabach. Frank York, J. Armstrong (1897), Ed Harty (1899–1905), prop men. Mgrs. W. M. Harmon (1896–1905), W. E. Smith (1907).

Town Hall, ca. 1883, seated 220. Stage was 18' wide × 12' deep.

Mitchell (*Mitchell*)

>Court House, ca. 1878 (1878–1886), seated 300. Stage was 40' wide ×
>20' deep (12' × 40', 1883).
>
>Mitchell Hall, ca. 1889, seated 300. Mgr. John Bartle.

Mitchellville (*Polk*)

>Pritchard's Opera House, ca. 1908. Ground-floor hall seating 200 in the
>balcony (no figure for main floor). Proscenium was 16' wide × 12'
>high; stage was 24' wide × 20' deep; 4' apron. 7' depth under
>stage. 1 trap, back of center. Gas light. No scene room. Cox Scenic
>Co., scenic artists. Mgr. J. W. Pritchard. Listed as "closed
>indefinitely" in 1912.

Modale (*Harrison*)

>Forester's Hall, ca. 1886. Seated 500. Mgr. A. Forester

Mondamin (*Harrison*)

>Klutts Opera House. Burned.
>
>Mondamin Hall, ca. 1886.

Moneta (*O'Brien*)

>**Moneta Town Hall.** A one-story building measuring 23'4" × 60'5".
>Currently it is used for storage.

Monmouth (*Jackson*)

>**Modern Woodman Hall**, ca. 1907. Two-story brick building, houses a
>grocery store. Owner wouldn't allow examination of the upstairs
>hall.

Monona (*Clayton*)

>**Monona Opera House**, ca. 1914, corner of Main and Center streets.
>Two-story brick building, 48'6" × 92'6"; the opera house was on
>the second floor above the present Monona Dry Goods Co. Interior
>measurements were impossible to get: an apartment, complete with
>four walls and a ceiling, has been built inside the hall, and extends
>from the back wall of the stage to the gallery, leaving only narrow
>storage passages on either side. In 1914 the stage was 24' deep ×
>28' wide × 30' high. Seating capacity 500. Mgr. G. S. Klotzbaugh.

Monroe (*Jasper*)

>GAR Hall, ca. 1889, seated 350. Mgr. J. R. Hall.

Montezuma (*Poweshiek*)

>Ritz's Hall, ca. 1889, seated 800. Mgr. John Ritz.

Monticello (*Jones*)

>Kinsella Hall, ca. 1889, seated 300.
>
>Monticello Opera House, ca. 1883 (1883–1921), ground-floor hall
>seating 800. Proscenium was 20' wide × 18' high; stage was 60'
>wide × 16' high × 20' deep; 5' apron. 5' depth under stage. Had
>2 traps, center and back. 16' high grooves. Electric light and steam
>heat (1898). Mgrs. Rosa & Foster, H. Tiarks (1889), G. E. Bishop
>(1896), A. Kempf (1903).

Montrose (*Lee*)

>Montrose Opera House, 100 block of Main St.
>
>Pastime Theatre, Main St. between 1st and River streets.

Moorland (*Webster*)

Moorland Opera House. Burned.

Moravia (*Appanoose*)

Moravia Opera House. Dated 1892, although the exterior carries the date "1918." Single-story, brick/stucco, 50′ × 100′. The interior was burned out in 1929, leaving only the exterior walls. Now the Van Dorin Implement Co.

Morning Sun (*Louisa*)

Finch's Hall, ca. 1889, seated 300. Mgr. J.W. Finch.

Morrison (*Grundy*)

Opera House, ca. 1900. Two-story frame; hall on second floor. Burned and/or razed ca. 1925.

Moulton (*Appanoose*)

Colonial Theatre/IOOF Hall, (1919–1920), Main Street. Currently housing the IOOF Lodge. The two-story brick building is 30′ × 90′, and has been completely remodeled inside to nontheatrical functions.

Moore's Opera Hall, ca. 1889, seated 400. Mgr. Ith Moore.

Mount Auburn (*Benton*)

Jenks Opera House.

Mount Ayr (*Ringgold*)

Mount Ayr Opera House.

Princess Theatre, ca. 1921, seated 300. "Plays Traveling Companies." Mgrs. Jobes Bros.

Cole and Pratt's Opera House, ca. 1883 (1883–1889). Size of stage 30′ × 16′. Seating capacity 300. "Seated with chairs. Fair ammount [sic] of scenery." By ca. 1889, seated 350. Mgrs. Cole and Pratt.

Mount Pleasant (*Henry*)

"No opera house at present (1904)."

Auditorium, 1843 (1912–1921), 119 E. Monroe St. Three-story brick building, 54′ × 70′, now remodeled into the Colonial Apartments (it had also been the Colonial Theatre). Although the building was built in 1843, it reportedly had been the Asbury Methodist Church, and was remodeled into a theatre ca. 1912. At that time the theatre was on the ground floor; the proscenium arch measured 28′ wide × 24′ high; stage was 55′ wide × 55′ high × 34′ deep; 3′ apron; 30′ between fly girders; 24′ to fly gallery. There were two grooves 22′ from the stage. 9 dressing rooms. The capacity was main floor 419, balcony 257, and boxes 48 (total: 724). Electric light by 1912. Mgrs. Geo. T. Hill (1912), C. H. Jackson (1914), G. Reddish (1921).

Bass' New Opera House, ca. 1886, seated 900. Piano. Proscenium was 26′ wide × 16′ high; stage was 51′ wide × 18′ high × 30′ deep. Had 10 scenes. Mgr. W. E. Bass.

Grand Opera House, ca. 1889 (1889–1904), ground-floor hall seating 650. Proscenium was 25′ wide × 14′ high; stage was 48′ wide × 14′ high × 33′ deep; 5′ apron; 4 sets grooves, 14′ high; 4′6″ depth under stage. 2 traps, center and right. R. McCoy, Carl Magdefraw

(1899), prop men. G. H. Sindray (1899), stage carpenter. Mgrs.
Frank E. McClary, O. J. Lindsay (1899).

Saunders' Hall, ca. 1878 (1878–1889), seated 1100. Stage was 30' wide
× 16' deep. Had 2 drop scenes. Mgrs. P. Saunders, W. E. Bass (in
1886, Bass "has no longer any connection with Saunders' Opera
House"), S. Saunders (1889).

Saunders' Opera House, ca. 1886, seated 1100. Stage was 30' wide ×
24' deep. Had 2 scenes. Probably the same as Saunders' Hall.

Union Hall, ca. 1840 (1878–1886), north side of square. Three-story
brick building, opera house was on the third floor. Building
measures 66' × 63'. In the 1880s the stage measured 40' wide ×
23' high, the seating capacity was 1000, and there were seven sets
of scenery. The theatre was "well-lighted with gas," and had "two
large and elegant side rooms." Mgrs. E. L. Penn, H. Ambler
(1879), W. E. Bass (1883).

Mount Sterling (*Van Buren*)

Opera House, north side of 1st St.

Mount Vernon (*Linn*)

Town Hall, ca. 1886 (1886–1889), "small."

Moville (*Woodbury*)

Sager Opera House.

Muscatine (*Muscatine*)

Columbia Theatre, ca. 1896 (1896–1902), seated 800. Ground-floor
house. Proscenium was 33' wide × 20' high; stage was 60' wide ×
50' high × 57' deep; 3' apron. 40' between fly girders; grooves can
be taken up flush. Had 5 sets, 18'–24' high grooves. 10' depth
under stage. Mgr. Carl Luendecker.

Gayety/Crystal Theatre, 303 E. 2nd. Three-story brick building, 18' ×
approx. 108'. Old.

Grand Opera House (or Grand Theatre), ca. 1903 (1903–1921). Ground-
floor house seating 407 on the main floor and 534 in 2 balconies,
plus 8 in the boxes (total: 949). Prices (1908), orchestra, $1 and
$1.50; balcony $0.50 and $0.75; gallery, $0.25. Proscenium was
33' wide × 40' high; stage was 56' wide × 56' high × 37' deep;
3' apron. 46' between fly girders, 26' to fly gallery. 10' depth under
stage. 8 dressing rooms. Gas and electric light. Wm. Hess (1908),
electrician. Jack Tunk (1908), prop man. Wm. Hess (1908), stage
carpenter. Julius Pandaur (1908), orchestra leader. Booking agent
(1914), J. Wingfield, Chicago. Mgrs. Chamberlain, Kint & Co. (C.
W. Kemble [1903], Frank Hurst [1904], Chas. H. Salisbury [1907],
resident managers); Shubert, Cort & Kindt (1912) (Chas. H.
Salisbury [1912], local mgr.), H. C. Wittmann (1921).

Hare's Hall, ca. 1886.

Old's Opera House, ca. 1878 (1878–1889), seated 650. Stage was 22'
wide × 18' deep (24' × 18', 1883). Had 8 sets scenery (12 in
1883). Mgr. L. W. Olds.

Princess Theatre, 1876, 227 E. 2nd. Three-story brick building, 18' ×
100'.

Stein's Music Hall, ca. 1879 (1879–1889), seated 700 in chairs ("perforated seats"). Stage was 38' wide × 17' deep. Had "twelve sets of new sliding scenery." "Two elegantly furnished dressing rooms." "Hall frescoed; its acoustic qualities are unsurpassed, and it is especially adapted for concerts, lectures and other entertainments." Mgr. S. G. Stein.

Tremont Hall, ca. 1879 (1878–1886), seated 650. Stage was 32' wide × 18' deep. Had 8 sets scenery. Mgr. S. G. Stein.

Turner Opera House, ca. 1889, seated 1200. Mgr. Turner Society.

Mystic (*Appanoose*)

Mystic Opera House, ca. 1914, ground-floor hall seating 600. Stage was 30' wide × 20' high × 25' deep. Mgr. A. J. Richardson.

Nashua (*Chickasaw*)

Butterfield's Opera House, ca. 1896 (1896–1900), ground-floor house seating 800. Proscenium was 20' wide × 12' high; stage was 12' high × 20' deep; 4' apron. 4' depth under stage. Had 4 grooves, 1 trap. Became Laird's Opera House in 1900. Mgr. H. L. Butterfield.

Granger Opera House, ca. 1912 (1912–1914), ground-floor house seating 450 on the main floor and 200 in the balcony. Proscenium was 24' wide × 10' high; stage was 44' wide × 12' high × 24' deep; 34' between fly girders. Electric light. Mgr. W. A. Granger.

Laird's Opera House, 1900 (1900–1905). Ground-floor house seating 600. Proscenium was 20' wide × 12' high; stage was 12' high × 20' deep; 4' apron. Had four 12' grooves, 1 trap. 4' depth under stage. Had been Butterfield's Opera House. Mgr. J. G. Laird.

Lampson's Opera House, ca. 1907 (1907–1909), seated 600. Dimensions and descriptions identical to Laird's Opera House. Mgr. R. M. Lampson.

Nashville

Little's Hall, ca. 1886 (1886–1889), seated 200.

Nemaha (*Sac*)

Nemaha Opera House, ca. 1910, Main St. One-story concrete-covered brick tile structure erected by George Ferguson. The building dimensions are 24'5" × 79'10". There was a raked stage at the south end. It had wings and a draw curtain and seated about 100. Currently used for storage.

Neola (*Pottawattamie*)

City Hall, ca. 1889, seated 300. Mgr. E. A. Foot.

Rink Hall, ca. 1889.

Nevada (*Story*)

Opera Hall, ca. 1883 (1883–1889), seated 600. Stage was 26' wide × 23' deep. Had 8 sets scenery. Mgrs. McCord & Briggs.

Opera House, ca. 1904 (1904–1914), second-story hall seating 700; 350 on the main floor and 350 in the gallery. Proscenium was 20' × 20'; stage was 48' wide × 15' high × 31' deep; 4' apron. 20' between fly girders, 15' to fly gallery. 4' depth under stage. No scene room. Had 2 traps. 3 dressing rooms. Gas and electric lighting. Mgrs. A. W. R. Boller, Dick Boller (1914).

New Hampton (*Chickasaw*)

Fireman's Auditorium (1897), 101 N. Locust Ave. Two-story brick building, 77'6" × 132'. Currently the Locust Ave. Offices-Apartments, the building has been completely remodeled inside. Building was designed by T. T. Carkeek of Dubuque and built by W. J. Zitterell, a Webster City contractor. There are some original fixtures stored in the basement.

Fireman's Theatre, 1916, two-story brick building, 60' × 110', 22 N. Locust Ave. Seated 600. Proscenium was 31'6" wide × 30' high; stage was 62' wide × 65' high × 24' deep; 6' apron with footlights. Pinrail. 6 dressing rooms. Main floor seated 303, balcony 223 (1983). Was a roll front drop above the stage. Were 2 light battens with original lamps. Was a bill on the side wall for *Birth of a Nation*. Was turned into a disco and burned in 1987. Mgrs. Savage & Martin.

Opera Hall, ca. 1886 (1886–1889), seated 600; folding chairs. Stage was 40' wide × 20' deep. Had 9 scenes. Mgrs. Mixer, Bennett & Bennett.

Opera House, ca. 1903 (1903–1913), seated 450. Prices, $0.35, $0.50. Electric light. Mgr. W. I. Turner.

New Liberty (*Scott*)

New Liberty Dance Hall. Two-story frame.

New London (*Henry*)

Fireman's Opera House, ca. 1880, north side of Washington St. Ground-floor hall seating 400 on the main floor and 100 in the gallery. Proscenium was 16' wide × 12' high; stage was 34' wide × 12' high × 20' deep; 6' apron. 16' between fly girders. 4 grooves. 2 dressing rooms. Electric light. Was originally a skating rink. Razed in 1919. Mgrs. F. L. Clawson, J. F. Pierson (1914).

New Sharon (*Mahaska*)

Auditorium, ca. 1914 (1914–1921), ground-floor hall seating 400. Stage was 34' wide × 20' high × 18' deep. Mgr. Chas. P. Roe.

Concert Hall, ca. 1883 (1883–1889), seated 400. Stage was 40' wide × 20' deep. Had "good scenery." Mgr. D. Stanton.

Grade School-Opera House, corner N. Elm and E. High. Two-story frame, 36' × 66'.

Opera House, (ca. 1900), 116 Main St. Two-story frame, 40' × 80' with embossed tin decoration. Could be the Concert Hall or the Rink Hall.

Rink Hall, ca. 1889. Mgr. John Pendland.

Star Theatre, E. Market St. Now the Capri Theatre, two-story brick.

Twentieth Century Theatre, ca. 1912, second-story hall seating 250. Proscenium was 18' wide × 11'6" high; stage was 24' wide × 23' deep; 3' apron. 2 dressing rooms. Electric light. Mgr. Grover C. Baker.

New Virginia (*Warren*)

New Virginia Opera House.

150

Newell (*Buena Vista*)
>**Union Hall.** A large meeting room above the first business building built in Newell and was used for theatricals. Currently it is remodeled into apartments.

Newhall (*Benton*)
>Opera House, 26 Main St.

Newton (*Jasper*)
>Lister's Opera House, ca. 1889 (1889–1914). Second-story hall seating 430 on the main floor and 400 in 2 balconies (total: 870–920). Proscenium was 26' wide × 24' high; stage was 64' wide × 16' high × 20' deep; 3' apron. Had four 14'–16' high grooves; could be taken up flush with fly gallery. 4' depth under stage. 2 traps, center and back. 2 dressing rooms. Oil light (electric light by 1912). A kerosene chandelier from here is in the Jasper County Museum. Booking agent (1914), J. Wingfield, Chicago. Mgrs. Arthur J. Wright, J. B. Lister (1897), A. Lister (1907).
>
>Rialto, ca. 1921. Stage was 20' wide × 18' high × 20' deep. Screen was 11' × 14'—throw was 85'. Simplex Projecting Machine; A. Burnett, operator. Mgr. Wm. Burnett.
>
>Union Hall, ca. 1878 (1878–1889), seated 600. Piano. Stage was 21' wide × 19' deep. Drop curtain and 6 sets scenery (1883). Mgrs. Will T. Lister, Larimer & Co (1889).

Nichols (*Muscatine*)
>**Nichols Opera House,** 1897. Two-story brick building, 65'4" × 66', housed the Elder Implement Co. Theatre was on the second floor. The stage was gone, but it could be seen that the proscenium was 22' wide; stage was 16' deep. There appeared to have been a 3-4' apron, and about 8' of wing space. There were borders still hanging from the ceiling, and two grooves on stage L. The *Nichols Iowa Centennial Book* (1984) reports that the hall, built by the Nichols Hall Association, had "2 sets flat scenery and 4 dressing rooms behind the stage." There also used to be an ad. front drop. On 9 June 1987 the second floor collapsed, killing one man. See *Waterloo Courier* and *Des Moines Register* for photos and description.

Nora Springs (*Nora Junction*) (Floyd)
>Trevett's Hall, ca. 1889, seated 350. Mgr. W. B. Trevett.

North English (*Iowa*)
>North English Opera House, ca. 1912. Became the Orpheum in 1927. Razed in 1982.

Northwood (*Worth*)
>Music Hall, ca. 1879 (1883–1889), seated 350. Stage was 16' × 16'. Had a drop curtain and wings. Mgr. R. C. Pike, F. C. White (1889).

Norway (*Benton*)
>Norway Opera House, 1904, on the south side of Railway St. A two-story brick–pressed tin building; hall was on the second floor. It was razed in 1962.

Oakland (*Pottawattamie*)
> Opera House, ca. 1914, ground-floor house seating 500. Stage was 33'
> wide × 16' high × 18' deep. Mgr. Phillip Cunnum.

Ocheyedan (*Osceola*)
> Ocheyedan Opera House.

Odebolt (*Sac*)
> **Mattes Opera House,** 1881, southeast corner 2nd and Main. Two-story
> brick building, erected by John Wright. The opera house was on the
> second floor. The seating capacity was 500 and there were plank
> benches in the rear of the main floor. The building dimensions are
> 55'5" × 100'2". Currently it is used for storage and business
> purposes.
> Wright's Opera House, ca. 1886, seated 300.

Oelwein (*Fayette*)
> Colonial Theatre, ca. 1921, seated 500. Prices, $0.25–$2.00. Prosceni-
> um was 28' wide; stage was 62' wide × 72' high × 18' deep.
> Screen was 10' × 12'. Mgr. J. W. Ridler.
> Opera House, ca. 1903 (1903–1909), second-story hall seating 700.
> Proscenium was 22' wide × 10' high; stage was 18' deep; 1' apron.
> Had 10 grooves. 2 traps. 2'6" depth under stage. No scene room.
> Electric light. J. Bittorf (1903), J. W. Ridler (1904), stage carpen-
> ters; D. M. Curten (1903), prop man; K. Boyd (1903, 1907), D. M.
> Auten (1904), stage managers. Mgrs. J. W. Ridler (1903, 1907);
> Ridler, Bennett & Auten (1904).
> Phillips Opera House, ca. 1896 (1896–1914), second-story hall seating
> 348 on the main floor, 150 in 2 balconies, and 12 in the boxes
> (total: 510). Proscenium was 17' wide × 9' high; stage was 27'
> wide × 10' high × 16'6" deep; 2' apron. 19' between fly girders.
> Grooves 9' high. 17' depth under stage. Had "one trap, under
> kitchen scene door." 7 dressing rooms. Electric light by 1912.
> Mgrs. R. B. Phillips, J. C. Tyler (1912).
> Wachtel's Hall, ca. 1889, seated 200. Mgr. A. Wachtel.

Ogden (*Boone*)
> Opera House, ca. 1883.
> **Ogden Opera House,** 1910 (1921). Built by the Ogden Amusement
> Company, it is a two-story brick building located on Fourth Street.
> The seating capacity was 500. Extensively remodeled. Now the
> home of the Bergstrom Company-AgServ. First appears in Cahn/
> Hill in 1921 with following statistics: Seating capacity 500. "Plays
> Traveling Companies." Mgr. W. C. Trelour.
> Rattray's Opera House, ca. 1889, seated 300. Mgr. P. Rattray

Olds (*Henry*)
> IOOF Hall. Two-story, hall on the second floor. "Where the post office
> now is."

Olin (*Jones*)
> **Opera House.** Now the Legion Hall.
> Opera House. Burned.

152

Ollie (*Keokuk*)
>**Latoska Opera House**, ca. 1915. Single-story brick building, 21' × 72'. Also apparently known as the **Fye Opera House**. The stage is still visible through the front door.
>**Ollie Opera House.** Two-story frame, 40' × 60'; hall was on the second floor. Nothing left upstairs; ground floor houses a hardware store.

Onawa (*Monona*)
>**Colby Opera House**, ca. 1889 or 1893 (also called **Whiting Opera House**), Iowa St. F. E. and E. W. Colby erected a two-story brick building with an opera house on the second floor and lodge rooms on the first. Measures 32'11" × 98'2". Seated 600. Currently storage for McFarland Furniture Store, which occupies the lower floor. Mgr. N. Whiting.
>Freeland and Cleghorn's Opera House, ca. 1886, seated 200.
>**IOOF Hall**, 1900 (also may have been called New Opera House or Onawa Opera House), Tenth St. A two-story brick structure with opera house on the first floor and lodge rooms upstairs, the building measures 56' × 116'. The stage was 30' × 52'. The proscenium opening was 20'; there were six dressing rooms, four downstairs and two on the stage floor. It had a seating capacity of 600. Currently it is Miller Furniture and storage.
>New Opera House, ca. 1903 (1903–1921), seated 545. Ground-floor house. Proscenium was 20' wide × 14' high; stage was 50' wide × 16' high × 20' deep; 6' apron. No grooves. No scene room. Electric light. By ca. 1904 seating capacity 560. Stage height 31'. Depth under stage 7'. By ca. 1914, seating capacity was 500. Stage 49' wide × 16' high × 26' deep. W. A. Bonhum (1903–1905), electrician. Charles Robinson (1903–1905), stage carpenter. Scy Moss (1903–1905), prop man. 4 to 7 in orchestra; leader, S. T. Skidmore (1903–1909). Mgrs. Len C. Sears, (1903–1905), S. T. Skidmore (1907–1909), Fred W. Wonder (1914–19??), M. McKinnon (1921). See IOOF Hall.
>Norton Opera House.
>**Whiting Opera House,** ca. 1889, seated 600.

Onslow (*Jones*)
>**IOOF Hall**, Lodge #398, 1895. Originally two stories, the Masons removed the upper story in 1960. 30' × 69'.

Orange City (*Sioux*)
>Lyric Theatre, ca. 1921, seated 500. Stage was 30' wide × 15' high × 17' deep. Mgr. C. Hales.
>Orange City Opera House, ca. 1896 (1896–1914), second-story hall seating 500. Proscenium was 22' wide × 14'6" high; stage was 43' wide × 15' high × 15'6" deep; 2' apron. Had three 11' high grooves, 2 traps, 3' and 4' from back wall. 32' between fly girders; 15' to rigging loft. 3'6" depth under stage. By ca. 1914, stage was 30' wide × 15' high × 17' deep. Electric light. F. Scott (1897), F. W. Michel (1904–1909), electricians; John A. Walraven (1896–1905), Vander Sluis (1907–1909), prop men. Mgr. D. Betten,

J. Van der Meide (1904–1905), G. L. Vander Steeg (1907–1914). Rink Opera House, ca. 1886, seated 400.

Osage (*Mitchell*)

Academy of Music, ca. 1879, seated 800. Stage was 50′ wide × 25′ deep. Drop curtain. Gas light. See Sprague's Academy of Music.

New Opera House, 1920, 607 Main. Two-story brick building, 21′ × 120′. The stage was 49′ wide × 22′ deep × 21′ high. Theatre was on the ground floor; seating capacity was 600. Was renamed Colonial at some time. Mgr. Roy Raub.

Sprague Opera House, ca. 1896 (1896–1914), second-story hall seating 1000. Proscenium was 24′ wide × 15′ high; stage was 30′ wide × 14′ high × 20′9″ deep; 1′3″ apron. 3′ depth under stage. Had three 12′ grooves, 1 trap, "about" center. In 1903, "grooves, none, lash stuff"; stage was 49′ wide × 21′ high × 20′ deep; 2′ apron. Mgrs. J. S. Detwiler, G. N. Symmes (1899), Goodall & Prime (1903), Katz & Gauss (1914).

Sprague's Academy of Music, ca. 1883 (1883–1889), seated 1600; "parquette, dress circle, gallery." Stage was 50′ wide × 25′ deep. Gas light. Same as Academy of Music.

Osceola (*Clarke*)

Opera House, ca. 1883 (1886–1989), seated 700. Stage was 22′ wide × 16′ deep. Had a "fair amount of scenery." Mgr. B. Pritchett.

Pritchett Opera House (1880), 200 W. Jefferson. Two-story brick building built for $7,000. The upper story housed the opera house while the lower floor was used for retail stores and various offices. It seated 400 people. The building dimensions are 44′5″ × 80′9″. Currently the upper story is storage for the Reynoldson law offices below. The building is called the Reynoldson Law Building.

Touet's Opera House, ca. 1903 (1903–1921), ground-floor house seating 1000. Proscenium was 26′ wide × 32′ high. Stage depth 21′, 3′ apron. Had 14′ grooves, 3 traps. Depth under stage 10′. Electric light. Mgrs. Dave A. Martin (1903–1905), Dave A. Martin, I. S. Touet (1907), I. A. Touet (1912).

Oskaloosa (*Mahaska*)

City Hall, ca. 1878 (1878–1879), seated 400. Stage was 38′ wide × 16′ deep; had a curtain and 3 scenes. Mgrs. Dutton & Lorins.

Hall, ca. 1889. Mgr. W. A. Seevers.

Mahaska Theatre, 115 So. Market. Converted from a retail sales building, perhaps always a movie theatre.

Masonic Opera House, ca. 1883 (1883–1909), ground-floor house, seating 1000 in a "parquette, dress circle, and gallery. Folding opera chairs"; prices (1896) $0.25–$1. "Stock concert grand piano." Proscenium was 30′ wide × 24′ high; stage was 60′ wide × 44′ high × 35′ deep; 6′ apron. 32′ between fly girders. 9′ depth under stage. Had "elegant" drop curtain, 14 sets scenery, five 16′ high grooves, 2 traps, center and side; 1 bridge, back. Grooves could be taken up flush with fly gallery. Gas and electric light (by 1889). Steam heat. O. P. Watkins, Harry Gilmore (1903), electricians; Harry Gillmore, stage carpenter; Harry Meyers, prop man; E. M. Fritze, orchestra leader; 9 in orchestra. Mgrs. G. N. Beechler, H. L. Briggs (1896), E. M. Fritze (1897), J. F. Jersey (1903), (Homer R. Kendig [1907], resident manager), Ray Wortman (1914).

New Masonic Hall, ca. 1879.

New Masonic Theatre, ca. 1912 (1912–1921), ground-floor house seating 546 on the main floor, 505 in 2 balconies, and 32 in the boxes (total: 1083). Proscenium was 28′ wide × 45′ high; stage was 60′ wide × 45′ high × 26′ deep; 46′6″ between fly girders; 18′ to fly gallery; 4′ apron. 9′ depth under stage. 15 dressing rooms. Electric light. Booking agents (1914), Klaw & Erlanger, New York. Mgrs. A. J. Busby (1912), (Roy Wortman [1912], local mgr.), Busby Bros. (1921).

Strand, 113. N. Market. Two-story brick building, 48′ × 118′. Difficult to tell the age; now remodeled into retail sales.

Ossian (*Winneshiek*)

Bullard Hall. Old; became Princess Theatre, then state liquor store. Single-story brick. Only the tin ceiling remains.

Ossian Opera House, 1893. Two-story frame, 40′ × 100′; now the Knights of Columbus Hall. Stage has been filled in—occasional outlines of proscenium arch can be detected. Appears to be approximately 20′ × 16′.

Ottumwa (*Wapello*)

Grand Opera House, ca. 1897 (1897–1921), brick building corner Main and Jefferson. Top floor has been removed; can't tell what it ever was. In 1897 it seated 1034. Proscenium was 35′ wide × 28′ high; stage was 74′ wide × 54′ high × 38′ deep; 5′ apron. 42′ between fly girders. There were four 20′ grooves, could be taken up flush with fly gallery. 14′ depth under stage. 5 traps (1 Hamlet, 1 in 1, 1 in 2), 1 bridge. Scene room. 12 dressing rooms. Gas and electric light (Edison system). D. Sullivan, O. Jones (1898), George Elkin (1900), electricians; Al. McDonald, Jos. J. Whippel (1898), Ada Abraham (1900), prop men; Wm. Corrigan, E. J. Smith (1898), stage carpenters. 6 in orchestra.

In 1912 the proscenium was 32′ wide × 28′ high; stage was 72′ wide × 54′ high × 36′ deep; 4′ apron. 42′ between fly galleries; 24′ to the fly gallery; 8′ depth under stage. 12 dressing rooms. Electric light. Booking agents, Klaw & Erlanger (1914), New York. Mgrs. J. F. Jersey (1897, 1904), L. T. Dorsey (1903).

Capitol Theatre, 233 E. Main.

Lewis Opera House, ca. 1878 (1878–1886), seated 300. Stage was 45′ wide × 22′ deep (30′ × 35′, 1883); 5 drop scenes. "Gas, water, etc." Mgr. Conn Lewis.

Market Street Opera House, ca. 1879 (1879–1886), seated 650. Stage was 27′ wide × 20′ deep; had 6 changes new scenery. Orchestra available. Mgr. Herm Wendt.

New Market Street Theatre, ca. 1903, ground-floor house, seated 1000.

Proscenium was 28' wide × 22' high; stage was 54' wide × 50' high × 31' deep. 46' between fly girders. 8' depth under stage. No grooves, 2 traps. Scene room. Gas and electric light. Geo. Elkin, electrician; Oda Abraham, prop man. 6 in orchestra. Mgr. J. F. Jersey.

Ottumwa Opera House, ca. 1896, seated 1200. Proscenium was 32' wide × 46' high; stage was 64' wide × 47' high × 34' deep; 6' apron. 41' between fly girders. 8' depth under stage. Had five 20' grooves, 4 traps, center, each side, and back. 1 bridge. Grooves could be taken up flush with fly gallery. Gas and electric light. W. Fisher, electrician; Chas. Dummler, stage carpenter; Chas. Pravalsky, prop man; Prof. T. H. Hand, orchestra leader. 6 in orchestra. Mgr. J. Frank Jersey.

Ottumwa Theatre, 229 E. Main. Perhaps the Ottumwa Opera House. Two-story brick building, approx. 36' × 126'; has been face-lifted and redesigned into a modern multimovie complex (Capri I, II, etc.)

Rialto, 223 Main. Two-story brick building, narrow front. Now a music store.

Strand, south side of Main between Green and Market, supposedly. Now reportedly houses the Daughters of the Nile/Rainbow.

Turner Opera House, ca. 1889, ground-floor house seating 900, "the only opera house in the city." Folding chairs. Piano. Proscenium was 22' wide; stage was 35' wide × 20' high × 35' deep. It was 15' to the grooves. 5 sets scenery. "All modern improvements." Mgr. Dick P. Sutton.

Oxford (*Johnson*)

Oxford Opera House, 1895, corner Augusta and Main. Three-story brick building, now a bank, measures 42' × 51'.

Oxford Junction (*Jones*)

Holup Hall, ca. 1879, seated 100. Stage was 20' wide × 10' deep. Mgr. D. Ferguson.

National Hall, ca. 1883 (1883–1889), seated 300. Mgr. F. Nowacheck.

ZCBJ Hall (ca. 1910). Three-story brick, 52' × 89', the theatre was on the ground floor. Used as a dance hall, the stage was ceilinged off, and enclosed by a box set made of old woodland flats by Sosman & Landis. Proscenium was 17' wide × 14' high; curtain line to back 16', with 6' of wing space on either side. The two roll drops above the stage are now in the Museum of Repertoire American, Mt. Pleasant (one is a gorgeous front drop, "A View of Prague"). A stack of flats backstage are by Sosman & Landis.

Panama (*Shelby*)

Legion Hall.

Zimmerman Hall. Located on the second story of a business building.

Panora (*Shelby*)

Opera House, ca. 1883 (1883–1889), seated 300. Stage was 40' wide × 18' deep. "No scenery. Have piano in house." By ca. 1889, proscenium opening was 12' × 20', height to grid 12'; to loft, 18'. Seated 350, with 3 scenes. Mgr. L. J. Pentacost.

Opera House, 105 N.E. 1st St. Now a laundromat and apartments.

Parkersburg *(Butler)*

Opera House, ca. 1904 (1904–1913), second-story hall seated 300. Had gas and electric lighting. Mgr. J. A. Foote.

Union Hall, ca. 1889, second-story of a two-story building, seated 300 on chairs and benches. No piano. Proscenium was 18' wide; stage was 44' wide × 10'6" high × 14' deep. Had 1 set scenery. Was above Foote & Mott's. Mgrs. Mott & Mahanke.

Patterson *(Madison)*

Patterson Opera House.

Paulina *(O'Brien)*

Paulina Opera House.

Pella *(Marion)*

Pella Opera House, ca. 1878 (1879–ca. 1900). In 1878 it had a 19' × 40' stage, a "drop curtain and four shifting scenes," and seated 400. Orchestra available (1883). Mgr. L. Bach.

Pella Opera House, 1900 (1903–1914), 611 Franklin. Three-story brick, 33' × approx. 100'. Theatre was on second and third floors; prior to restoration the building had been reduced in height, a floor had been put in at balcony level and the interior completely altered to nontheatrical function. In 1903 the proscenium was 18' wide × 18' high; stage was 35' wide × 28' deep. One trap, 8' under stage, no grooves, one bridge. Electric lighting. A. J. Burwalder (1903), electrician; John Van Maren (1903), scenic artist; H. J. Bootsma (1903), stage carpenter; Josh Mann (1903), prop man. Mgr. H. S. Rhynsburger (1903). In 1984 there were remains of rigging in the third-floor ceiling; a roll drop was found, which turned out to be an advertising front drop. A restoration project has recently been undertaken: the exterior has been restored to its original appearance; the interior is restored and the theatre reopened in 1990. The theatre now seats 328 in reproduction opera chairs on a main floor and horseshoe balcony (original balcony was straight-fronted); the original light green and gold color scheme has been followed, the original pressed-tin ceiling has been restored and painted, and a modern stage has been installed.

Perry *(Dallas)*

Breed Opera House, ca. 1889, seated 600. Stage was 40' wide × 20' deep. Had 4 scenes. Mgr. Allen Breed.

Grand Opera House, 1903 (1903–1921). Built by Col. E. Young of Chicago. It was a two-story brick building with box seats and a balcony. Remodeled throughout the years, it is currently used as a movie house. In 1903 it seated 772. The proscenium was 31' wide × 23'6" high; the stage was 65' wide × 47' high × 35' deep; 3' apron. 2 traps. Electric light. Depth under stage 9'. No grooves. By ca. 1904, seating capacity was 800. By ca. 1907, proscenium height 24'6". Theatre on ground floor. In ca. 1914, stage was 62' wide × 46' high × 38' deep. In 1921 it seated 390 on the main floor, 354 in 2 balconies, 48 in the boxes (total: 792). Proscenium was 31' wide × 46′ high; stage was 62′ wide × 46′ high × 33′ deep; 4′ apron. 10 dressing rooms. Clif Hain, Frank Roberts (1904–1905), Keno Myers (1907–1909), electricians. 5 in orchestra; leader W. W. Wallis, (1903–1905), Mrs. Perle Snyder (1907–1908). Mgr. R. M. Harvey (1903–1908), A. W. Walton (1912).

Newport's Hall, ca. 1879, seated 250. Stage was 20′ wide × 12′ deep.

Smith's Opera House, ca. 1886, seated 600. Piano. Stage was 29′ wide × 20′ deep; had 4 scenes and a drop curtain. Mgrs. Haskins and Wales.

Union Hall, ca. 1883, seated 500. Stage was 35′ wide × 12′ deep. Had a drop curtain and 6 flies. Seating capacity 500. Mgrs. Lunt and Neaton.

Peterson (*Clay*)

Peterson Opera House.

Pierson (*Woodbury*)

Home Room Opera House, ca. 1921. Was used as a skating rink in 1921.

Pilot Mound (*Boone*)

Pilot Mound Opera House. A two-story brick building originally built as Odd Fellows Lodge. Remodeled. Currently Masonic Lodge upstairs and Community Hall downstairs. The building dimensions are 80′ × 30′.

Pisgah (*Harrison*)

Pisgah Opera House, 1909. According to resident Mrs. Pauline Fairchild Seabury, it was a one-story frame building constructed in 1909 by Oscar Peasley. The dimensions were 25′5″ × 86′6″; dressing room 16′2″ × 25′; stage 16′ deep × 25′ wide. It had folding seats and wings and drops. Extensively remodeled it currently is Post 408, American Legion.

Plano (*Appanoose*)

IOOF Lodge Hall. Second-story brick, 50′ × 59′. The second floor has been sealed off. The building now houses the post office.

Pleasant Plain (*Jefferson*)

Eck's Opera Hall, 1884. Building was 40′ × 50′.

Pleasanton (*Deactur*)

Pleasanton Opera House.

Plymouth (*Cerro Gordo*)

Borman Hall, ca. 1912 (1912–1914), ground-floor hall seating 275. Stage was 16′ wide × 9′ high × 12′ deep. Gas light. Mgr. W. H. Borman.

Pocahontas (*Pocahontas*)

Hornek Opera House, 1900. According to the 1970 *Pocahontas Centennial* and the 1982 *Pocahontas City History,* it was a two-story brick building with opera house on the second floor, it was built by F. E. Hornek. The proscenium was 20′ wide × 16′ high, with dressing rooms on either side. The main floor was 50′ × 54′. There were several drop curtains. All scenery was painted by the Jesse Cox Company of Estherville, Iowa. Currently it is an appliance store.

Polk City (*Polk*)
> City Hall Theatre, 1904 (1904–1909), second-story hall. Proscenium was 16' wide × 13' high; stage was 16' deep; 1' apron. Depth under stage 3'6". Gas and electric light. May still be extant. Mgr. H. Eggleston.

Pomeroy (*Calhoun*)
> Pomeroy Opera House. Burned.

Popejoy (*Franklin*)
> Opera House. Burned.

Portsmouth (*Shelby*)
> Woodman Opera House, ca. 1921, seated 600. Mgr. Don Sarggen.

Postville (*Allamakee*)
> City Hall, ca. 1889 (1889–1921), seated 300. May still be extant. Mgrs. Bayless, Douglass & Co.
> Turner Hall, ca. 1883 (1883–1889), seated 500. Mgrs. John Thoma, Secretary of the Turner Society (1889).

Prairie City (*Jasper*)
> **American Theatre.** Single-story frame, 30' × 71'. Now houses a machine shop.
> **Union Hall**, ca. 1886 (1886–1889). Two-story brick/stucco; hall was above the barber shop–fabric store. The stage is reportedly gone. It was originally 22' × 18'. There were four scenes, and the hall seated 500. Mgr. W. G. Clements.

Prairieburg (*Linn*)
> Opera House, Main St.

Primghar (*O'Brien*)
> Opera House, ca. 1921, seated 450. "Plays Legitimate and Picture Performances." Mgr. J. A. Klink.

Pulaski (*Davis*)
> Townsend Theatre, ca. 1910 (1921), second-story hall seating 400. Proscenium was 25' wide; stage was 12' high × 14' deep. Screen was 10' × 14'; throw was 62'. Was nicknamed "The Titanic" because of its size, apparently without intended irony. Mgr. Bush Milligan.
> Walther's Hall, ca. 1889, seated 200. Mgr. A. Walther.

Quasqueton (*Buchanan*)
> Budinger Opera House, 1902, Dubuque and Water streets. On the second-story of a two-story 36' × 80' building, seated 225. Stage was 18' deep. Razed 1967.

Quimby (*Cherokee*)
> Quimby Opera House, ca. 1914, second-story hall seating 400. Stage was 30' wide × 20' high × 16' deep. Mgr. Issac Clark.

Radcliffe (*Hardin*)
> Blum's Hall, ca. 1886 (1886–1889), seated 200. Mgr. M. L. Blum.
> Finn Hotel and Opera House, 1894. Razed in 1930.

Randolph (*Fremont*)
> **Sells Opera House.** One-story brick building erected in 1917 by Miles Sells; 96'2" × 32'. Current use is storage.

Red Oak (*Montgomery*)
> Beardsley Opera House, 1880–1881. Three-story brick building measuring 45′ × 112′, seated 1000. Stage was 28′ wide × 24′ deep.
>
> Beardsley Theatre, ca. 1912 (1912–1921), ground-floor house seating 550 on the main floor, 400 in 2 balconies, 36 in the boxes (total: 986). Proscenium was 30′ wide × 22′ high; stage was 60′ wide × 60′ high × 34′ deep; 3′ apron. Electric light. 7 dressing rooms. By ca. 1914, seating capacity was 900. Stage was 60′ wide × 50′ high × 35′ deep. By ca. 1921, seating capacity was 986. Mgr. L. M. Beardsley.
>
> Bishop's New Opera House, ca. 1886, seated 1000. Probably the same as Beardsley Opera House.
>
> Bryson's Hall, ca. 1879 (1879–1883), seated 500. Stage was 40′ wide × 25′ deep. Had 1 drop curtain. By 1883 had 2 drop curtains and "good stock of scenery." Mgrs. Bryson and Sons.
>
> Evans Theatre, ca. 1898 (1898–1904), seated 1000. Proscenium was 23′ wide × 16′ high; stage was 45′ wide × 23′ deep; 3′ apron. Had 2 traps. Depth under stage 8′. Probably the same as Beardsley Opera House. Geo. Eiler, Art Johnson (1900), Joe Zuber (1901), Emmit Harding (1903), prop men. M. Smith (1898), E. O. Pace (1900–1902), stage carpenters. Mgrs. Priesman and Clark, Frank Hathaway (1900), W. H. Evans (1903).
>
> Opera House, ca. 1897, second-story hall seating 600. Proscenium was 20′ wide × 16′ high; stage was 45′ wide × 14′ high × 20′ deep; 5′ apron. Had fifteen 14′ high grooves, 2 traps. Geo. Eiler (1897), prop man; Wm. Redman (1897), electrician. Mgrs. Prussman and Clovis (1897).
>
> Roach's Hall, ca. 1878, seated 350. Stage was 32′ wide × 14′ deep. Had a drop curtain.
>
> Rynearson's Hall, ca. 1889 seated 600. Proscenium was 20′ wide; stage was 42′ wide × 13′ high × 25′ deep. Had 12 scenes. Probably the same as the Opera House. Mgr. M. N. Spencer.
>
> Rynearson's Opera House, ca. 1904 (1904–1909). Seating capacity 1000. Proscenium 24′ wide × 16′ high. By ca. 1908, seating capacity 750. Proscenium 23′ wide. Stage 44′ wide × 14′ high × 24′ deep. No rigging loft. H. O. Beardsley, orchestra leader. Mgrs. L. M. Beardsley and Son (1904–1905), L. M. Beardsley (1908). Could be Evans Theatre.

Redding (*Ringgold*)
> **Redding Opera House.** The second story of a two-story brick building. The building dimensions are 25′ × 71′. According to resident Barton Abarr, the stage was about 16′ × 14′. There was no balcony and the seating capacity was about 100. Currently it is used for storage.

Reinbeck (*Grundy*)
> Rink Hall, ca. 1889, seated 200. Mgr. J. F. Sherralt.
>
> Therratt's Opera House, ca. 1886, seated 500. Could be the same as Rink Hall if "Sherralt" is a misprint in the guide for "Therratt," or

"Therratt" for "Sherralt."

Rembrandt (*Buena Vista*)

Rembrandt Opera House, 1912. One-story brick structure. The building dimensions are 32'6" × 80'1½". The auditorium is 55'5" × 34'9". The proscenium height is 10'7" at sides and 11'6" in the middle. The curtain line to back wall is 16'. The proscenium width is not measurable. Current use: storage.

Remsen (*Plymouth*)

Falke Block. The opera house was located on the second story of this two-story brick building. Currently it is storage for Jack Thiel Tire Center.

Remsen Grand Opera House.

Renwick (*Humbolt*)

Renwick Opera House, ca. 1886, Main St. Single story. This may be the same building that, according to local residents, was constructed between 1912 and 1915, so identification is uncertain. The outside dimensions of the extant structure are 30'6" × 90'2". The seating capacity was about 150. It had three small balconies and wings and drops. Extensively remodeled it currently is Jeri's Cafe.

Small Hall #1, ca. 1889. Seated 150.

Small Hall #2, ca. 1889. Seated 150.

Riceville (*Howard*)

Brown's Opera House, 1902, corner Woodland Ave and 2nd St. Two-story brick, 67' × 80'. Hall was on the second floor; nicknamed "Rainbow Hall" because of the multiplicity of stenciled and painted wall and ceiling decoration: the overall color scheme was rose with lime green and rose trim. The proscenium arch is unique: it is framed with stenciled decoration and light bulbs, and across the top it reads "All the World is a Stage [sic]." It measures 21' wide × 11' high; curtain to back is 19'2". The curved apron measures 4'6"; wing space R is 14', L is 12'. The stage has one trap; there is a footlight trough with 12 lights. There are 2 dressing rooms. The original lighting control panel is situated off L. There are 12 flats still backstage. There is a seascape mural R of the proscenium and a mountain/waterfall scene on the L: both painted by M. Smith. The original wood-burning stove is in place. The ceiling leaks, and the hall is in an advanced state of decay. However, in a room added on especially for the purpose, the Riceville Public Library displays six original, restored roll drops behind a replica of the original proscenium arch. A main front drop, with painted drapery and an exotic Middle Eastern harbor scene, and a fancy advertising drop, with a center panel depicting a lake and castle, measure 13'6" × 23'6". Three other drops measure 13'6" × 20': they are a Street, a Country Road, and a Rocky Mt. Pass. In addition, the library displays a plaque listing admission prices: e.g., "Adults .18, War Tax .02, Total .20."

Richland (*Keokuk*)

Bridger's Opera House, ca. 1889, second-floor house seating 400.

Proscenium was 16' wide × 11' high; stage was 44' wide × 11'
high × 18' deep; 3' apron. Had 3 grooves, 1 trap. Mgr. A. F.
Bridger.

Opera House, ca. 1896 (1896–1914). Second-floor house, seated 500.
Proscenium was 16' wide × 11' high; stage was 44' wide × 11'
high × 18' deep. Had 3 grooves 11' high, 2'6" depth under the
stage, 1 trap, center. By 1914 the stage was 60' wide × 14' high ×
18' deep, and it seated 500. Probably the same as Bridger's Opera
House. Mgrs. W. A. Shaffer, F. W. Smith (1899), J. W. Hollowell
(1914).

Richland Opera House, ca. 1914, second-story house seating 500. Stage
was 60' wide × 14' high × 18' deep.

Richmond/English River Township (*Washington*)
Casino Hall. Now Holy Trinity Hall, used by church for social functions, etc.

ZCBJ Hall.

Ridgeway (*Winneshiek*)
Ridgeway Town Hall, ca. 1923. Two-story brick, 27'6" × 90'6".
Ceiling has been lowered, stage removed and a kitchen built.

Ringsted (*Emmett*)
Ringsted Opera House, 1912, Maple. St. Built for $5,000 through the
sale of stock. The building dimensions are 40'3" × 74'. Completely
remodeled it currently is the Community Center.

Riverton (*Fremont*)
Riverton Opera House, Main St. According to resident Ralph A. Fox,
it was a one-story hollow-tile brick building, 100' × 24'. The
seating capacity was 150 and the stage was 15'–20' deep. Part of the
building still stands and is used as city storage.

Rockford (*Floyd*)
Leigh's Hall, 1877 (1889), second-floor house in a two-story building,
seated 400. Mgr. Charles Lee.

Rockford Opera House, 1903, Block 11, lots 16, 17. Razed 1937.

Rock Rapids (*Lyon*)
Armory Theatre, ca. 1912 (1912–1914), first-story house seating 440 on
the main floor and 150 in the balcony (total: 590). Proscenium was
20' wide × 16' high; stage was 43' wide × 23' deep; 2' apron. 5
dressing rooms. By ca. 1914, seating capacity was 600. Stage was
45' wide × 18' high × 25' deep. Mgrs. Tonne and Anderson
(1912), E. A. Tonne (1914).

Lyon Theatre. A three-story brick building with a basement, built
sometime after World War I by E. A. Hunt. It could accommodate
movies as well as live shows. The theatre is in the greater part of
the first and second stories. On the third story is a very large room
once used for dances and basketball games. It has a raised platform
at one end for an orchestra and several smaller rooms in back of
that. The building is 41'6" × 93'. The proscenium is 24'5" wide ×
18' high. The curtain line to back wall is 21'4". The fly gallery
offstage right is 17'5" high and has 21 slots in the pinrail. There are

three dressing rooms in the basement. The seating capacity was 600. Currently there is a retail shop in front and the theatre proper is used by the Community Theatre. (Probably also called **Lyon Opera House**.)

Lyon Opera House, ca. 1921. Seating capacity 650. Stage 45' wide × 18' high × 25' deep. Mgr. E. J. Anderson.

Union Opera House, ca. 1889, seated 600. Mgr. D. H. Shannon.

Rock Valley (*Sioux*)

Orpheum Theatre, ca. 1921, seated 350. Mgrs. Dahl Bros.

Rock Valley Opera House, ca. 1921, seated 350. Mgrs. Dahl Bros.

Rockwell (*Cerro Gordo*)

City Hall, ca. 1889, seated 500. Mgr. J. A. Felthous.

Odd Fellows Hall, ca. 1889, seated 600. Mgr. C. P. Kenyon.

Rockwell City (*Calhoun*)

Empress Theatre. See Golden Buckle Theatre.

Golden Buckle Theatre, on the north side of the square. Became the Empress Theatre.

Joe Palmer's Opera House, late 1800s.

Johnson's, ca. 1914. Second-story house, seated 500. Stage was 20' wide × 11' high × 20' deep. Mgr. A. L. Johnson.

Old Opera House, ca. 1906.

Rodney (*Monona*)

Rodney Opera House, ca. 1920. Built shortly after World War I, is completely altered: current use is honey storage.

Rolfe (*Pocahontas*)

Bruce's Hall, ca. 1886, seated 175.

Rolfe Lecture Hall, 1889, seated 350. Proscenium was 12' high; stage was 24' wide × 12' high × 16' deep. Proscenium opening 12'; height to both grid and loft 12'. Mgr. J. F. Benson.

Rolfe Opera House, ca. 1912 (1912–1914), second-story hall seating 450. Proscenium was 20' wide × 14' high; stage was 18' deep. Gas light. 2 dressing rooms. By ca. 1914, stage was 25' wide × 18' high × 20' deep. Mgrs. Joe Weiwel (1912), Rosenkranz and Damborg (1914).

Shirley's Hall, ca. 1886, seated 300.

Rossie (*Clay*)

Rossie Opera House.

Rowan (*Wright*)

Opera House, Main St., on the upper floor of the Bingham Building. Razed 1976.

Rudd (*Floyd*)

Schraders Opera House, 513 Chickasaw St.

Runnells (*Polk*)

Brown's Hall, ca. 1889, seated 300.

Ruthven (*Palo Alto*)

Ruthven Opera House, ca. 1912 (1912–1914), seated 350. Ground-floor house. Proscenium was 18' wide × 12' high; stage was 30' wide × 27' deep; 24' between fly girders; 3' apron. Had four 10'6" high grooves. 2 dressing rooms. Oil light. Mgrs. Jas. Ruthven, L. T. Clark (1914).

Sabula (*Jackson*)

Blenner Hall, ca. 1883 (1883–1889), seated 500. Mgr. Jerry Blenner.

Sac City (*Sac*)

Opera House, ca. 1886, seated 700. Piano. Stage was 50' wide × 24' deep. Had 5 scenes. May be the Opera House Clothing Store, which is still standing. Mgr. A. J. Miller (1886).

Sac City Opera House, ca. 1904 (1904–1909), seated 600. Proscenium 21' wide × 19' high; stage 48' wide × 25' deep, 1 trap. Depth under stage 3'. Five 13' grooves. No scene room. Theatre was on second floor. Gas lighting. By ca. 1907, electric lighting. Mgr. Charles L. Early.

Salem (*Henry*)

Rialto, 1906. Two-story brick, 22' × 76', now houses a feed store. This may have been only a site for early movies. There was reportedly an opera house in town which has been torn down.

Salix (*Woodbury*)

Salix Opera House. Burned.

Salix Opera House, 1913, corner Poplar and Tipton. According to resident Fayann Hubert, it was a two-story brick building, 31' × 100', built by hardware dealers Senecal and Every. The upper story housed the opera house, which had a stage at the north end, removable chairs, and a kitchen, ticket office, and coat room in the south half. Currently the building has a tavern below and is empty above.

Sanborn (*O'Brien*)

Citizen's Opera House, ca. 1914, seated 700. Stage was 50' wide × 20' high × 40' deep. Mgr. A. R. West.

Roden Hall, ca. 1883, seated 300. Mgr. A. H. Roden.

Sanborn Opera House, 1905, 110 Main St. A brick building erected at a cost of $5000, opened in 1906. May have been on the second floor. The building dimensions are 48' × 104'. The seating capacity was 1200. There were many exits. The interior was decorated in Alice Blue. The stage was 35' × 60'. There were six dressing rooms. There was a check room 18' × 30' to the left of the main entrance. Currently the bottom floor is Roth TV with storage upstairs.

Scarville (*Winnebago*)

Opera House.

Schaller (*Sac*)

Schaller Opera House, ca. 1900 (1912–1921). Three- or possibly four-story frame. The upper floors were used for meeting rooms and the lower floor was the opera house. The building dimensions are 89' × 36'. First appears in Cahn/Leighton 1912–1913. No details. By ca. 1914 it seated 400 and the stage was 40' wide × 15' high × 25' deep. Currently Thompson Hardware is below and apartments are above. Mgr. J. I. Murray.

Scranton (*Greene*)
> IOOF Opera Hall, ca. 1889, seated 450. Proscenium was 16' wide; stage
> was 30' wide × 12' high × 14' deep. Had 8 scenes; grooves were
> 8' high. "Only hall in town with stage." Mgr. B. F. Roberts.
>
> Public Hall, ca. 1886, seated 500.

Searsboro (*Poweshiek*)
> **IOOF Hall**. Two-story brick.

Sergeant Bluff (*Woodbury*)
> Knights of Pythias Hall. Burned.

Seymour (*Wayne*)
> Lowrey Opera House, 5th and Wall streets.

Sheffield (*Franklin*)
> Town Hall, ca. 1889, seated 250. Mgr. James Borst.

Shelby (*Shelby*)
> Shelby Opera House. Burned.

Sheldon (*O'Brien*)
> D. S. White Jr.'s Hall, ca. 1883, seated 400. Stage was 48' wide × 14'
> deep. No scenery. Seating capacity 300–400. "Do not play on
> shares." Mgr. D. S. White, Jr.
>
> GAR Hall, ca. 1889, seated 600. Mgr. E. C. Brown.
>
> Royce Opera House.
>
> Sanders' Hall, ca. 1889, seated 800. Mgr. C. Sanders.
>
> Sheldon Opera House, ca. 1914, second-story hall seating 600. Stage was
> 40' wide × 30' high × 25' deep. Mgr. William H. Sleeper, Jr.
>
> **White's Hall,** 1879. Built by Dan White, it was a two-story brick
> building with a meeting hall on the second floor. The seating
> capacity was 500. The building dimensions are 48' × 80'. Currently
> there are apartments above and Zenith Radio and TV Center below.
>
> Lyric Theatre, ca. 1921. Seating capacity 600. Stage 40' wide × 15'
> high × 25' deep. Mgr. J. I. Murray.

Shell Rock (*Butler*)
> Wilson's Hall, ca. 1889, seated 300. "No stage, no scenery." Mgr. E.
> Wilson.

Shellsburg (*Benton*)
> Opera House, Main St. Burned.

Shenandoah (*Page*)
> Empress Theatre, ca. 1921, seated 700. Proscenium was 15' wide; stage
> was 20' wide × 20' high × 30' deep. Mgr. J. B. Wicks.
>
> **McComb Opera House,** ca. 1896 (1896–1909). According to resident
> C. W. Fishbaugh, it was the second story of a two-story brick
> building erected by John McComb. Seated 600. Proscenium was 22'
> wide × 16' high; stage was 50' wide × 18' deep; 6' apron. Had 1
> trap. Depth under stage 4'. Electric light. 8 in orchestra. G. Becker
> (1896–1902), stage carpenter. Was remodeled in 1903 and called
> The Opera House, seating capacity 800. By ca. 1904, called
> McComb Opera House again. Proscenium opening 22' wide × 22'
> high. 5 in orchestra. Mgrs. J. H. McComb (1897–1902), J. L.
> Gwynn (1903). Currently it is retail and apartments.

Norton & West's Opera House, ca. 1883, seated 600. Stage was 50' wide × 24' deep. Had good scenery. Mgrs. Norton and West. By 1889 had become West's Opera House. Mgr. A. B. West.

Williams' Hall, ca. 1883, seated 300. No scenery.

Sibley (*Osceola*)

Academy of Music, ca. 1883 (1883–1889). By ca. 1889, seating capacity was 600. Mgrs. Close Brothers (1883 –18??), Matt Dodsworth (1889).

Campbell Opera House, ca. 1921. See Sibley Opera House.

Sibley Opera House, ca. 1914 (1914–1921), second-story hall seating 450. Stage was 44' wide × 16' high × 26' deep. Was Campbell Opera House in 1921. Could be the Academy of Music. Mgrs. Ellerbroek and Dixon (1914–??), Geo. E. Dixon (1921).

Sidney (*Fremont*)

Sidney Opera House, ca. 1914 (1914–1921), first-story house seating 450. Stage was 34' wide × 14' high × 22' deep. Mgrs. S. N. Mosier (1914–??), Trewett (1921).

Sigourney (*Keokuk*)

Fridays, ca. 1914, second-story hall seating 310. Stage was 24' wide × 12' high × 12' deep. Mgr. F. S. Wertz.

Yerger's Opera House, ca. 1879 (1879–1989), seated 300. Stage was 20' wide × 18' deep. 4 scenes and a drop curtain. An orchestra available. In 1889, "nothing else but churches in town that can be used even for lectures." Mgrs. Theo Robinson, J. P. Yerger (1883), Silas McClure (1889), F. S. Yerger.

Silver City (*Mills*)

Plumer Opera House.

Silver City Opera House, 1891. It cost $10,000 and was originally owned by Chris Plumer and George Pullman, Sr. The opera house was located on the second floor. The auditorium was about 50' × 50'. It seated about 350. It was later remodeled and the second story was taken off. The building is currently owned by the Masons.

Sioux Center (*Sioux*)

Sioux Center Town Hall. Was used for entertainments. It has been remodeled and is used by the city.

Sioux City (*Woodbury*)

Gertz and Doss Hall, ca. 1868.

Groningers' Hall, ca. 1868.

McElhaney's Hall, #1, ca. 1868.

McElhaney's Hall, #2, ca. 1869.

Olympic Theatre, ca. 1869.

Varieties Theatre, ca. 1869–1871.

Theatre Comique, ca. 1870–1871.

O'Connor's Variety Hall, ca. 1871.

The Varieties Theatre, ca. 1872.

H. C. McDannell's Olympic Theatre, ca. 1872.

Olympic Theatre, ca. 1879. Mgr. John Coonce.

Hedges' Hall, ca. 1880.

Vaudeville Variety Theatre, ca.1885. Mgr. Ed. Tinerney.

Standard Variety Theatre, ca. 1885–1887. Mgr. James Kelly.

Theatre Comique, ca. 1887 Mgr. W. M. Mitchell.

The Pavilion Theatre, ca. 1890–1894.

Eden Musee, ca. 1890. Dime Museum, formerly the Academy of Music.

The Riverside Aerial Casino, ca. 1894–1902. Mgr. A. B. Beall.

Olympic Theatre, ca. 1892–1893. Mgr. John McGoffin.

Pearl Street Theatre, ca. 1892–1893. Mgr. A. O. Trudell.

People's Theatre, ca. 1894.

Soo Theatre, ca. 1895. Mgr. M. M. Powers.

The Riverside Pavilion, ca. 1902–1903.

Palace Family Theatre, ca. 1904. Mgrs. Gooch and Getty.

New Family Theatre, ca. 1906. Seating capacity 600. By 1909, seating capacity was 540. Mgrs. Nathaniel Blossom (1906), Wm. Marshall (1907), G. G. Lehman (1908), Geisel and Tappan (1909), N. H. Nelson (1910).

Lyric Theatre, ca. 1907. Seating capacity 1200. Mgr. J. E. Jackson.

Scenic Theatre, ca. 1908. Seated 300. Mgrs. Tierney and Cameron (1908).

Unique Theatre, ca. 1908 Mgrs. Tierney and Cameron.

The Family Park (Airdome), ca. 1907. Seating capacity 2000. Mgr. F. H. Bradstreet.

Crystal Theatre, ca. 1908. Seating capacity 300. By 1909, seating capacity was 325. Mgrs. F. B. Donahue, E. A. Rodenbaugh (1909).

Kluff Theatre, ca. 1909. Seated 225. Mgr. O. E. Dunn.

Olympic Theatre, ca. 1909. Seated 300. Mgr. C. E. Wirick.

Magestic Theatre, ca. 1910. Seated 300. Mgrs. C. W. Melcher, H. B. Groves (1914), J. H. Gould (1916).

The Big Airdome Theatre, ca. 1909–1911. Mgr. O. E. Dunn.

Colonial Theatre, ca. 1912 Seated 1000. Mgrs. W. H. Dance, H. L. Holmes (1913), Dubinsky Bros. (1916).

Mizzou Theatre, ca. 1912. Seated 500. Mgrs. Lander and Lowe.

Empress, ca. 1913. Seated 500. Mgrs. G. J. Schaefer, Jose Kohlberg (1916).

Gem Theatre, ca. 1913. Seated 230. By 1920, seated 200. Mgrs. J. K. Huffman, Katherin Huffman (1914), Gus and Mabel McKay (1920).

End Theatre, ca. 1914. Seated 220. Mgr. Wm. Dixon.

Park Place Theatre, ca. 1913. Seated 200. Mgrs. Postin and Heald, Robert Heald (1914).

Lyric Theatre, ca. 1914. Seated 367. Mgrs. McLean and Waters.

National Theatre, ca. 1915. Seated 850. Mgrs. F. E. Murphy, J. H. Marshall (1916).

Princess Theatre, ca. 1915. Seated 1600. By 1920, seated 1356. Mgrs. Harry L. Holmes, John Biegger, Jr.(1916), J. E. Schlank (1918), J. S. Shortly (1919), Frank Wood (1920).

Royal Theatre, ca. 1915. Seated 700. Mgrs. Louis Weil, J. C. Hosteller (1920).

Palace Theatre, ca. 1916. Seated 220. Mgr. L. E. Carnes.

Park Theatre, ca. 1917. Seated 300. Mgrs. Lucile Bros.

Strand Theatre, ca. 1917. Seated 800. Mgr. Leon Weil.

U.S.A. Theatre, ca. 1917. Mgrs. Hammitt Bros.

Gayety Theatre, ca. 1919. Seated 1200. Mgr. J. E. Schlank.

Rivoli Theatre, ca. 1921. Seated 1200. Mgr. J. E. Schlank.

Academy of Music, ca. 1870–ca. 1890, seated 800. Originally called Hubbard Hall. Changed to Academy of Music in 1871. Stage was 24' wide × 22' deep. Had 6 scenes. By 1879, size of stage increased to 22' × 50', seating capacity dropped to 700. By 1883, seating capacity was 650 with 5 scenes. Gas. Mgrs. Selden M. Irwin (1870–1871), Hubbard, Hoskins and Stone (1878–ca. 1883), William Grady (1883–18??), E. M. Lord (1889–18??), W. I. Buchanan (1886–1887).

Auditorium, ca. 1910. Seated 3500. First mentioned in Cahn/Hill in 1921. Seated 523 on the main floor, 678 in 2 balconies, 56 in the boxes (total: 1257). Proscenium was 36'6" wide × 79' high; stage was 72' wide × 60' high × 32' deep, 10' apron. Mgrs. W. H. Barnes (1910), H. S. Baker (1912–19??), A. B. Beall (1919).

New Grand Theatre, ca. 1907 (1907–1914), ground-floor house seating 1500. Proscenium was 32' wide; stage was 70' wide × 60' high × 36' deep; 8' apron. Had tormentor grooves, 5 traps, 1 bridge. Electric light. Depth under stage 9'. 10 in orchestra. By ca. 1914, seating capacity was 1250. Stage was 70' wide × 66' high × 40' deep. Mgrs. H. H. Talman (1907), Maurice Jencks (1910), Morgan Wallace (1917), Herman Galinsky (1919). In 1919, the New Grand ceased being a theatre and was given over to commercial ventures. It burned in 1931. (See Peavey Grand Opera House).

Orpheum, ca. 1908 (1912–1921). In 1908 seated 1200. By 1912, ground-floor house seated 696 on the main floor, 331 in the balcony, 60 in the boxes (total: 1087). Proscenium was 20' wide × 19'6" high; stage was 47' wide × 40' high × 29' deep. Electric light. 10 dressing rooms. By ca. 1921, proscenium opening was 36' wide. Stage was 71' wide × 56' high × 34' deep. Mgrs. David Bechler (1908), C. E. Wilder (1910), General Mgr. Martin Beck; Local, C. E. Wilder, (1912), G. S. Riordan (1916), R. C. Emery (1918), C. S. Harris (1919).

Peavey Grand Opera House, 1888 (1888–1907), ground-floor house seating 1500 (main floor, balconies, boxes). Also called Grand Opera House. By ca. 1896, seating capacity 1369. Proscenium was 32' wide; stage was 70' wide × 60' high × 34' deep; 8' apron. Had tormentor grooves, 5 traps, 1 bridge. Depth under stage 9'. Gas light. J. H. Carmody (1896–1902), carpenter. 10 in orchestra. By ca. 1901, gas and electricity. Seating capacity back to 1500. By ca. 1902, electricity only. Mgrs. W. J. Buchanan (1888), E. L. Webster (1892), T. F. Boyd (1894), A. B. Beall (1895), Woodward and Burgess Amusement Company (1904), T. F. Boyd (1905). By 1907 it was the New Grand Theatre.

Sioux Rapids (*Buena Vista*)

Sioux Rapids Opera House, 1894 (1903–1909). Opened in 1895. It is a 2½-story brick structure, seating 572 (main floor and balcony). The current dimensions are 44' × 89'. It was remodeled in 1901. Auditorium 44' × 50'; gallery 18' × 44'; proscenium was 24' wide × 12' high; stage including wings was 42' wide × 13' high × 20' deep; 3' apron. Electric illumination. Twenty 10'6" grooves. May be taken up flush with fly gallery. No traps, no scene room. Theatre on second floor. N. H. Crowell (1903–1905), W. J. Pulford (1907–1909), electricians. T. M. Murdock, prop man. Mgr. Thos. Murdock It was remodeled again in 1914 and taken over by the Masons.

Sloan (*Woodbury*)

Lee & Spencer's Hall, ca. 1886, seated 300.

Smithland (*Woodbury*)

Smithland Opera House. Burned, 1910.

Smithland Opera House, 1912 (1912–1914), Main St. The first Smithland Opera House, located over a drugstore, burned in 1910. The second was located on the second story of a two-story frame building, 72'2" × 41'5½". There are two entrances; one on the north side and one on the south. The main floor is 34'8" × 46'. The proscenium is 22'9" wide × 9'5" high. The curtain line to back wall is 14'. The stage height is 30" from the main floor. There is a dressing room stage right 12'9" × 4'7". It is 7'6" in height. There is a small ticket booth at the front of the main floor. First listed Cahn/Leighton 1912–1913. No details. By ca. 1914, seating capacity 300. Stage 36' wide × 11' high × 14' deep. Mgr. G. E. Wendel (1914). Torn down in 1991.

Solon (*Johnson*)

CSPS Hall, 301 N. Dubuque. Two-story brick, 58' × 78'. Theatre on the second floor above Ruzicka's Meat Market. There had been alterations inside, but the stage measured 38' between side walls, and was 17' deep. The main floor was 48' × 38'; the gallery was 15' × 38'. There were stacks of old flats with interior and some exterior scenes. There were three roll drops hung above the stage—unable to get them down. Helen Urbanek reportedly has main front drop. Some remnants of painted drapery borders still hung from the ceiling. Building burned 11/04/88, destroying opera house interior.

South English (*Keokuk*)

Opera House/IOOF Hall, 1896. Two-story brick on the west end of Ives St. on the south side; 32'6" × 64'. Opera house was on the ground floor; apartments for actors and meeting rooms were on the second floor. Ground floor has been gutted.

Spencer (*Clay*)

Grand Opera House, ca. 1904 (1904–1921), second-story house, seated 750. Proscenium was 35' wide × 20' high; stage was 73' wide × 42' high × 30' deep; 7' apron. No grooves, 4 traps. Electric light.

Depth under stage 5'. By ca. 1907, stage was 73' wide × 46' high × 32' deep; 7' apron. By ca. 1912, seating capacity was 743, stage height 44'. 8 dressing rooms. By ca. 1921, seating capacity was 738. Proscenium 40' wide. Stage 75' wide × 33' deep. John Broadgate (1904–1905), Francis Hebert (1907–1909), electricians. E. Montgomery (1904–1908), prop man. L. Hagerty (1904–1905), R. H. Wilkins (1907–1908), stage carpenters. 5 in orchestra; Leader P. M. Ingold (1904–1905). Mgrs. Ackley Hubbard (1904–1905), Franklin Floete (1907–1909), E. R. Mauss (1912–1914), L. H. Rasmuson (1921).

Rink Hall, ca. 1889, seated 500. Mgr. F. Floete.

Spirit Lake (*Dickinson*)

Pearsoll's Hall, ca. 1889. Mgr. Geo. E. Pearson.

Rice Opera House, ca. 1883 seated 400. Stage was 42' wide × 17' deep. Four sets of scenery. Mgr. G. W. Rice.

Spring Hill (*Warren*)

Hall, second-story, southeast corner of 2nd and Carson streets. Razed in 1936 or 1937.

Springville (*Linn*)

Springville Opera Hall, 1898, 273 Broadway St. Two-story brick, 57' × 83'; theatre was on the second floor. The proscenium is 20' wide × 12' high; stage is 34' wide × 18' deep; 4' curved apron. It appears that there used to be a balcony; the main floor measures 34' × 35'. There are some old flats and several old roll drop rollers, one marked "J.S. Butler & Son, Springville, Iowa." The main curtain is in the collection of the Museum of Repertoire Americana, Mt. Pleasant.

St. Ansgar (*Mitchell*)

City Opera House, ca. 1896 (1896–1921), ground-floor house seating 400. Proscenium was 20' wide × 11' high; stage was 34' wide × 10' high × 18'6" deep; 1'6" apron. 3'6" depth under stage. Had three 10' grooves. 4 traps, 1 each side, 2 in center. By ca. 1912, seating capacity 450. Proscenium 20' wide × 12' high. Stage 34' wide × 16' high × 19' deep; 3' apron. Six 12' grooves, 2 dressing rooms. By ca. 1914, stage was 34' wide × 14' high × 20' deep. By ca. 1921, proscenium 22' wide. Stage 36' wide × 22' deep. Seating capacity 350. Mgrs. O. H. Koch (1896–1909), Koch & Sherman (1912–1914), Lewis C. Moe (1921).

St. Olaf (*Clayton*)

St. Olaf Auditorium, 1939. Built by the WPA. It is two-story stone construction, 38'8" × 76'2". The proscenium measures 24' wide × 14'6" high; the stage is 34' wide × 14' deep with no apron, although there are footlights. The main floor measures 44' × 34'; there are dressing rooms under the stage.

Staceyville (*Mitchell*)

Opera House, Main St.

Stanwood (*Cedar*)

Opera House, second-floor hall. Burned.

State Center (*Marshall*)

    Bell's Hall, ca. 1889, seated 300. Mgr. R. Bell.

    Grand Opera House, ca. 1907 (1907–1921), 40′ × 100′ brick. Second-story hall seating 400–500. Prices $0.75, $0.50, $0.35, $0.25. Proscenium was 20′ wide × 14′ high; stage was 40′ wide × 14′ high × 16′ deep; 4′ apron. 2 dressing rooms. Electric light; 226 lights with 3 dimmers; 48 lights on stage hangers. In 1907, proscenium was 20′ wide × 12′ high; stage was 24′ deep. 3 dressing rooms. Mgrs. Coe & Gohlke, F. C. Rohde (1912), Cowan & Rohde (1914), B. H. Grey (1921). See State Center Opera House.

    Liston Building/IOOF Hall, ca. 1912, 102 E. Main. Two-story concrete block, 27′ × 102′. Interior converted into apartments and a NAPA store.

    Masonic Hall, 121 E. Main. Two-story frame, 36′ × approx. 80′. May have been used as an opera hall.

    Manwaring's Hall, Main St. Remodeled inside; a floor added. Two-story brick, old enough to be Bell's Opera House. Inside are posters and playbills.

    State Center Opera House, ca. 1904, 40′ × 100′ brick building, seated 320; prices $0.50, $0.35, $0.25. Proscenium was 20′ wide × 12′ high; stage was 24′ deep. Oil light. In 1907 lighting was electric; 226 lights with 3 dimmers; 48 lights on stage hangers. Probably the same as the Grand Opera House. Mgrs. S. M. Brimhall & Co.

    Star Theatre, ca. 1919, 201 W. Main. Two-story brick, 72′ × 80′; theatre on first floor. Stage is about all that's left after remodeling. Proscenium measures 17′3″ wide × 12′6″ high. Stage is 29′ wide. Stage is too full of junk to measure from curtain line to back.

Stewart (*Adair/Guthrie*)

    Stewart Opera House, ca. 1883. "Elegantly frescoed and lighted with gas. Complete stock of new scenery." Seating capacity, 600. Mgrs. Savage and Ryan.

Stockport (*Van Buren*)

    Stockport Opera House.

Storm Lake (*Buena Vista*)

    Brown Brothers' Hall, ca. 1883, seated 225. Stage was 21′ wide × 12′ deep. "No piano in hall." Mgrs. Brown Brothers.

    Empire Theatre, 1921. See Opera House.

    Opera House, ca. 1889, ground-floor hall seated 800. Proscenium was 27′ wide × 13′ high; stage was 30′ wide × 20′ deep; 4′ apron. By ca. 1912, seating capacity was 601. By ca. 1914, seating capacity was 700. Stage was 30′ wide × 16′ high × 22′ deep. By ca. 1921, seating capacity was 601. Stage was again 20′ deep. Was Empire Theatre by 1921. Mgrs. E. E. Mack (1889–18??), W. C. Skiff (1912–1914), M. E. Tries (1921).

    Rawson's Opera House, ca. 1886, seated 1000. Proscenium was 22′ wide; stage was 48′ wide × 18′ high × 20′ deep. Had 8 scenes. Mgr. C. E. Rawson.

Story City (*Story*)

City Hall, ca. 1889, seated 500. Mgr. S. Larson.

Story City Auditorium, 1913, 512 Broad St. Two-story brick, 50' ×
90'. The proscenium measures 27' wide × 20' high (originally 30'
high). Stage is 50' wide × 19'6" deep. The orchestra pit was
floored over in the 1930s. Dressing rooms off R and L. The main
floor seats 296, the balcony 100. There is a 26' × 13' front curtain
which can't be lowered because of the movie screen. Original cost
was $12,163.41. May also have been called The Auditorium. Mgr.
Iver Egenes.

Stratford (*Hamilton*)

Johnson's Hall, ca. 1907 (1907–1914), seated 200. Proscenium was 20'
wide × 8' high; Stage was 10' wide × 3' deep, 7' apron. Gas and
electric light. By ca. 1914, called Opera House. Seating capacity
250. Stage 44' wide × 10' high × 10' deep. Mgr. J. H. Johnson.

Stratford Opera Hall, ca. 1881, seated 500. It was "well-ventilated [with]
good stage and scenery."

Strawberry Point (*Clayton*)

Davis Auditorium, ca. 1914, ground-floor house, seated 500. Stage was
32' wide × 16' high × 20' deep. Mgr. Oscar Davis.

Kingsley's Opera House, 106 W. Mission.

Opera House, ca. 1914, second-floor theatre, seated 600. Stage was 40'
wide × 15' high × 20' deep. Mgrs. Opperman & Nace.

Orpheum, Commercial St.

Stuart (*Guthrie*)

Bates' Opera House, ca. 1889. Mgr. J. R. Bates.

Ryan's Opera House, ca. 1889. Mgr. M. Ryan.

Sumner (*Bremer*)

Cass Opera House, ca. 1889 (1889–1921), ground-floor house seated
600; "only opera house in the city." "The latest improved 'La Belle'
upholstered folding opera chairs, hat racks, foot rests, etc." Organ
and piano. Proscenium was 20' wide × 14' high; stage was 40'
wide × 16' high × 30' deep; 1' apron. 34' between fly girders. 8'
depth under stage. Had a "complete outfit of scenery from the
studio of Sosman & Landis," 4 grooves, 1 trap, center. Ample
rooms under stage. Gas light (gas and electric light by 1904). In
1921 screen was 9' × 12'; throw was 70'. Mgrs. J. F. Cass, H. W.
Bathke (1914).

Sumner Opera House, ca. 1886, ground-floor house seated 500. Stage
was 36' wide × 14' high × 30' deep. Mgr. C. Forrsmann.

Sutherland (*O'Brien*)

Nott Opera House, 1921. See Sutherland Opera House.

Sutherland Opera House, ca. 1912 (1912–1921), Main St. Two-story
brick. Seated 325. Proscenium was 16' wide × 8' high; stage was
32' wide × 14' deep. Gas and electric light. 3 dressing rooms. By
ca. 1914, stage was 32' wide × 10' high × 16' deep. By ca. 1921,
seating capacity was 350. Was the Nott Opera House in 1921. It
currently is an unused movie theatre. Mgr. C. L. Nott.

Opera House, ca. 1904 (1904–1909). Seating capacity 300. Gas and electric light. Proscenium 16' × 8'. Stage 14' feet deep, 1 trap. Theatre first floor. Depth under stage 2'6". By ca. 1907, gas light only. Mgrs. Peter Seeman (1904–1905), D. W. Elliott (1907), J. W. Pickrell (1908). Probably the **Sutherland Opera House.**

Swaledale (*Cerro Gordo*)

Opera House. Burned.

Swea City (*Kossuth*)

Swea City Opera House.

Tabor (*Fremont*)

Tabor Opera House, 713–719 Main St. Two-story brick, theatre on the second floor. It had a main floor but no balcony. The interior is irregularly shaped. Currently it is empty.

Tama (*Tama*)

Merchant's Hall, ca. 1883 (1883–1889). No scenery. Mgr. I. Merchant.

Rink Hall, ca. 1889, seated 1200. Electric light. Mgr. E. L. Carmichael.

Soleman Opera House, ca. 1886 (1886–1921), ground-floor hall seated 500. Proscenium was 23' wide × 14' deep; stage was 48' wide × 26' high × 18' deep; 2' apron. 8' depth under stage. 4 dressing rooms. Scenery was from Jesse Cox studio. Electric light by 1904. Van Durmark (1904), prop man; Shaw (1904), stage carpenter. In 1921 stage was 46' wide × 26' high × 20' deep. Mgrs. H. Soleman, M. Hyland (1914).

Templeton (*Carroll*)

Templeton Opera House, ca. 1890. Located on the second story of a brick building on Main St. Its current dimensions are 44'5" × 50'9". The main floor auditorium may have been 42' × 49'5". Remodeled, it currently is the Halbur Templeton Hardware.

Thor (*Humboldt*)

Thor Community Hall. Burned.

Tingley (*Ringgold*)

Opera Hall, ca. 1886.

Tingley Opera House. According to resident Billy Breckenridge, it was the second story of a two-story brick building located at the west end of the business district. The stage was 4' up from the main floor. There were wings and drops and the seating capacity was probably 250. Sources conflict as to building dimensions. It was either 60' × 80' or 50' × 100'. It was rebuilt in 1945 and currently is the Community Hall.

Tipton (*Cedar*)

City Hall, ca. 1879 (1879–1889), seated 500. Stage was 12' wide × 11' deep (44' × 12', 1883) . Had 6 sets scenery. Orchestra available. Mgrs. J. C. Reichert, Wm. Dean (1889).

Hardacre Hall, 1916, 112 E. 5th St. Two-story brick, built by the estate of Jacob L. Hardacre to serve as an IOOF hall. Currently it is a movie house, the Hardacre Theatre. The frontage measures 48'. A permanent movie screen box fills the stage, which has a 28' wide × 15'6" high proscenium. Stage is 40' wide × 20' deep. There are five dressing rooms below the stage. The main floor seats 270; the gallery seats 132. The exterior marquee was added in 1937.

Opera House, ca. 1904 (1904–1921), second-story hall. Proscenium was 20' wide × 14' high; stage was 50' wide × 20' high × 10' deep; 5' apron. Had seven 15' high grooves, could be taken up flush with fly gallery. 5' depth under stage. 15' to fly gallery. 2 traps. Electric light. C. Hinkhouse (1904), Billie McCabe (1907), electricians; Ingman (1904), scenic artist; Merriam (1904), J. Doyle (1907), prop men; Baxter (1904), Bill Doyle (1907), stage carpenters; Smith, orchestra leader—6 in orchestra. Mgr. Grant Ingman.

Titonka (*Kossuth*)

Hanson Opera House. Burned.

Toeterville (*Mitchell*)

Toeterville Town Hall. Two-story frame; there were a few scenes around a couple of years ago.

Toledo (*Tama*)

Baker's Opera House, ca. 1896 (1896–1901), ground-floor hall seated 700. Proscenium was 22' wide × 14' high; stage was 45' wide × 45' deep. 10' depth under stage. Scenery was by Sosman & Landis. Electric light. E. N. Wing, electrician and prop man; P. L. Swirringin, orchestra leader; 6 in orchestra. Mgr. S. E. Baker.

Opera House, ca. 1886 (1886–1889), seated 600. Mgrs. Churchill & Warren.

Toledo Opera House, ca. 1889, seated 500. Proscenium was 23' wide; stage was 25' wide × 13' high × 23' deep. Had 8 scenes by Sosman & Landis. Had good dressing rooms. Mgr. Hiram Baldwin.

Toledo Opera House, ca. 1903 (1903–1913). Ground-floor house seated 700. Proscenium was 22' wide × 14' high; stage was 45' wide × 45' deep. Depth under the stage was 10'. Sosman & Landis scenery. Electric light. R. E. Johnson (or Johnston), electrician and prop man. Art Lever (1907), electrician. Jerry Eberhart (1907), prop man. Mgr. Fred Dragoun.

Wieting Theatre, 1912 (1914–1921), corner of Church and E. High. Two-story brick, 50'6" × 100'. Proscenium is 29' wide × 20' high; stage is 48' wide × 40' high × 26' deep. The apron is 8' with footlights. 10' of wing space. A 4' × 6' trap, center, has been covered over. The orchestra pit is covered over. Dressing rooms are off R and L and in basement. The front asbestos curtain is by Twin Cities Scenic Studio (may have been repainted). Other artifacts are in the theatre office and in the local History Museum. Seating capacity was 650. Mrs. James Snyder (works at the post office) has the blueprints. Booking agent (1914), J. Wingfield, Chicago. Mgrs. J. G. Wieting, N. J. Fullendorf (1921).

Traer (*Tama*)

Bowen's Opera House, ca. 1886 (1886–1889), seated 800; stage was 45' wide × 20' deep. Mgr. W. H. Bowen.

Traer Opera House, ca. 1896 (1896–1904), Main Street. Ground-floor house seated 800. Proscenium was 20' wide × 20' high; stage was 46' wide × 24' high × 27' deep; 3' apron. 5' depth under stage.

Had four 20' grooves, 1 trap, "located on main street." 4 dressing rooms. Mgr. T. J. McGinnis.

Traer Opera House, 1904 (1904–1921), two-story brick, ground-floor theatre. Seated 482 on the main floor and 160 in the balcony (total: 642); prices $0.15–$0.75. Proscenium was 28' wide × 20' deep; stage was 19' deep. In 1907 stage was 48' wide × 35' high × 24' deep; 4' apron. 34' between fly girders; 22' to fly gallery; 8' depth under stage. 1 trap, center. "All scenery goes up." No scene room. Mgrs. T. J. McGinnis, F. E. (or E. E.) Taylor (1907).

Treynor (*Pottawattamie*)

Treynor Opera House, on Highway 72. One-story frame, 48' × 96'. According to a local inhabitant the building has been moved three times. Currently it is American Legion Post 725.

Tripoli (*Bremer*)

City Hall, ca. 1886, seated 500. Mgr. W. C. Rockwood.

Tripoli Opera House, 1912, 108 First Ave. S.W. Single-story wood frame. The building measures 36' × 99'. The interior has been totally remodeled, and the building is now the Tripoli Bowl-Inn bowling alley.

Truro (*Madison*)

Truro Opera House, 1916. Built by Walt Roby. A two-story brick building, currently empty.

Union (*Hardin*)

Union Opera House, ca. 1896 (1896–1901), second-story hall seated 250. Stage was 21' wide × 11' deep; 1' apron. Mgr. O. E. Lawrence.

New Opera House, 1902, on second floor of a 40' × 80' building "to be erected this summer."

Vail (*Crawford*)

Vail Opera House.

Plaza Theatre, ca. 1921. See Woodman Theatre.

Woodman Theatre, ca. 1904 (1904–1921), ground-floor house seated 500. Proscenium was 22' wide × 18' high; stage was 30' wide × 10' deep; 10' apron. Gas light. Depth under stage 4'. By 1907 lighting was acetylene gas. By ca. 1912, seating capacity 400. Stage 32' wide × 18' deep. 2 dressing rooms. In 1921 it was the Plaza Theatre. Allbrook (1904–1909), scenic artist. Stork (1904–1909), prop man. Mgrs. J. P. Duffy (1904–1905), P. J. Monaghan (1907), A. J. Monaghan (1908), J. J. Dugan (1914–19??), E. T. Quirk.

Van Horn (*Benton*)

Griese's Theatre.

Van Horn Opera House.

Varina (*Pocahontas*)

Varina Opera House.

Villisca (*Montgomery*)

Opera Hall, ca. 1883, seated 350. Had a fair amount of scenery. By ca. 1886 it was called Opera House and seated 400. Stage 16' × 30'. Mgr. H. D. Dolson.

Villesca Opera House, ca. 1903 (1903–1909), ground-floor theatre seated 600. Proscenium was 19' wide × 14' high; stage was 36' wide × 12' high × 21' deep; 5' apron. Had six 12' high grooves. May be taken up flush with fly gallery. Depth under stage 6'; 1 trap. No scene room. 9 in orchestra. Electric light. Mgrs. E. C. Gibbs (1903), Dr. F. M. Childs (1908).

Vining (*Tama*)

CSPS Hall, 1913. Two-story frame, 68'6" × 96'8". Proscenium is 23' 11" wide × 12'8" high; stage is 47' wide × 14'9" high × 11' deep; 3' apron. The main floor measures 69'10" × 47'1". Advertising front drop similar to Westgate and Chelsea, measures 24'7" × 13'.

Vinton (*Benton*)

Palace Theatre, ca. 1921, ground-floor hall seated 650. Stage was 30' wide × 18' high × 24' deep. Same as Vinton Opera House. Mgr. Geo. Jackson.

Vinton Opera House, ca. 1914. Ground-floor house seated 500. Stage was 30' wide × 18' high × 24' deep. Mgr. J. F. Brechner.

Vinton Theatre, ca. 1912, ground-floor hall seated 335. Proscenium was 20' wide × 15' high; stage was 14' deep. Had four 14' high grooves. 6 dressing rooms. Electric light. Mgr. J. F. Breckner.

Watson's Hall (Watson's Opera House), ca. 1878 (1878–1889), seated 600. Piano. Proscenium was 24' wide × 22' high; stage was 49' wide × 24' deep. Had 16' high grooves, 10 scenes. "Entirely refitted for season of 1883–1884. New stage, scenery, opera chairs, etc."

  In 1889 the proscenium was 22' wide × 16' high; stage was 40' wide × 16' high × 25' deep; 11' to grooves. Had Thos. Kane & Co. opera chairs. 12 sets scenery. 2 proscenium boxes. 4 elegant dressing rooms. Piano. "Is only house here and is modern in every detail." Mgrs. Sam H. Watson, C. Watson (1889).

Watson's Parlor Opera House, ca. 1896 (1896–1909), second-floor house seated 500; prices $0.25–$0.75. Proscenium was 23' wide × 20' high; stage was 42' wide × 25' high × 20' deep; 2' apron. 3' depth under stage. Grooves could be taken up flush with fly gallery. Had four 15' high grooves, 1 trap, center. Scene room. Electric light. Ita Hahn, prop man; Fred Rose (1898), Christ. Wenner (1904), Bert Gee (1907), prop men and stage carpenters. Mgrs. C. Watson, Matt Gaasch (1899), Geo. D. McElroy (1904), F. T. Primus (1908).

Viola (*Linn*)

Viola Community Building. Originally two-story frame, the second floor, where the hall was located, has been removed. The building is 20' × 60'.

Volga (*Clayton*)

Volga Opera House, 1913, Washington Street. Two-story brick, 45' × 100'10". The opera house is on the first floor. The proscenium is 24' wide × 14' high; stage is 42'6" wide × 30 high × 19'6" deep; 5' curved apron. There is a pinrail stage R, and a 3' × 4' trap.

Dressing rooms are below the stage. The flat-floor hall measures 41' × 65'6"; there is a horseshoe-shaped hanging gallery. Backstage are some old flats, some graffiti, a few playbills on the walls, and some remnants of stage rigging. A permanent, 2" × 4" drywall-construction 3-wall set has been built on the stage. The current owner is performing some restoration of the audience area. The building presently houses the Redwood Inn in the basement.

Wadena (*Fayette*)

Wadena Opera House. Now the Wadena Locker, the single-story frame and stucco building measures 30'2" × 68'5". Now in a state of disrepair and used for storage, it is possible to determine that the proscenium measured 20'4" wide, the stage was 28'4" wide × 8' deep. The Wadena Museum has the front curtain.

Walker (*Linn*)

Spencer's Hall, ca. 1889, seated 250.

Wall Lake (*Sac*).

Wall Lake Opera House, 1912, on 2nd St. Two-story brick, 40'1½" × 72'7". According to residents and the *Wall Lake Centennial,* it had a balcony, a main floor with moveable chairs, drops, probably flats, and dressing rooms in the basement. Currently it is the Wall Lake Community Building.

Walnut (*Pottawattamie*)

Walnut Opera House, ca. 1886 (1886–????), on Central Ave. A two-story brick building, now in the renovation process. Mgr. O. M. Bruce (1889–18??).

Wapello (*Louisa*)

Garrett's Hall, ca. 1889, seated 250. Mgr. A. Garrett.

Keck Theatre, ca. 1921, seated 475. Mgr. W. E. Harrick.

Myron Hall, ca. 1896 (1896–1909), second-floor hall seated 400. Proscenium was 20' wide × 15' high; stage was 17' deep; 3' apron. Mgrs. John Keck, Jr.; Frank Van Loon (1907).

Van Loon's Hall, ca. 1889, seated 400. Mgr. Mrs. W. G. Van Loon.

Washington (*Washington*)

Everson's Opera House, ca. 1878 (1878–1886), seated 800. Stage was 22' wide × 19' deep. Had 7 "slide scenes" and a drop curtain. See Music Hall. Mgr. N. Everson.

Graham Opera House, 1893 (listed continuously from 1889–1921; there might have been two with the same name), E. Washington and S. 2nd Ave. Two-story brick, 54' × 100', seated 783; "'It is the finest little house in the State,' and only house in the city used for theatrical purposes." Prices (1896) $0.25–$1. Now houses the State Theatre. Measurements today conform generally to those of 1896: proscenium is 32' wide × 29' high; stage is 62' wide × 42' high × 28' deep; 4' apron. Grooves (now only on L) are 18' from stage (originally four 12' grooves) (no grooves listed for 1908); distance between fly galleries, 50'. 10' depth under stage. 1 trap, center. Gas and electric light (and still listed as such as late as 1921). Baggage elevator. Ample exits. 7 "fine" dressing rooms off R and L. "All modern conveniences." W. Mannhardt, F. Dupuis (1897), W. Mannhardt (1903), electricians; A. F. Beitel (1896), John W. Long (1903), Ben Miller (1904), George Clapper (1908), stage carpenters; J. Long (1893, 1900), J. Boling (1897, 1899), I. Hall (1898), prop men; John F. Mackin (1896), L. Mintle (1899), H. McConnoughey (1897), D. Donovan (1900), Prof. Brown (1903), Lou Galyean (1904), orchestra leaders; 5-6 in orchestra. Original capacity was 360 on the main floor, 388 in 2 balconies, 12 in the 2 boxes (total: 760): now seats 310 on the main floor and 215 in the balcony. Playbills, posters, clippings offstage R and L, and on fly gallery. Bills from Chase-Lister Co., Mae Abbott in *My Dixie Girl,* etc. Library has portfolio (text and pictures) on opera house. Mgrs. A. H. Wallace, Warren Moore (1896), Washington Opera House Co. (1907), J. E. Lemmon (1908), W. F. Brinton (1912), L. Moorissey (1921).

Music Hall, ca. 1878 (1878–1886), seated 800. Stage was 22' wide × 19' deep. Had 4 scenes. Probably the same as Everson's Opera House. Mgrs. Chilcote & Scofield.

Waterloo (*Black Hawk*)

Brown's New Opera House, "new, bright, convenient and comfortable. Metropolitan in every respect." In 1889 (1889–1905), ground-floor house, seated 1200; parquette, dress circle and 2 balconies; prices (1896) $0.25–$1. "Suburban street cars connect with outside towns, giving 17,000 to draw from." Proscenium was 30' wide × 26' high; stage was 60' wide × 60' high × 40' deep; 4' apron. 38' between fly girders. 8' depth under stage. Had five 18' high grooves, could be taken up flush with the fly gallery (no grooves by 1903). 1 trap, center. Scene room. Gas and electric light. John Mantel (1896, 1903), H. G. Brown (1898), stage carpenters; Prof. Knapp (1896), Prof. Marcuson (1898), Prof. J. Power (1904), orchestra leaders; 9 in orchestra. Mgr. C. F. Brown, East Waterloo.

Burnham's Opera House, ca. 1878 (1878–1886), ground-floor house, seated 895. Chickering piano. Stage was 60' wide × 28' deep (60' × 34', 1883). It was "completely fitted with scenery." Gas light. "No snaps allowed on any terms." Orchestra available. "Theodore Thomas, Emma Abbott, Lawrence Barrett, Thos. Keene, Thatcher, Primrose & West and equally strong attractions play here." Mgr. C. W. Burnham.

Goodwin's Opera House, ca. 1889, seated 1000; Burnham folding opera chairs. Piano. Proscenium was 30' wide; stage was 60' wide × 40' high × 30' deep. Grooves were 16' high. Had 12 scenes. Mgr. L. C. Goodwin.

The Waterloo, ca. 1907 (1907–1921). Brick. Ground-floor house seated 600 on the main floor, 400 in balcony, 400 in gallery. Prices: orchestra, $1.50; general admission, $0.25. Proscenium was 34' wide × 30' deep; stage was 63' wide × 65' high × 34' deep; 10' apron; no grooves, 1 trap. 44' between fly girders, 22' to fly gallery. 9' depth under stage. Scene room. Gas and electric light. F.

E. Doxey, electrician; C. Kennedy, scenic artist; John Mantle, Gerald Hess (1908), stage carpenters; C. C. Crawford, Maxim de Grosz (1908), orchestra leaders—7 in orchestra. Razed ca. 1984. Booking agents (1914), Klaw & Erlanger, New York. Mgrs. H. D. Haffa, A. J. Busby (1908), Busby Bros. (1914), Bresley Bros. [sic]. (1921).

Theatre (ca. 1908), seated 500 on the main floor; balcony, 286; gallery, 400 (total: 1186). Proscenium was 42' wide × 40' high; stage was 70' wide × 68' high × 52' deep; 6' apron. 60' between fly girders; 12' depth under stage; 35' to fly gallery. No grooves. No scene room. Gas and electric lighting. Howard Tuttle, scenic artist. Roy Dunkleberg, prop man. Harle Hileman, stage carpenter. Geo. Bagby, orchestra leader; 7 in orchestra. The listing in the 1908 Cahn gives no name other than "Theatre." Mgr. A. J. Busby.

Union Hall, ca. 1879 (1878–1879), seated 700. Stage was 40' wide × 20' deep. Had 7 scenes. Mgr. Geo. Mason.

Waucoma (*Fayette*)

Waucoma Opera House, 1912. Single-story, false-front frame building, 37' × 100'. Currently functions as the American Legion Hall. Has been completely remodeled inside—no stage. M. J. Blong has some of the share certificates for the original opera house company— belonged to M. H. Blong.

Waukon (*Allamakee*)

Armory Opera House, ca. 1903 (1903–1913), second-floor hall, seated 600; prices $0.25, $0.35, $0.50. Proscenium was 22' wide × 16' high; stage was 44' wide × 12' deep; 4' apron. 7' depth under stage. Had 2 grooves, could be taken up flush with fly gallery. 2 traps. No scene room. Electric light. M. Howard, electrician; Royal Pratt, Rafael (or Raphael) Banon (1907), stage carpenters; Sam Peck, Clem Hoag (1907), prop men. Mgrs. J. H. Hager, A. S. Bowen (1907).

Boomer's Opera House, ca. 1883 (1883–1889), seated 600; chairs. Piano. Stage was 40' wide × 16' deep. Had 18 sets scenery. Orchestra available. Mgrs. J. H. Boomer, Boomer Bros. (1886).

Cota, ca. 1914 (1914–1921), ground-floor hall, seated 330. Stage was 32' wide × 20' high × 12' deep. Mgr. Dennis Cota.

Waukon Opera House, ca. 1914–1916, 14 Allamakee. First-story brick, 62' × 140' with a fly loft. The stage is now fitted with a false ceiling. Backstage is still equipped with a fly gallery. The asbestos fire curtain is still in place, marked "Johns-Manville Co., 55, 57 and 59 High St., Boston, Mass." The proscenium width is 30'; stage is 62' wide × 26' deep. Five dressing rooms remain backstage left. The building currently functions as a community hall/bar.

Waverly (*Bremer*)

Moulds' Opera House, ca. 1921, ground-floor house seated 700. Stage was 42' wide × 30' high × 20' deep. Probably the same as the Opera House. Mgr. Geo. Moulds.

Nichols Theatre, ca. 1903 (1903–1914), second-floor house. Proscenium was 25' wide × 15' high; stage was 42' wide × 45' high × 16' deep; 4' apron. 25' between fly girders. 6' depth under stage. Had four 14' high grooves, could be taken up flush with fly gallery. 2 bridges. Scene room. Electric light. Healey, electrician; Roy Kemp, Clide Andrews (1904), orchestra leaders; 7 in orchestra. Mgr. H. G. Nichols.

Opera House, ca. 1878 (1878–1889), seated 700. Stage was 44' wide × 22' deep. Had 10 complete sets scenery. Probably the same as Moulds' Opera House. Mgrs. C. H. Burrows, W. R. Switzer.

Wayland (*Henry*)

City Hall, ca. 1889, seated 200.

Wenger Hall, ca. 1886 (1886–1889), seated 200. Mgrs. Wenger Bros.

Webster City (*Hamilton*)

Armory Opera House, ca. 1907 (1907–1921), ground-floor hall seated 825. Proscenium was 28' wide × 17' high; stage was 44' wide × 40' high × 23' deep; 38' between fly girders; 20' to fly gallery; 5' apron. 12' depth under stage. 2 traps. Gas and electric light. Electric only by 1908. By ca. 1912, seating capacity: ground floor 462, balcony 176, gallery 139 (total: 777). Proscenium 28' wide × 18' high. Stage 25' deep, 3' apron. 7 dressing rooms. By ca. 1914, seating capacity was again 825. Stage was 24' deep. G. H. Maffit (1909), electrician; W. S. Norton (1909), stage carpenter; J. C. Jenkinson, orchestra leader (1907–1909); 6 in orchestra. Booking agent (1914), J. Wingfield, Chicago. Mgr. N. P. Hyatt.

Willson's Opera House, ca. 1883 (1883–1905), seated 700 until ca. 1896, when seating capacity fell to 600; prices (1896) $0.25–$0.75. In ca. 1886 stage 23' × 66'. In 1896, proscenium was 30' wide × 16' high; stage was 66' wide × 24' high × 18' deep, 6' apron. Four 16' high grooves. 5' depth under stage. 2 traps. Grooves could be taken up flush with fly gallery. 5 in orchestra. Theatre on second floor. By ca. 1904 stage was 20' deep, 4' apron. O. E. Simmons (1896–1901), stage carpenter. Had full stock of scenery. Electric light (ca.1896). Mgrs. F. E. Willson (1883–1886), W. C. Willson (1889), F. E. Willson (1900), F. W. Heron (1901).

Weldon (*Clarke*)

Opera House. Second floor of a two-story building; the second floor has been removed.

Wesley (*Kossuth*)

Kunz Opera House, ca. 1900, 108 E. Main. Located on the second story of a two-story brick building. The building is 56' × 70'. The proscenium is 20'5" wide × 8'7" high on either end and 10'9" in the middle; curtain line to back wall 14'3"; stage height 3'2" above the main floor. The main floor is 39'5" × 57'. The balcony is 32'11" × 8'3" and 7'9" high. It may have been added later. There are two rooms auditorium right measuring 12'10" × 10'4½" and 50'8" × 10'5½". Two doors provide access. They also may have been added later. Currently empty, it has been used as a meeting room by various organizations. The lower floor, formerly Johnny's

Market, is also empty.
West Bend (*Palo Alto*)
    West Bend Opera House.
West Branch (*Cedar*)
    Macomber (?) Opera House, 1895, N. Downey St. Part of the two-story brick C. A. Macomber Opera Block/Masonic Hall. We assume the opera house was on the second story, which is now apartments. The building measures 60' × 63'. Currently undergoing some renovation.
    Union Block. Two-story brick, (date unknown, probably late 1800s). Accounts differ as to whether there was an opera house in the building. If there was, it was obviously another second-floor opera hall. Dimensions unknown. Condition of interior unknown.
West Liberty (*Muscatine*)
    Liberty Hall, ca. 1883 (1883–1889) Mgrs. McLinn Bros. (1889).
    New Theatre (Strand), 1910 (1912–1921), 3rd St. Three-story brick, 39' × 96'. Seated 550 on the main floor and 216 in the balcony (total: 766). Proscenium was 24' wide × 20' high; the stage was 41' wide × 20' deep; 3' apron. 5 dressing rooms. Electric light. In 1921 proscenium was 26' wide × 20' high; stage was 41' wide × 23' deep; 3' apron. Now a movie theatre. Mgrs. G. B. Embree & Co., John N. Miller (1914).
West Point (*Lee*)
    West Point Opera House, ca. 1900 (1921), frame. 1 block north of the town square. Originally a Methodist church and library. Burned 1941. Mgr. B. Brink (1921).
West Union (*Fayette*)
    Princess Theatre, ca. 1920, North Vine St. Two-story brick, with a 25' front. It looks old enough to be Ziegler Hall. In 1921 it had a seating capacity of 300; Ziegler's was listed with a capacity of 400. Mgr. Mr. Simpson.
    Ziegler Hall, ca. 1878 (1878–1909), second-story house, seated 400. "Only house in town." Assembly seats. Proscenium was 18'10" wide; stage was 40' wide × 15' deep; 4' apron. Had 7 scenes. Mgrs. Joseph Johnson, J. Hobson (1886); Wallace, Lathrop & Woodard (1889); R. O. Woodard (1897).
Westfield (*Plymouth*)
    Westfield Opera House.
Westgate (*Fayette*)
    Westgate Opera House, 1911, Cass St. Single-story, false-front, tin-covered frame building, completely lined inside with tin panels as well. Measures 36' × 80'. Proscenium is 14' wide × 11' high; curtain line to back 16'6" with 9'6" offstage R and L. The top half of the proscenium is covered with a basketball backboard and hoop. Four sets of grooves. Nine flats from Kansas City Scenic Studio; one advertising front drop (amateur); one "Westgate Street" roll drop by Kansas City Scenic Co. (addressed on back to E. W. Lusby, Mgr.); scenery now in collection of the Museum of Reper-

toire Americana. Remnants of a gas lighting fixture backstage L: "Perfection Lighting System, American Gas Machine Co., Albert Lea, Minn., Style A, No. 3." The main floor measures 34'6" × 53". One trap, center. Mgr. E.W. Lusby. In 1990 there was a restoration project under way.

Westphalia (*Shelby*)

Parochial School. Entertainments were given here. It is still standing.

Westside (*Crawford*)

Germania Verein, 1893, 207 1st. St. A one-story frame structure, measuring 48'4½" × 90'. The main floor is 69'6" × 45'. There is a balcony on three sides approx. 9'7" high and 6'–9' deep. It is reached by a stairway to the left of the front entrance. The proscenium height is 10' at either side and 11'9" in the middle; proscenium width is 20'; curtain line to back wall is 17'6". Currently it is used as a storage area for old gas station equipment and supplies. The building is in extremely poor condition.

What Cheer (*Keokuk*)

New Masonic Opera House, 1893 (1896–1921). One of the best examples of a restored midsize opera house in Iowa. Three-story brick, 48' × 94'. The proscenium today is 21'9" wide × 24' high; stage is 46' wide × 20' deep; 6' apron. Originally the proscenium was 24' wide × 24' high. The distance between fly girders was 38'; there were four grooves 15' above the stage; the rigging loft was 18' high; 38' between fly girders; 10' depth under stage. There is a trap (6'6" × 4'10"), center. Seating capacity was originally 850; today the main floor seats about 383 while the horseshoe-shaped balcony seats 217 (total: 600). The building appears to have its original seats. There are dressing rooms offstage R and L. Posters for a production of *Quo Vadis* on stage R fly gallery are dated 1901. Mgrs. Peter M. Flaherty, Geo. A. Poff (1903), F. L. Adams (1921).

Opera House, ca. 1883 (1883–1889), seated 640. 4 sets scenery (1883). Mgrs. Lortscher Bros.

Wheatland (*Clinton*)

Hinrichsen's Theatre, ca. 1904, seated 300. Mgr. Peter Hinrichsen.

Kroeger's Hall, ca. 1886 (1886–1889), seated 200. Mgr. Peter Kroeger. "No theatre at present" (1907–1913).

Whiting (*Monona*)

Kroon's Hall, 1904, corner Whittier and Blair streets. Seated 650. The Cassady and Whiting Company built a two-story brick structure. The south half of the top floor was the opera house. It measured 56' × 46'. The stage was located on the west end with dressing rooms on either side. There were three sets of flats and three different drops. You can see where the stage had been torn out. The following dimensions are based upon that perspective: stage width 44'10"; curtain line to back wall 16'2½". Currently the space is storage for the community bank located below.

Koon's Hall, ca. 1889. Seated 650. Possibly the same as Kroon's Hall above. Mgr. W. A. Koon or W. C. Whiting (1889).

Whittemore (*Kossuth*)

Opera House, ca. 1921, seated 400. Mgr. Wm. Huckenberry.

Williams (*Hamilton*)

Hurd's Hall, ca. 1889, seated 200. Mgr. H. N. Hurd.

Williamsburg (*Iowa*)

Trojan Opera House, 1894 (1914), southwest corner of Welsh and Elm. Frame with brick veneer; ground-floor hall, seated 425. Probably was the Latona Theatre in 1921. Was originally a skating rink. Mgr. T. T. Osborne.

Latona Theatre, ca. 1921, ground-floor theatre, seated 450. Mgr. T. T. Osborn.

Williamson (*Lucas*)

Opera House.

Wilton (*Muscatine*)

Johnson's Opera Hall, 1878 (1889), 117 W. 4th. Two-story brick. The stage is gone, but there are still 2–3 sets of grooves, a backstage elevator, and the walls are "papered" with old drops. Decorative stenciling remains. The distance between side walls is 27′6″; curtain line to back was about 18′.

Winfield (*Henry*)

Pratt's Theatre, 1919. Story and a half brick, 40′ × 100′. Was the community building most recently, now being remodeled into a plastics company. Jeffery for 1889 mentions only that Winfield had two "halls."

Small Hall #1, ca. 1889, seated 500.

Small Hall #2, ca. 1889, seated 500.

Winterset (*Madison*)

Opera Hall, ca. 1879, seated 400. Stage was 24′ wide × 18′ deep. Had 6 scenes. Mgr. M. R. Tiduck.

Iowa Theatre, ca. 1921. Seating capacity 340. Electric lighting. Proscenium opening 16′ wide. Stage 22′6″ wide × 23′ deep. Mgr. A. B. Pettit.

Winthrop (*Buchanan*)

Winthrop Theatre, 1901, Madison St. Single-story frame, 36′ × 81′. Interior has been completely remodeled into Towne-House Apartments.

Woden (*Hancock*)

Woden Town Hall. Housed community and school plays, and the Tilton and Guthrie Players, according to the Woden librarian.

Woodbine (*Harrison*)

Mathews and Kling Opera House. On the second floor of the Mathews Building, a two-story brick structure. The building was destroyed by a tornado in 1915 and rebuilt. Currently all that is left of the original building is the basement of what is now the Boyer Valley Lumber Company and that measures 40′ × 56′5″. It is close to the railroad tracks.

Woodbine Opera House, ca. 1904 (1904–1909), second-floor house, seated 300. Proscenium was 22' wide × 11' high; stage was 38' wide × 11' high × 17' deep; 3' apron. Had grooves, 1 trap. Grooves may be taken up flush with fly gallery. Gas light. Depth under stage 4'. No scene room. J. L. Templin (1904–1908), prop man. Mgr. G. C. Mathews. Could, of course, be Mathews & Kling Opera House.

Woodstock (*Wright*)

Opera House.

Worthington (*Dubuque*)

Worthington Opera House. Dilapidated single-story frame structure, 33' × 82'10", now serving as a feed shed. The interior has been gutted, but the outlines of the stage and proscenium can still be seen; the proscenium width was about 15', and curtain line to back wall was about 18'. There was 8–10' of offstage room on either side. The main floor measures 60' × 31'. By climbing a pile of baling twine spools to get to the old stage level, graffiti can be seen dated between 1909 and 1923: "Ray E. Curtis, Curtis Comedy Co., one wk., April 16, '23, good biz." Building was scheduled for demolition and may now be down.

Wyoming (*Jones*)

Wyoming Opera House, ca. 1900 (1912–1921), Main St. Two-story brick, the opera house was on the second floor. Building is 75' × 60'. The room is now used for storage—the stage has been removed. The Citizens' State Bank, on the ground floor, has an oil painting of the building as the opera house. Originally the proscenium was 20' wide × 18' high; stage was 30' wide × 18' high × 19' deep; 4' apron. Grooves were 13'6" above the stage. 2 dressing rooms. In 1921 stage was 40' wide × 18' high × 14' deep. Mgrs. W.G. Krouse, Wyoming Amusement Club (1921).

Yorktown (*Page*)

Yorktown Opera House. According to resident Mrs. Marvin Mc-Elhiney, it originally was a schoolhouse that was moved into town and was remodeled into an opera house. Later the building was sold, moved again, and remodeled into a private residence, which is its present use.

References

Ade, George. 1908. *History of Union County from the Earliest Historic Times to 1908*. Chicago: S. J. Clarke Pub. Co.

Allen, Reynolds Keith. 1981. "Nineteenth century theatre structures in Iowa and Nebraska 1857–1900: A classification of selected general utility halls, opera halls and opera houses as described in local newspapers and histories." Ph.D. diss., Florida State University.

Andrews, Clarence A. 1982. The trouping Trousdales. *The Iowan* (Summer): 23–27.

Atlantic News and Telegraph. 1884.

The Bicentennial History of Little Sioux Township. 1976. Shawnee Mission, Kans: Inter Collegiate Press.

Brown, Mabel Nair. 1967. Final curtain call for opera house. *Ogden Reporter*, 16 March.

Bureau of the Census. n.d. *Historical Statistics of the United States, 1789–1945*.

Cahn, Julius. 1896–1909. *Julius Cahn's Official Theatrical Guide*, containing information of the leading theatres and attractions in America. New York: n.p.

The Cahn-Leighton Official Theatrical Guide, 1912–1913. 1912. New York: n.p.

Chautauqua, lyceum, opera, circuses and movies provided entertainment. 1968. *Estherville Daily News*. 29 October.

Cosgrove, Luke. 1952. *Theatre Tonight*. Hollywood: House-Warven Pub.

Cox revolutionized early scenery. 1966. *Estherville Daily News*. 3 October.

Cunning, Tracy. 1987. *Opera Halls and Opera Houses: Evolution of Stage-focused Structures in Iowa, 1850–1925*. Des Moines: Bureau of Historic Preservation, Iowa State Historical Society.

Deemer, Lee. 1980. *Esther's Town*. Ames: Iowa State University Press.

Donahoe, Ned. 1953. "Theatres in central Illinois—1850–1900." Ph.D. diss., University of Illinois.

Dunbar, Willis F. 1943. The opera house as a cultural institution in Michigan. *Michigan History Magazine* 27 (Oct.–Dec.): 661–72.

Frick, John W., and Carlton Ward, eds. 1987. *Directory of Historic American*

Theatres. New York: Greenwood Press.

Glenn, George D. 1988. Steyer's opera hall, Decorah, Iowa, and its existing 1875 grooves, flats, and wings. *Theatre History Studies* 8.

_____. 1988. The opera houses of Iowa: an introduction. In *Opera Houses of the Midwest,* ed. Judith Zivanovic. Mid-America Theatre Conference.

Gus Hill's National Theatre Directory, 1914. 1914. New York: n.p.

Henderson, Mary C. 1986. *Theatre in America.* New York: Harry N. Abrams.

Holmes, Marjorie. 1973. *You and I and Yesterday.* New York: William Morrow.

Hornblow, Arthur. 1965. *A History of the Theatre in America.* Vol. 1. New York: Benjamin Blom.

In and around George. 1975–1976. George, Iowa: n.p.

Jeffrey, John B. 1879–1890. *Guide and Directory to the Opera Houses, Theatres, Public Halls, Bill Posters, etc., of the Cities and Towns of America.* Chicago: n.p.

Julius Cahn–Gus Hill Theatrical Guide and Moving Picture Directory, 1921. 1921. New York: n.p.

Kramme, Michael. 1990. Opera House Illusions: Jesse Cox and Theatrical Scenery. *The Palimpsest* 71 (Winter).

Lipsitz, George. 1987. Theatre space as social space: The twin city scenic collection. *The Twin City Scenic Collection.* Minneapolis: University Art Museum, University of Minnesota.

McNamara, Brooks. 1976. *Step Right Up.* New York: Doubleday.

Mickel, Jere C. 1974. *Footlights on the Prairie.* St. Cloud, Minn.: North Star Press.

The name opera house. 1885. The *Dramatic Mirror.* 7 March.

Nelson, William. 1983. *Wilton, (illegible) & Yesteryear.* n.p.

Nichols Iowa Centennial Book. 1984. n.p.

Nicoll, Allardyce. 1980. *The Garrick Stage: Theatres and Audience in the Eighteenth Century.* Manchester: Manchester University Press.

The Opera House Reporter. 1910. Estherville, Iowa.

Our Life. A Little Gleam of Time between the Eternities, 1882–1982. 1982. Akron, Iowa: Akron *Register-Tribune* and *LeMars Daily Sentinel.*

Poggi, Jack. 1968. *Theatre in America: The Impact of Economic Forces, 1870–1967.* Ithaca, N.Y.: Cornell University Press.

Quimby 75th Anniversary Book. n.d. Quimby, Iowa: n.p.

Slout, William. 1972. *Theatre in a Tent.* Bowling Green, Ohio: Bowling Green University Press.

Sweet, Oney Fred. 1940. An Iowa county seat. *The Iowa Journal of History and Politics* 38 (October).

Toll, Robert C. 1974. *Blacking Up: The Minstrel Show in Nineteenth-Century America.* Shawnee Mission, Kans.: Inter Collegiate Press.

Zivanovic, Judith, ed. 1988. *Opera Houses of the Midwest.* Mid-America Theatre Conference.

Index